The Insider's View on Corporate Governance

The Insider's View on Corporate Governance

The Role of the Company Secretary

Gertrud Erismann-Peyer,
Ulrich Steger,
and
Oliver Salzmann

palgrave macmillan

IMD INTERNATIONAL
Real World. Real Learning®

First published in 2008 by
PALGRAVE MACMILLAN
Houndmills, Basingstoke, Hampshire RG21 6XS and
175 Fifth Avenue, New York, N.Y. 10010
Companies and representatives throughout the world.

PALGRAVE MACMILLAN is the global academic imprint of the Palgrave Macmillan division of St. Martin's Press, LLC and of Palgrave Macmillan Ltd. Macmillan® is a registered trademark in the United States, United Kingdom and other countries. Palgrave is a registered trademark in the European Union and other countries.

ISBN-13: 978–0–230–51597–0 hardback
ISBN-10: 0–230–51597–5 hardback

This book is printed on paper suitable for recycling and made from fully managed and sustained forest sources. Logging, pulping and manufacturing processes are expected to conform to the environmental regulations of the country of origin.

A catalogue record for this book is available from the British Library.

A catalog record for this book is available from the Library of Congress.

10 9 8 7 6 5 4 3 2 1
17 16 15 14 13 12 11 10 09 08

Printed and bound in Great Britain by
CPI Antony Rowe, Chippenham and Eastbourne

Contents

List of Tables vii

List of Illustrations viii

List of Abbreviations x

Acknowledgments xi

Foreword xii

Notes on the Authors xv

Executive Summary xvii

1 The Evolution of Modern Corporate Governance **1**

1.1 The corporate governance earthquake and where we stand today 3

1.2 The role of the company secretary 6

1.3 Overview of recent research and literature 9

1.4 Roadmap through this book 11

2 Study Design **14**

2.1 Scope and framework 14

2.2 Method 15

2.3 Samples 18

2.3.1 Interviews 18

2.3.2 Self-completion questionnaires 22

3 Descriptive Evidence **26**

3.1 Drivers for corporate governance 26

3.1.1 Regulation 26

3.1.2 Stock markets 30

3.1.3 Public pressure 31

3.2 Organization of the board 33

3.2.1 Board characteristics and composition 33

3.2.2 Executive and nonexecutive chairmen 35

3.2.3 Executive and independent board members 36

3.2.4 Internal organization 39

3.3 The company secretary 43
3.3.1 Career 45
3.3.2 Reporting lines and discretion 54
3.3.3 Working relationship and allegiance 60
3.3.4 Resources 69
3.3.5 Tasks and responsibilities 71
3.3.5.1 Board support 74
3.3.5.2 Committee work 90
3.3.5.3 Corporate governance 103
3.3.5.4 Management support 117
3.3.5.5 Shareholders 118
3.3.5.6 Compliance and legal responsibilities 126
3.3.5.7 Other responsibilities 128
3.4 A look at recent developments 130
3.4.1 Changes in companies' corporate governance 131
3.4.2 Effects on the role of the company secretary 138

4 Analyzing Causal Effects 145
4.1 Which factors determine how the company secretary views his/her setting? 145
4.2 Which factors shape the secretary's tasks and responsibilities? 149
4.3 Which factors influence corporate governance performance? 152

5 Conclusion – Where Are We Heading? Making Sense Out of Diversity 153
5.1 Future dynamics of the corporate governance officer 157
5.1.1 Board information improvements 159
5.1.2 External and internal compliance management 161
5.1.3 The governance process manager 162
5.2 Where shall we go? What has to be done? 163

Appendix 166
A.1 Interview guide 166
A.2 Project description 170
A.3 Self-completion questionnaire 172

Additional References 178

Glossary 179

Index 183

List of Tables

ES.1	Improvements in corporate governance	xxiii
2.1	Distribution of geographical regions targeted	16
2.2	Interview sample – companies represented	19
2.3	Sample distribution (interviews) – industries	20
2.4	Sample distribution (interviews) – location of headquarters	21
2.5	Sample distribution (questionnaire) – company size	24
3.1	Board characteristics	34
3.2	Educational background	45
3.3	Prior engagement	48
3.4	Prior positions	48
3.5	Reporting line	55
3.6	Working relationship	61
3.7	Secretaries' involvement in board committees	94
3.8	Corporate governance performance	132
3.9	Improvements in corporate governance	133

List of Illustrations

Figures

ES.1	Typology of company secretaries	xxv
1.1	Book structure	12
2.1	Conceptual framework	15
4.1	Causal effects tested	146
5.1	Clusters of company secretary roles	154

Charts

ES.1	Importance of tasks and responsibilities	xxi
2.1	Sample distribution (questionnaires) – industries	22
2.2	Sample distribution (questionnaires) – location of headquarters	23
2.3	Sample distribution (questionnaires) – location of listings	23
2.4	Sample distribution (questionnaires) – ownership structure	24
3.1	Corporate governance drivers (strength of effect)	27
3.2	Career opportunities (level of agreement)	52
3.3	Support from the chairman (level of agreement)	57
3.4	Strategic and operational discretion (level of agreement)	58
3.5	The secretary's primary accountability (level of agreement)	63
3.6	Conflicts between management and board (level of agreement)	64
3.7	Staff support (level of agreement)	70
3.8	Importance of tasks and responsibilities	72
3.9	Supporting board meetings (task importance)	77
3.10	Continuously informing board members (task importance)	89
3.11	Supporting board committees (task importance)	91
3.12	Defining corporate governance structure and approach (task importance)	104
3.13	Influence on corporate governance process and structure (level of agreement)	105
3.14	Supporting board evaluation (task importance)	112
3.15	Formulating codes of conduct and ethics (task importance)	113
3.16	Whistle-blowing (task importance)	116

3.17 Supporting management meetings (task importance) 117
3.18 Contributing to AGM (task importance) 119
3.19 Contributing to the annual report (task importance) 123
3.20 Continuously informing key shareholders (task importance) 126
3.21 Taking legal responsibilities (task importance) 127
3.22 Reporting on management transactions (task importance) 129
3.23 Engaging in corporate communication (task importance) 130
3.24 Creating visions and ideas (task importance) 131
3.25 Developments strengthened company secretary role (level of agreement) 139

List of Abbreviations

ADR	American Depositary Receipt
AGM	Annual General Meeting of Shareholders
BIS	Board Information System
CEO	Chief Executive Officer
CFO	Chief Financial Officer
CGO	Corporate Governance Officer
COO	Chief Operating Officer
HR	Human Resources
LSE	London Stock Exchange
NASDAQ	National Association of Securities Dealers Automated Quotations
NYSE	New York Stock Exchange
OECD	Organization for Economic Cooperation and Development
PLC/plc	Public Limited Company
Q&A	Questions & Answers
SEC	Securities and Exchange Commission (US)
SOX	Sarbanes-Oxley Act of 2002
SWX	Swiss Stock Exchange

Acknowledgments

We are extremely grateful to Peter Lorange, Jim Ellert, Philip Koehli, and the IMD-community for their generous material and intellectual support.

We also express our sincere gratitude to Lindsay McTeague and Anita Hussey for getting the manuscript in shape, as well as Roxanne Perrinjaquet for supporting our extensive mail survey.

The completion of this study obviously owes a lot to our respondents. They are very busy individuals and we greatly appreciate their support. Special thanks go to the 68 companies, their company secretaries and general counsels who agreed to provide an in-depth view of the organization and the working methods of their boards, and, last but not least, shared their personal experiences about handling this crucial function. We also express our thanks to a great number of chairmen and board members in large international companies who supported our research, mainly through opening the doors for our information gathering. Our participation in the Essentials Seminar "Critical Lessons for Corporate Secretaries & Governance Professionals" in January 2007 contributed a great deal to our better understanding of the broad array of activities of US corporate secretaries. We thank the Society of Corporate Secretaries and Governance Professionals for their willingness to make this participation possible.

We hope that all find the results worthwhile.

Gertrud Erismann-Peyer, Ulrich Steger, and
Oliver Salzmann

Foreword

A book that claims to provide "The insider's view on corporate governance" is making an interesting promise. Who are these "insiders" and what do they tell us – board members, chairmen, CEOs, interested shareholders, and the public at large? As the subtitle of the book specifies: Company secretaries are providing their intimate view on what they are doing, how they are supporting boards at work, and how they are dealing with the increasing challenges of today's corporate governance requirements – requirements that are often driven by political and public pressure rather than by the real needs of the companies and their striving for success. The company secretaries are also talking about how they are trying to help internal and external board members in performing their roles better. And, last but not least, they talk about their dilemmas, their conflicts of interests and loyalties.

A great number of books have been published in the recent past about corporate governance, focusing on areas such as the roles and duties of the boards, the chairman and the CEO, and on board information, board conflicts, checks and balances, internal and external control, and board members' independence. Little research, however, has been done so far on those working with the boards behind the scenes – the people who quite often stay much longer in their function than the chairmen and the CEOs and often even longer than most of the board members.

This in-depth view on board practices in various jurisdictions, industries, and different types of companies allows for a number of interesting conclusions. Why do regulators and corporate governance organizations around the world put enormous emphasis on director's mostly very formally defined independence, whereas nobody seems to care that those supporting these "independent directors" are in no way independent of management? Why are a majority of company secretaries still reporting to the CEO, despite their important role of supporting the board and its work? And why – last but not least – does it seem typical that company secretaries in various jurisdictions have completely different roles and responsibilities, whereas boards are under pressure to become more and more uniform around the world?

Today's definition of "independence" for directors is clearly a result of the US system of a combined chairman-CEO role, whereas in a number of European countries these two top leadership positions have been bestowed on two different people, thus providing an automatic separation of powers. And where the legal system even provides for two strictly separate boards, one supervising the other, supervisory board members' independence has a different quality. Because the CEO and other members of the executive management have no say in selecting the members of the supervisory body, directors can far more openly express their views, even if the CEO might not like them. In my view, being independent of the company is anyhow much less important than being independent of management and, even more so, having an independent mind. External directors, who know the business due to their former employment with the company can make independent judgments and take independent, well-informed decisions without having to fully rely on what management wants them to know. A strong character and the willingness to express independent views is thus much more important than formal independence qualification. In two-tier board structures, board performance could well be improved if directors, who due to their independent mind and their in-depth knowledge, were allowed to also assume important committee responsibilities even if they were not meeting all of the formal independence requirements. Companies, and first and foremost, all regulators and corporate governance activists, should rethink the real reasons behind the call for "independent boards," which are indeed well-functioning checks and balances through the separation of powers between different corporate bodies. Strict formal rules will not avoid future corporate scandals and failures if the people involved are not able to take decisions based on independent reflections. But inflexible rules, driven by form rather than substance, might hinder companies from achieving better performance.

What is now the role of the Company Secretary in this context? I am convinced that a strong personality, with the clear will to serve the company in its striving for excellence, can add much value. Yet it is crucial that the function becomes more and more independent of management. In my view, company secretaries – and even more so, the "corporate governance officers" as described in the book – should have a direct reporting line with the chairman. They must be in a position to provide independent information to the external directors and they must also be the clear and undisputed confidants of the chairman. If any conflicts arise between board and management, between chairman and CEO, this should not lead to a conflict of loyalty for the company secretary.

The authors of the book, in their conclusions, state that the company secretary role requires a high degree of discretion due to the important and often sensitive issues involved. And I could not agree more with what they say at the very end of the book: "People matter – not structures. This is true for the boards as well as for the secretary." I hope that this book, which is based on comprehensive research and rich personal and professional experience of the authors, will contribute to a broader understanding of what is really important for companies and their boards' structures and working methods. May it also contribute to an open discussion on the essence of the independence of boards and the support they get from their secretaries!

Marcel Ospel
Chairman of UBS AG

Notes on the Authors

Gertrud Erismann-Peyer

Gertrud Erismann-Peyer joined International Institute for Management Development, Lausanne, Switzerland (IMD) as Executive in Residence with a primary responsibility for an empirical study on the role of the company secretary, after her retirement as the Company Secretary of UBS AG. She assumed the Company Secretary function of the Swiss financial services group for eight years, after having been in charge as head of the Group Corporate Communications Department with responsibility for media relations, employee communication, investor relations, and marketing communication at Union Bank of Switzerland. Prior to that, she was responsible for the Political Public Relations Department of the Organization for the Promotion of Swiss Economy in Zurich. She holds a Master of Law from the University of Zurich. Since her retirement she also serves as an independent board member for a Swiss medium-sized, internationally active engineering company.

Ulrich Steger

Ulrich Steger joined IMD in 1995. He has directed various top management programs (e.g. for DaimlerChrysler, Allianz, Yukos) and the Board Program. Currently his main involvement is with Board Programs for the Malaysian Academy of Directors and similar events around the world. He leads IMD's research on Complexity, Corporate Sustainability and Global Corporate Governance. Since 1983 he has served as Chairman, Vice Chairman or Member of (Supervisory) Boards in Germany, Switzerland, and the UK. He was also Member of the Managing Board of Volkswagen. Before that he was a professor at the European Business School in Oestrich-Winkel and a Minister of Economics and Technology in the State of Hesse. He is the author of numerous publications, most recently: *Inside the mind of stakeholders* (2006), *Managing Complexity in Global Organizations* (2007), *Corporate Governance – Concepts and Cases* (forthcoming early 2008).

Oliver Salzmann

Oliver Salzmann is a research associate at IMD. He holds a Master's degree in Industrial Management from Dresden University of Technology and a Ph.D. in Engineering from Berlin University of Technology. Since he joined IMD in 2001, he has conducted empirical research in various areas such as corporate sustainability management, stakeholder relations, and corporate governance.

Executive Summary

Context and research design

Since the mid-nineteenth century, corporate governance rules have always evolved after serious breakdowns in the trust of investors. Financial markets are especially prone to bubbles and when the inevitable burst occurs, the "hangover" leads to government interventions. The individual topics under the aegis of corporate governance change, as do the names of the players involved, but the pattern has remained the same since the modern corporation evolved more than 150 years ago – that is, powerful insiders taking advantage of naive investors for their own financial gain. We owe most of the resulting regulations to efforts that governments have made to restore "investors' confidence" (primarily after stock market turbulences or corporate scandals): accounting rules, external independent certification, stock market listing requirements, reporting, and transparency rules. The "principal–agent" theory provides the underlying conceptual framework for these changes.

The backlash after the 2001 dot-com bubble was extremely powerful. Today, investors are no longer predominately small "retail" shareholders but instead are powerful institutional investors, for example, pension funds or hedge funds with an agenda to be able to look closely into a company without becoming insiders (which would impede their trading ability). For the first time, company boards and their work also became a focus of regulatory intervention. Boards of directors worldwide appointed a majority of independent directors and established independent committees. New responsibilities were added to the boards' rosters (e.g., risk management and control, compensation policy and management performance assessment, corporate responsibility, codes of ethics, board self-assessments). Boards have become more active and involved – they have moved from a "Lap Dog" to a "Watch Dog" style of management supervision.

As the board's workload proliferates – and becomes more elaborate in an effort to meet an increased number of regulatory and capital market requirements – the processes behind the board meetings also become more complex and sophisticated. There has to be someone responsible for "oiling the board machine."

At IMD we have always been interested in the inner workings of the board, its leadership role and the conflicts and dilemmas that it is confronted with. As a result, it was only natural that in 2002 we began to look into the work of those people who keep the board machinery functioning – those primarily referred to as the "company secretary." It is important to be aware, however, that the job was and still is executed under a wide variety of titles. The position's content differs considerably depending upon the country and the company in which the company secretary works. As the importance of these duties grew and the job description broadened, we decided to launch a global research project on the role of the company secretary – a function that is increasingly developing into what we call the "corporate governance officer (CGO)." On the basis of extensive discussions with company secretaries, especially at an IMD Discovery Event in October 2004, we formulated the following key research questions:

- What are the corporate governance drivers and to what extent do they influence the work of the company secretary/CGO in particular?
- What is the profile of such a function (previous job, education, hierarchical position)?
- What is the corporate governance setup with regard to board processes and compositions? What is the job of the company secretary/CGO in terms of responsibility, support structure, activities, and so on?

We conducted 68 in-depth personal interviews mostly in large, global companies and analyzed quantitative data obtained from 330 questionnaires worldwide (for details of the study design and methodology see Chapter 2). In the following paragraphs, we will provide an overview of the main findings.

Corporate governance dynamics and structures

It is not at all surprising that regulation is regarded as the main driver of corporate governance. And there is certainly no lack of new legislation around the world – a lot of it in forms that are "softer" and nontraditional, for example, stock market listing requirements (mentioned as second driver in importance by company secretaries responding to our questionnaire). Public pressure was seen as the least important driver; this may, however, merely reflect a certain short-term view not taking the "history" of many corporate governance laws and regulations into consideration. Public pressure, after all, is very often the trigger for new or more intensive regulations (see Section 3.1 for more detail on this subject).

One important aspect of corporate governance is, of course, the way boards are organized. Whether the company has a one-tier or a two-tier board is a significant factor, even if decision-making processes are shaped primarily by the composition of the board and the working relations between internal and external, independent and executive directors. In all cases, however, the reporting line of the company secretary tells a great deal about his/her position within the organization and the importance attached to the independence of the secretary function. Company secretaries are often highly ranked within the internal hierarchy with more than two-thirds reporting directly to either the chairman or the chief executive officer (CEO). A reporting line to the CEO automatically places more emphasis on the executive side of the company whereas reporting to the chairman, whether executive or not, can be a clear sign of the board's desire to be more independent of management. Supervisory boards in two-tier systems, however, sometimes do not have any dedicated staff support making it difficult, or even impossible, to have a secretary reporting to the external, nonexecutive chairman. This can potentially lessen the board's overall independence.

The relationship between the chairman and other board members, in addition to the overall internal organization of the board, are other key factors when it comes to defining the company secretary's role; they determine how much support the secretary gives to the board as a whole or just to the chairman as an individual. Furthermore, the full board's meeting frequency, in addition to the number of board committees (both of which have gone up in recent years), hold significant importance. Both factors are "multipliers" of the secretary's workload (there are more details about this in Section 3.2).

Background, career opportunities, and challenges for the company secretary

Given their past and current role, it is no surprise that an educational and professional background in legal affairs is the predominant experience for company secretaries. More surprising, nearly half of our respondents were recruited externally to fill a job where confidence is key and networking across the company a must. We can only conclude that in many cases no adequate internal talent existed (probably especially true in smaller companies). The widespread perception of the function being a rather technocratic, legalistic administrator might further reduce the chances for internal recruiting on a high level. Future career advancement also seems to be rather restricted. Few of the secretaries have experience in line management and would therefore not easily find an adequate business function within the company. Moving to another, probably larger, corporation as a company secretary may be a good solution. Owing to the secretary's broad experience in corporate governance, assuming a board seat in other medium-sized companies after early retirement might be a promising and challenging move but it is not yet a common one.

Both job duration and job satisfaction are high for company secretaries; factors which serve as indications of the job's "richness" and importance. It became clear through our interviews and questionnaire responses that the job of the company secretary is often fairly unstructured. There is significant discretion in terms of how to fulfill the task. The interpretation of the role is shaped by the personality of the office holder, how he/she is networking, building relationships, and so on. This should not be surprising because the issues that the secretary has to deal with are generally not the chairman's or the CEO's (to whom they primarily report) favorite topics. The chairmen and CEOs are generally happy to leave the complicated, sometimes boring, but important legal and compliance "stuff" to someone they trust and who will take care of it competently. This paves the way to a pretty influential job ("éminence grise") as long it is done with discretion and tact. Ultimately, of course, the board makes the decisions, not the secretary.

Life can be difficult for the company secretary. In most cases, at least outside of the United States, the roles of chairman and CEO are assumed by two different individuals. Secretaries, however, are often accountable to both the chairman and the CEO. This can result in a variety of demands both in process and in overall job assignments (some of which, of course, are legally mandated). During "normal times" this dual accountability is not a problem but it can become a significant challenge for the secretary in the case of fundamental differences between the chairman and the CEO and/or between the board and management. Loyalty conflicts are the unpleasant result of these situations (see Section 3.3.3 for more about this topic).

Tasks and responsibilities

Both the company secretaries who were interviewed and those who responded to our questionnaire reported having a wide variety of tasks and responsibilities (Chart ES.1).

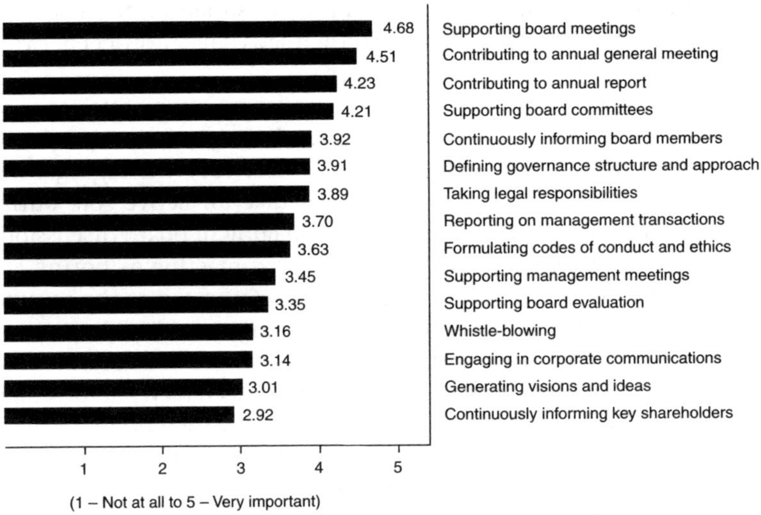

Chart ES.1 Importance of tasks and responsibilities

Providing support to the board of directors is, of course, one of the primary tasks of the company secretary. But the way that support is executed in terms of intensity and priority differs widely. The company secretary is involved in setting the board's agenda to varying degrees. Most secretaries have to ensure that the documents for the board book are ready on time (requiring considerable "herding" efforts). Some set specific criteria for the necessary papers, edit the texts, and/or add additional information (to help the outside directors understand the topic). Other secretaries simply compile the necessary paperwork that has been delivered to them. The only commonality is that electronic distribution of board papers is not widely utilized (it is employed by only 10 percent of respondents).

We know from the results of a previous study that there is significant room for improving board information management (Steger and Amman, 2008). Basically, board information is too often seen from the perspective of a "rear view mirror" and remains internally focused; examining more external and forward-looking information (e.g., regarding competitors, industry trends, and technology dynamics) is desirable. However, few boards take the trouble to clearly define what information they want and need. This can leave management guessing and adding information "organically" as requests come up. Over time, this results in a growing information flood without becoming more helpful to the decision maker. In this type of situation, the company secretary may be able to play an important role as liaison-officer between the chairman/board and CEO/management.

When it comes to board meetings, some company secretaries write "scripts" for the chairman beforehand (including decision proposals) while others just "whisper in his/her ear" if necessary (mostly regarding procedural issues). Only a few secretaries take an active role during meetings, making presentations or even engaging in board discussions. Some regard writing the minutes of the board meeting as boring and routine, happy to delegate it to someone else. Others view the minutes as one of their most important tasks, spending considerable personal time and effort to ensure a systematic follow-up. We also found a similar variety of responses regarding the company secretary's involvement during so-called Executive Sessions (meetings at which no executive is present) and the recording of the results of those meetings.

With respect to the secretaries' activities with board committees, the range of involvement is even broader. Responsibilities range from pure administrative support to clearly defining activities such as the drafting of documents or even the submission of their own proposals. Participation in committee meetings also differs significantly from company to company. On average, involvement is strongest in relation to nominating/corporate governance committees (where secretaries sometimes even actively support the preselection of new external directors) and least intensive in conjunction with compensation committees. When it comes to audit committees, the activities of company secretaries are often rather administrative in nature.

It appears that company secretaries rarely serve as a direct interface to shareholders. But most of them do play a significant role in the Annual General Meeting (AGM). Their involvement ranges from both administrative and technical meeting preparations (including the handling of proxy statements and proxy voting), to acting as the "master of ceremonies" (overseeing internal support staff and backroom experts as well as the external service provider) and being present during the meeting (helping the chairman with the handling of procedures, voting, and other legal issues). As corporate governance experts, many secretaries are responsible for drafting the Annual Report chapters on corporate governance; this includes compensation reporting and also, in part, the coordination of the whole reporting process when it comes to ensuring compliance with legal and regulatory requirements.

In an increasing number of cases, the secretary job is enriched through involvement with compliance activities (which often go beyond legal compliance and include company standards), "whistle-blowing" processes, and certifications required by the Sarbanes-Oxley Act of 2002 (SOX). Other types of involvement can include an active role in supporting the board's self-assessment (however, this is an exception and is generally relegated to data collection and/or shaping the discussion), designing codes of business conduct and ethics and/or specific communication responsibilities.

We found a huge diversity in responses concerning the area of responsibility because in the majority of cases the company secretary's sphere of influence correlates with the company specific situation. For example, the secretary's competence and tasks clearly reflect the influencing factors of personalities, capital markets, exposure and public scrutiny (in listed companies more so than in family business), size or complementary regulation, for example, for the financial services industry where any noncompliance has more serious repercussions than in other industries (for more details on the diversity in tasks and responsibilities see Section 3.3.5).

How have recent developments influenced the job of the company secretary?

Responses to our question about the companies' corporate governance performance relative to peers showed the usual bias in surveys: A large majority of respondents believed that their company's corporate governance is "above average" and that it has also improved significantly over the past two years. It is certainly more interesting to see what changes were reported (see Table ES.1), and then to discuss the impact of these changes on the role of the company secretary.

Table ES.1 Improvements in corporate governance

Which of the following improvements in corporate governance structure and processes have occurred over the last two years in your company? (Mark all that apply)	**% of respondents**
CEO is no longer chairman	12.0
Majority of board members are now independent	27.0
New board committees	47.6
Only independent members now on audit committee	31.5
Company secretary has become more independent	23.2
Code of conduct designed and implemented	60.0
Other	23.2

On the basis of the quantitative and qualitative data collected, we have ascertained the following impact of changes in governance structures and processes on the job of the company secretary:

- Work load and responsibilities for company secretaries (e.g., through additional committees, more meetings, and new responsibilities of the boards) have increased supporting a trend to split the role of company secretary from that of the general counsel/head of legal affairs.
- Company secretaries have become more independent from management as a result of the stronger position of independent directors; this has also strengthened the role of the secretary. More professional and independent information supplied by the company secretary has become a necessity.
- Board members, especially independent directors, request more and more focused support from the secretary; this has led to new and growing responsibilities, as well as different working processes.
- The title "corporate governance officer" has begun to emerge making the job more managerial and attractive – the time for "legal only" and primarily administrative secretaries is over.

Making sense out of the diversity

In general, companies are free to set their own rules and tasks for a company secretary or CGO (aside from some basic legal prescriptions for company secretaries, e.g., in the United Kingdom). This explains the wide variance of roles and responsibilities we have found in our empirical investigation. By stepping back and not getting bogged down with all of the diverging details, we detected a pattern: A typology emerged in practice, depending upon the nature and strategy of the corporation. Four company secretary types differ across two criteria (see Figure ES.1).

1. The organizational positioning in terms of reporting line. The options are either to report to the board or to top management; in practice, the most common case is a reporting line to the chair or to the CEO.
2. The overall level of competence of the company secretary is an overriding factor. The (high or low) level of competence associated with the secretary runs parallel to the importance of the secretary's tasks and is therefore a useful indicator of his/her impact on the governance of the company.

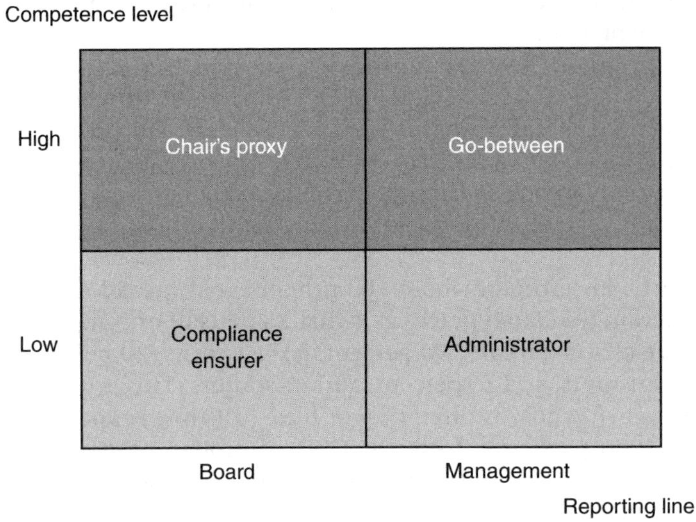

Figure ES.1 Typology of company secretaries

Each type of company secretary has a different basic job description, different tasks, and ultimately a different impact on the company's corporate governance (for a detailed description of the four different types see Chapter 5):

1. Chair's proxy: The "chair's proxy" is a secretary with considerable competence, who reports to the board's chair and functions as his/her "eyes and ears." If the chair is a strong personality, this type of CGO is an influential person, perhaps even an "éminence grise" at the helm of the company.
2. Go-between: With a high competence level the "go-between" reports to top management and is a confidant of the CEO with the additional task of providing top-level support to the board. The go-between's objective is to ensure that the board accepts the proposals from the CEO and the management board. The go-between controls process rather than content.
3. Compliance ensurer: The "compliance ensurer" holds a position with a lower level of competence and reports to the board (mostly to the chair). In general, the compliance ensurer does not control or influence the preparation of board meetings or the processes during the meetings. Instead, this type of secretary responds to individual

requests, for example, from the chair and prepares the requested documentation.

4. Administrator: The "administrator" role does not comprise major competencies and is characterized by a direct reporting line to management. The tasks of this type of secretary are predominantly administrative. "Administrators" are often seconded to the chair's office from among staff members of the corporate legal department and only temporarily delegated to the chair's office.

Roughly, an estimate about the proportional breakdown of each job function (in actual practice) is that 25 percent of company secretaries are chairs' proxies, 40 percent, go-betweens, 20 percent, compliance ensurers, and 15 percent, administrators. This is underscored by the fact that boards often do not have full-time support staff but must rely on personnel from the CEO-controlled headquarters. We conclude overall that today the majority of secretaries have considerable competence, as well as an influential role in their companies. Also, a significant percentage of them report to management. Dynamics in the corporate world are likely to lead to further shifts between the four types of company secretaries. The percentage of compliance ensurers and administrators will most probably drop with their respective job descriptions becoming increasingly comprehensive. Accordingly, more secretaries will be chair's proxies and go-betweens.

A look into the crystal ball

In the future, boards will require even higher levels of support. As a result the role of what has been known as the company secretary in most companies will be elevated in terms of hierarchy and support staff to a full CGO. Owing to the increasing demands on boards, three particularly important challenges surface for the CGO:

1. Improving board information: The CGO must make sure that board information is timely, of high quality and delivered in a useful way. External board members cannot work their way through an exhaustive management report that they may have received only shortly before a board meeting. The CGO might challenge management to provide sound, convincing summaries of such reports which are targeted to the specific needs of external board members; he/she might also write the summaries himself/herself. The tasks of the CGO

might also include providing information from external sources since CEO-influenced sources might be somewhat biased. In the future, the CGO will have to ensure that external directors have direct access to high-level management for collecting additional, supporting information.

2. Managing external and internal compliance: The CGO must make sure that the company complies with external regulations – laws, stock exchange requirements, and rules set by other authorities. It is also the job of the CGO to monitor compliance with internal, that is, self-imposed regulation. Most modern companies have implemented business guidelines, corporate values, and codes of conduct/ethics that they promote extensively to investors and other stakeholders, which makes strict compliance even more important.
3. Managing the governance process: Finally, the CGO will have to ensure efficiency and quality results in the company's governance processes. Board work is becoming more complex and now includes extensive risk management and control efforts. Risks have to be managed and controlled no longer primarily in the financial domain but equally importantly in the fields of tax, legal, technology, and corporate reputation. The CGO must therefore propose effective rules and clear criteria about how the board and its various committees assume their responsibilities in defining and overseeing the company's risks. It is the CGO's responsibility to make certain that the board work remains transparent and that the board members have a shared understanding about the necessary processes.

Standard CGO job description or permanent change?

This leads to a set of "must" tasks for every CGO especially at listed companies:

- Facilitating governance processes: This involves helping the chair set the agenda, not just for individual meetings but also for board work in general. It entails presenting management reports to the board and its committees, as well as ensuring that the board follows established procedures.
- Supporting board and committee meetings: The CGO is responsible for preparing board and committee documents and making sure that they meet directors' needs. Writing the minutes and handling the follow-up after the meetings are key tasks.

- Ensuring compliance: The CGO must propose the framework for ensuring compliance with internal and external rules and regulations applicable to the company. Compliance of the board with best practice standards of corporate governance is a crucial part of this.
- Shareholder management: This entails managing the process for the AGM of shareholders and looking to make sure that shareholders' rights are guaranteed. The drafting of corporate governance reports and proxy statements is part of this engagement.
- Integrating new directors: The CGO facilitates the induction of new, nonexecutive directors into the business and their roles on the board. The CGO also assists with the ongoing training and development of directors.
- Keeping track of changes in the environment: The CGO must be able to read emerging trends in the political and legal environments and provide an early warning to the board and management with regard to any changes that may affect the company, for example, the current debate on social responsibility.

Corporate governance is, of course, not static and pressures will continue to shape and change the role of the CGO. As companies continue to grow and globalize they also become more complex, confronting the CGO with even-more demanding responsibilities. Legal expertise will certainly continue to be helpful but mastering the complex processes within a company's supreme corporate bodies requires different and much broader skills. Today's job description for the company secretary may no longer be adequate for the challenges companies will be facing tomorrow.

Therefore, CGOs must be forward-looking and should have flexible mindsets. Governance plays an increasing role in a company's success – debates about how to manage companies will be more animated, even heated, in the future. Conflicts between the chairman and CEO and between board and management are no longer the exceptional cases they were in the past; the CGOs will more often find themselves involved in such conflicts. Reporting lines and the independence of CGOs may also become a topic over time. Successfully managing the corporate governance processes of the company – a crucial precondition for companies' compliance with legal and regulatory requirements and the continuous adaptation to upcoming trends – is only possible if the CGO is adequately positioned within the organization. He/she must have a broad set of professional and ethical skills, be well integrated in the entire firm and respected as the person able to lead the board to successful structures and working methods. It is not a result of he/she wanting to play a more "political" role; it is an effect of the development of the CGO role that we have described. In light of this evolution, are today's company secretaries ready for these tough choices and challenges? (For more details see Chapter 5.)

1
The Evolution of Modern Corporate Governance

The roots of corporate governance go back to the emergence of capitalism and modern stock corporations, the rise of world trade and the big multinational companies that grew up during the "Industrial Revolution" in the early nineteenth century. The discussion about good and bad corporate governance has been ongoing for many years (under a variety of monikers) and has culminated during various crises – most importantly the bursting of speculative "bubbles" which have occurred since 1852 (for more details see Steger and Amann, 2008). External auditing practices and rules on published balance sheets – everything we consider standard procedure today – are a result of these dynamics. The emergence of, and current responsibilities attributed to, the "Company Secretary" is no exception.

The company secretary's first legally prescribed role originated in the United Kingdom in 1948; the United States and other countries with Anglo-Saxon legal systems followed thereafter. The detailed legal administrative tasks associated with corporate law or stock exchange regulations provided only a basic framework for the job description compared to how it functions today. Job titles and descriptions are numerous and vary depending upon each country and its traditions, overall corporate structure, and hierarchy. This is a clear reflection of the discrimination each company exhibits in determining how it organizes and supports the work of its board.

Although legislation regarding corporate governance can differ considerably, for example, the classical one-tier (board) versus two-tier (board and management) governance systems, the legal framework has only a small influence on how boards actually work. It is widely accepted, nevertheless, that the origins of corporate governance go back to the United States with the early emergence of its capital markets, growing stock corporations, and economic significance. For better or worse, it is, and continues to be, the world's leading economy and not, of course, just in the area of corporate governance.

Of paramount importance is the "Principal–Agent Theory" which dates back to the classic research of Berle and Means[1] on the separation of ownership and control in stock corporations. Managers steer the company although owners (i.e., shareholders) ultimately should have the control over their assets; ideally, corporate managers should be working on behalf of shareholders. However, as global companies emerged and grew in terms of revenues and employees, and as their subsidiaries were established around the world, organizations became more complex as did corporate governance. When it became increasingly difficult to control a global company's operations and govern its management, company owners began to worry about the separation of ownership and control. Analyzing this dilemma led Berle and Means to assume that the fiduciary management system, having to be accountable to the shareholders, was inadequate and would cause inefficiencies.

Whereas the basic corporate governance problems were the same in all growing economies, the exploitation of owners by managers was far more prevalent in the United States. As the economy grew considerably in the first half of the twentieth century, business units became larger and more global. The vast majority of shareholders were interested in investing and not in exercising control over a company – ownership became dispersed. As a result, shareholder control diminished and few individual shareholders had sufficient stakes to influence the composition of supervisory or management boards. The reasons for the early emergence of this dilemma and its serious nature in the United States, rather than in other parts of the world, were that large firms in Northern Europe and Asia, for example, were controlled primarily by just a few wealthy families or major investors. In addition, financial needs were satisfied with bank loans rather than through issuing securities on equity markets.

A relatively lax corporate law system led to simple and, for the most part, effective corporate governance systems located within the top executive office suite. The Chief Executive Officer (CEO) usually also chaired the board, managing both the company and running the board. This type of CEO-centered governance system allowed for quick and nearly unrestricted decisions. The board rarely contradicted the CEO, and it had little impact on the company's trajectory. As cynics have argued, a typical US board at that time consisted of the CEO, his five friends from the golf club, a woman, and an Afro-American. Electing other board members was only possible through a lengthy, costly, and risky proxy process. In most annual meetings, the chair (which means the CEO) was not even challenged regarding the appointment of new board members.

Short of a full-blown shareholder revolution, which rarely happened, the board was often a self-perpetuating body to rubberstamp CEO decisions. When it came to the control of management, the US system put their trust in the market rather than in the board. If a company was poorly managed, the prevailing thought was that the declining share price would provide investors with the opportunity to buy the company inexpensively and subsequently remove the ineffective management. The argument was therefore that CEOs would work on behalf of shareholders, allocating business resources to optimize their use and reach the ultimate goal of increasing shareholder value. This "market for corporate control" was one of the drivers for subsequent merger and acquisition waves and frequent hostile takeovers.

The emergence of institutional investors did not have much impact on this pattern until 2000. Although pension funds considerably raised the financial stakes in big companies, most institutional investors assumed the role of "outsiders looking in." When performance problems arose, investors quickly adapted their portfolios by divesting, regardless of good or bad governance. Later on hedge funds became more powerful but their interests were also focused on financial gains rather than optimizing the corporate governance system. Both types of investors avoided becoming "insiders" because it would have meant being distracted from their actual business of trading. Generally, these investors were not represented on the board or involved in the formal control of management. If their interests were not considered, however, lengthy and costly proxy fights could occur. Furthermore, as long as share prices were moving in the right direction no one objected and CEO salaries multiplied tenfold, mostly through generous stock options. Certainly, in this regard one of the most prominent cases is The Walt Disney Company's CEO, Michael Eisner. In 1998 he was paid USD 590 million, making him one of the highest paid executives in corporate history.

1.1 The corporate governance earthquake and where we stand today

The dramatic failures of the dot-coms during 2000 and 2001 are a certain confirmation of the saying "recession reveals what the auditors didn't." In addition to a series of high-profile corporate bankruptcies, many of them resulting in criminal charges, there was also a broad range of misconduct and unethical behavior which extended to some of the icons of the US economy.

These events, added to tensions that had been building around ownership and control over the years, were more than unacceptable; the result was that stakeholder groups called for radical changes in corporate governance. This caused a corporate governance earthquake – a dramatic shift in the way corporate governance was viewed and carried out in America. The consequences of this earthquake were most severe and apparent in the United States – the Sarbanes-Oxley Act (SOX) was quickly pushed through Congress in 2002. The legislation changed accounting, corporate law, and stock market regulations considerably and ultimately the face of corporate governance. In 2003 and 2004 alone more than half of the S&P 500 firms had to restate their earnings and many managers were required to testify in the subsequent criminal investigations. The prosecution hit its peak when former WorldCom CEO Bernard Ebbers was sentenced to 25 years in prison in July 2005.

Institutional investors in the United States then discovered that they could use corporate governance to improve corporate transparency and install independent directors as their proxies. Powerful new audit committees, made up solely of independent directors, were set up to scrutinize top management and the organization's every financial detail. Independent directors also often held all the seats on the compensation and nomination committees.

Against strong CEO opposition, investors demanded that the job of chairman and CEO be split (a change which is still far from being completed in the United States). As an intermediate step, a "lead director" would often organize the work of independent directors on the board and limit the power of the chairman-CEO. Less than three years after the corporate crises commenced, one-third of the companies in the United States had split the position of chairman and CEO.[2] This brought US corporate governance closer to the European checks and balances system that had been deemed more appropriate for big companies.

Europe already had many checks and balances in place, for example, the classic German supervisory boards that were mainly in charge of scrutinizing top management. In most of Northern Europe, one-tier systems were supported by appointing a mandatory nonexecutive chairman. In the United Kingdom and Ireland, the majority of board members had to be nonexecutive. Europe also had its share of corporate crises (e.g., Parmalat), however, even though they were less significant than those in the United States. The orientation of checks and balances within its governance systems, in addition to a greater involvement of banks, prevented scenarios from being worse. Nevertheless, Europe and other major economic players followed the United States by enhancing their rules and regulations. Blue ribbon panels flourished and documented best practices in codes of conduct. The basic idea was to "comply or explain" – there was no more room for corporations to ignore or oppose emotionally charged issues such as the transparency of management remuneration.

The enormous changes in corporate governance have affected all positions within the top echelon of companies but none more so than the board of directors. With legal empowerment, boards were assigned stronger competencies and new tasks, significantly increasing the board's importance.

Companies were forced to reconsider and rework the way they were dealing with corporate governance. The task of understanding, and complying with, all of the new regulations became more intricate; companies had to invest in new competencies and resources. They learned in the wake of the corporate disasters that investors, employees, and consumers would reward them if they exhibited superior corporate governance, resulting in enhanced reputations and stock market valuations. To tap into this opportunity, companies began to create the position of a "corporate governance officer." In doing so, the scope of work and competencies of former company secretaries were enhanced, many of whom already had responsibilities in a lot of the fields that began to emerge as mandatory for modern companies. In addition, the company secretaries became most closely linked with the critical core of corporate governance – the supervisory and the management boards.

Prior to the corporate governance earthquake, the roles and responsibilities of the company secretary had varied widely. In most companies, however, the company secretary had already assumed a vital role in the day-to-day governance at the company's helm by being a close personal confidant and indispensable aid to the chairman of the supervisory board. In several, mainly Anglo-Saxon, countries the company secretary also had considerable responsibility as a result of specific company secretary legislation prescribing a minimum scope of aims and duties.

It is widely considered that the position of the UK company secretary is the most obvious starting point in a discussion about the officer in charge of corporate governance and its regulations.

1.2 The role of the company secretary

Great Britain – forerunner in codification

The United Kingdom has been the leader in developing and codifying the role of the company secretary and it continues to play a leading role today. In 1948 the Companies Act, which first mentioned and defined the position, was passed – the company secretary was given an officer-level position in the company. Today other countries, particularly those with Anglo-Saxon legal systems (e.g., United States and India), also legally mandate that there be a company secretary position.

The UK Companies Act of 1985[3] mandates that the board appoint a company secretary in all UK companies. The position of the company secretary is, along with that of a director that runs the company's day-to-day business, the only obligatory function. Combining both offices is allowed only if there is more than one director running the company. Also, there may be more than one person running the company secretary's office in a so-called joint secretaries' office. Because the company secretary is positioned as an officer in the company, he/she may be held personally responsible for not complying with the Companies Act, the corporate articles of association, or any other regulation the company is subject to. This may also extend to a criminal liability.

The UK Companies Act does not provide a comprehensive overview of the tasks and responsibilities of a company secretary. Since management responsibility is reserved for directors, there is an initial assumption that the company secretary's basic tasks are administrative. In practical UK business life, however, the company secretary's role is usually enhanced by an additional employment contract – a strengthening of the company secretary's role widely perceived as resulting from this regulation (several other sections in the UK Companies Act and other acts mention tasks a company secretary "may" also have). Generally these assignments extend to keeping the company's records (including transfer of share ownership and issuing of share certificates), the register of members, the register of charges, the directors' meetings and shareholder assembly minutes, and their provision at the request of auditors or shareholders.

Depending upon the size and nature of the company, the company secretary's responsibilities in most companies usually involve the actual writing (not setting) of directors' meeting agendas, sending them out, compiling meeting minutes, and keeping statutory company documents. In addition, he/she might be responsible for a wide variety of other tasks that may be further detailed in the company's articles of association or the above-mentioned employment contract.

The position of the company secretary in a public (rather than private) company (PLC) is subject to additional requirements: The directors must make certain the company secretary has the necessary knowledge and experience and is properly qualified. Proper qualifications are assumed when the person is, for example, a member of the Institute of Chartered Accountants or the Institute of Chartered Secretaries and Administrators (ICSA).[4] The UK's Combined Code of Corporate Governance[5] of 2006 – to which compliance is a prerequisite for being listed on the London Stock Exchange – states:

> All directors should have access to the advice and services of the company secretary who is responsible to the board for ensuring that board procedures are complied with. Both the appointment and removal of the company secretary should be a matter for the board as a whole.

The Code also describes as one of its principles that the company secretary, under the direction of the chairman, should be responsible for ensuring good information flows within the board and its committees and between senior management and nonexecutive directors, as well as facilitating induction and assisting with professional development as required. The company secretary should also be responsible for advising the board through the chairman on all governance matters.

Rather surprisingly, given the ever-increasing importance of corporate governance, a legislative project is currently under discussion in the United Kingdom aimed at easing the rules for the organization of companies by eliminating the mandatory secretary function in private companies. This change, although possibly advantageous to smaller companies, may well have an impact on the general understanding of the secretary's position. In the future there may be companies in the United Kingdom who no longer have a secretary who is an "authorized signatory."

Codification in other countries

Although US corporate secretaries exercise quite significant influence in general, the US codes on corporate governance explain very little about this function. Most US state company laws, however, mandate the appointment of a "secretary" with a number of corporate responsibilities but provide no details about the job description. Their definition is the responsibility of individual companies. Switzerland is another country where the company law requests the appointment of a "secretary to the board of directors" but again without saying anything about the responsibilities of this function.

We find some more specific mentions of the "secretary" in the corporate governance codes of Australia and some European countries. The Australian Code[6] states:

> The company secretary plays an important role in supporting the effectiveness of the board by monitoring that board policy and procedures are followed and coordinating the timely completion and dispatch of board agenda and briefing material.
>
> It is important that all directors have access to the company secretary.
>
> The appointment and removal of the company secretary should be a matter for decision by the board as a whole.
>
> The company secretary should be accountable to the board, through the chair, on all governance matters.

The Dutch Corporate Governance Code[7] provides a similar description of the responsibilities of the company secretary. The role of the secretary, with regard to assisting the chairman in the actual organization of the affairs of the supervisory board, is further defined as "information, agenda, evaluation, training programs etc." Although the secretary's role is clearly defined as "assisting the chairman of the supervisory board," the Code provides that the secretary be appointed and dismissed by the management board but only after the approval of the supervisory board has been obtained.

Fairly detailed provisions about the role of the company secretary are contained in the Spanish Principles of Good Corporate Governance issued by the Institute of Directors-Administrators and the Spanish Unified Code on Good Corporate Governance.[8] The secretary has a responsibility of his/her own in conjunction to a number of compliance issues. He/she has to ensure that the board's actions

- Adhere to the spirit and letter of laws and their implementing regulations, including those issued by regulatory agencies.
- Comply with the company bylaws and the regulations of the general shareholders meeting, the board of directors and others.
- Are informed by the good governance recommendations of this Unified Code and adhere to the letter and spirit of those accepted by the company.

In order to safeguard the independence, impartiality, and professionalism of the secretary, his/her appointment and removal must be proposed by the nomination committee of the board and approved in a full-board meeting.

The most comprehensive codification of the company secretary's responsibilities is most likely in the Russian Code of Corporate Conduct of 2002.[9] It contains numerous provisions that define the role of the secretary including the tasks of preparing for and holding shareholders meetings, preparing for and holding board of directors meetings, and guaranteeing the disclosure of information about the company and the maintenance of corporate records. The Russian Code also mandates that the secretary ensure that the company give due consideration to shareholder petitions and the resolution of conflicts arising out of shareholder rights violations, as well as making him/her accountable for notifying the chairman of all corporate procedure violations. Given this range of duties, it is not surprising that the Code requests that the secretary be vested with sufficient authority and have a broad knowledge to perform properly within the function. The Code even suggests that the secretary should not be charged with any other functions within the company but be able to devote all his/her energy to ensure strict compliance.

The requirements cited above are not conclusive for all companies. But it is evident that the company secretary function can have significant influence within the realm of company leadership. Their responsibility can clearly reach beyond ensuring compliance with all corporate-governance-related regulations. From a business point of view, he/she may also be a facilitator of governance processes at the company's helm and act as one of the links to shareholders and external stakeholders. Nevertheless, surprisingly little is known about this position throughout the corporate world.

1.3 Overview of recent research and literature

An initial look at studies available in this area quickly revealed a significant research gap. Obviously, we found a sizeable body of literature on corporate governance. Various studies focused on individual areas such as

- The role and duty of boards and the directors
- Board information
- Board conflicts

- Executive compensation
- Whistle-blowing and
- Codes of conduct

We also saw an increase in research since the beginning of 2000 primarily reflecting renewed interest in the subject (often by country and region) after the big corporate governance scandals. However, the studies clearly ignored (or at least lacked a specific focus on) the role of the company secretary.

Only a very few contributions – including handbooks and manuals – actually focused on the role and tasks of the company secretary or related positions such as the general counsel, for example,

- Siekmann (2003) discusses the contribution the general counsel can make to corporate governance and board support.[10]
- Smith (2000) similarly outlines a more evolved role of the corporate secretary in the United States.[11]
- Lamm (2003) elaborates on the emergence of what he calls the corporate governance officer, his/her responsibilities, and impacts on the business culture.[12]
- Gangl (2006) focuses on the potential harm of backdate stock option grants for corporate secretaries.[13]

All these contributions are highly valuable, although they are

- Based on the author's professional experience rather than a comprehensive empirical survey.
- Limited to one country or region and thus do not provide any comparison across different corporate governance regimes and types of companies (e.g., in terms of ownership, board structure, listed versus nonlisted).
- Unable, by design, to provide further depth and breadth with regard to the background and the tasks of company secretaries as well as explanation (e.g., for certain commonalities and differences across corporate governance regimes).

The field of corporate governance simply lacks a comprehensive empirical study on the company secretary including his/her background and profile, tasks and responsibilities, and expert views on the key challenges of corporate governance as well as how they can be met. We set out to fill this void with this study.

1.4 Roadmap through this book

In this section, we provide a brief overview of the book's structure and content (see Figure 1.1). An essential context to our study was presented in this chapter. Section 1.1 included a brief analysis of the current significance of corporate governance and the reasons behind it (e.g., the burst of the dot-com bubble, the increasing importance of shareholder activist groups). In Section 1.2 we outlined the emergence and role of the company secretaries across a variety of countries and corporate governance regimes. Section 1.3 provided an overview of related studies and literature and points to a significant research gap.

Chapter 2 features a comprehensive description of our study design. We outline the study's scope and framework in Section 2.1, our method in Section 2.2, and our samples (both with regard to our interviews and the self-completion questionnaire) in Section 2.3, respectively.

In Chapter 3 we present our descriptive evidence. We start with corporate governance drivers (regulation, stock markets, and public pressure) in Section 3.1. In Section 3.2 we discuss the significance and characteristics of the board – as the company's supreme governance body. This includes an analysis of board composition and board work (e.g., board committees).

Section 3.3 features our key findings regarding the company secretary in particular:

- His/her career (see Section 3.3.1), that is, educational and professional background, job duration, and future career opportunities.
- Reporting lines and discretion (see Section 3.3.2), that is, to what individuals or departments the secretary reports and how much freedom he/she has at his/her job.
- Working relationship and allegiance (see Section 3.3.3), that is, for what individuals or function the secretary primarily works and to whom he/she is accountable. Furthermore, we discuss potential loyalty conflicts and with whom the secretary' s allegiance lies.
- Resources (see Section 3.3.4), primarily the secretary's staff support.
- Tasks and responsibilities (see Section 3.3.5). We highlight and discuss key tasks in various areas such as board and management support, committee work, corporate governance and shareholders, and so on.

In Section 3.4 we outline key trends we came across in our data, namely developments in corporate governance (see Section 3.4.1) and how they affect the role of the company secretary (see Section 3.4.2).

1 The Evolution of Modern Corporate Governance

1.1 The corporate governance earthquake
1.2 The role of the company secretary
1.3 Overview of recent research and literature
1.4 Roadmap through the book

2 Study Design

2.1 Scope and framework
2.2 Method
2.3 Samples
  2.3.1 Interviews
  2.3.2 Self-completion questionnaires

3 Descriptive Evidence

3.1 Drivers for corporate governance
  3.1.1 Regulation
  3.1.2 Stock markets
  3.1.3 Public pressure
3.2 Organization of the board
  3.2.1 Board characteristics and composition
  3.2.2 Executive and nonexecutive chairmen
  3.2.3 Executive and independent board members
  3.2.4 Internal organization
3.3 The Company secretary
  3.3.1 Career
  3.3.2 Reporting lines and discretion
  3.3.3 Working relationship and allegiance
  3.3.4 Resources
  3.3.5 Tasks and responsibilities
3.4 A look at recent developments
  3.4.1 Changes in companies' corporate governance
  3.4.2 Effects on the role of the company secretary

4 Analyzing Causal Effects

4.1 Which factors determine how the company secretary views his/her setting?
4.2 Which factors shape the secretary's tasks and responsibilities?
4.3 Which factors influence corporate governance performance?

5 Conclusion – Where Are We Heading?

5.1 Future dynamics of the corporate governance officer
  5.1.1 Board information improvements
  5.1.2 External and internal compliance management
  5.1.3 The governance process manager
5.2 Where shall we go? What has to be done?

Figure 1.1 Book structure

In Chapter 4 we analyze causal effects to determine which factors influence the working environment of the company secretary (see Section 4.1), which affect his/her tasks and responsibilities (Section 4.2), and which influence governance performance (see Section 4.3).

We conclude this book in Chapter 5 by synthesizing our findings and providing an outlook for the future challenges and roles of the company secretary.

Notes

1. A. Berle and G. Means, *The Modern Corporation and Private Property* (New York: McMillan, 1932).
2. Robert F. Felton and Simon C.Y. Wong, "How to Separate the Roles of Chairman and CEO" *McKinsey Quarterly*, Iss. 4 (2004) 58–69.
3. *Companies Act of 1985:* General positioning of the secretary (section 744), personal union of director and company secretary position (section 283), appointment of several company secretaries (section 290), additional requirements for PLCs (section 286).
4. The ICSA also provides specimen job descriptions for the corporate governance role of the company secretary (see also Additional References).
5. The *Combined Code of Corporate Governance* is the written and codified combination of the corporate governance recommendations of three UK investigative corporate governance committees – Cadbury (1992), Greenbury (1995), and Hampel (1998). The Combined Code was established by all UK stock exchanges as mandatory, beginning in 1998 and updated last in 2006. Mandatory compliance means there is a "comply or explain" rule leading to a factual "comply" requirement for all companies since most competitors comply as well.
6. *Revised Corporate Governance Principles and Recommendations (Australia) of 2007*, issued by ASX Corporate Governance Council.
7. The *Dutch Corporate Governance Code* (The Tabaksblat Code) of 2003, issued by the Corporate Governance Committee.
8. *Principles of Good Corporate Governance of 2004*, issued by Instituto de Consejeros-Administradores (Spain) and the *Draft Unified Code of Recommendations for the Good Governance of 2006*, issued by Comision Nacional del Mercado de Valores (CNMV).
9. *The Russian Code of Corporate Conduct of 2002*, issued by the Co-ordination Council for Corporate Governance.
10. Thomas C. Siekmann, "The General Counsel: Invaluable Resource for Boards" *Directorship*, Vol. 29, Iss. 4 (April 2003) 12–15.
11. David W. Smith, "The Case for a Chief Governance Officer" *Insights: The Corporate & Securities Law Advisor*, Vol. 14, Iss. 6 (June 2000) 2–3.
12. Robert B. Lamm, "The Emergence of the Corporate Governance Officer" *Investment Guides Series: Corporate Governance* (Fall 2003) 86–89.
13. Walter T. Gangl, "Back-Dated Options = Back-Dated Minutes" *Corporate Governance Advisor*, Vol. 14, Iss. 5 (September/October 2006) 21–23.

2
Study Design

In this chapter we will outline the design and methods of the study in more detail. In Section 2.1 we will present (1) the framework and (2) our research questions and subsequently in Section 2.2 we will shed light on to our methodology, that is, our means of data collection (direct interviews, self-completion questionnaires) and analysis (content analysis and statistical techniques). Finally in Section 2.3 we will describe our sample across a variety of characteristics such as industries covered, the location of headquarters, listings, and so on.

2.1 Scope and framework

Our aim is to provide a reasonably comprehensive picture of corporate governance, in general, and to provide a detailed analysis of the company secretary in particular: This has resulted in focusing on four key concepts (see Figure 2.1):

- Drivers of corporate governance: What factors influence or drive corporate governance, for example, regulation, listings, public pressure?
- Profile of the company secretary: What are his/her roles prior to the engagement as a company secretary? What is his/her educational/ professional background?
- Companies' corporate governance setup: What is the general setup with regards to board processes and composition? How are companies set up in terms of activities, responsibilities, authorities, support structure, career opportunities, and so on, of their company secretaries?
- Corporate governance performance: How has corporate governance evolved over recent years? Which specific improvements were made and why? And what was the impact on the role of the secretary?

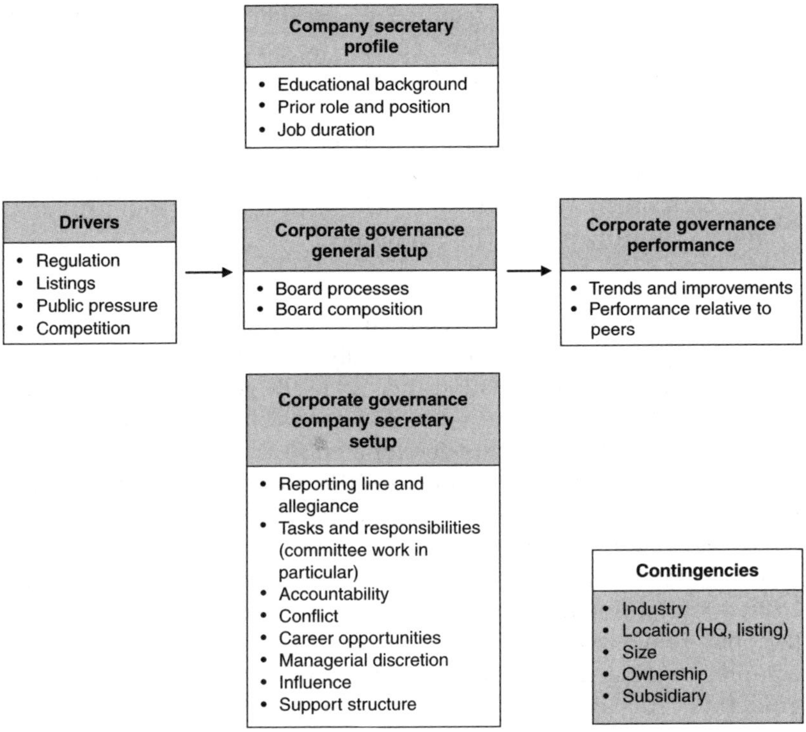

Figure 2.1 Conceptual framework

The concepts are likely to be contingent on a variety of factors such as the location of headquarters and listings (since they determine regulation), the company size, ownership, and so on. Hence we designed the study, and the questionnaire in particular, so that we could detect and control for such so-called contingencies (for more detail, also refer to Section 2.3 and Chapter 3).

2.2 Method

We employed a mixed method design based on personal semistructured interviews and self-completion questionnaires. This method allowed us to

- Collect data that complement each other: Whereas the questionnaires guarantee the breadth of the study (primarily due to large samples) which is also required to provide insight into the key contingencies, the interviews ensure the necessary depth and provides us the opportunity to discuss causal relationships, key events, and outcomes.

- Benchmark findings against one another: Are findings obtained from the interviews and questionnaires congruent or do they contradict each other? We can then check the plausibility of our findings and successfully triangulate our results.

Interviews

The interviews were semistructured (see interview guide in the Appendix) giving the interviewer the ability to probe and search for rich and compelling information and, as a result, get an in-depth picture of the role of the company secretaries – responsibilities, impact on board work, challenges facing future developments.

Between November 2005 and June 2007 we conducted 68 personal interviews with company secretaries, assistant secretaries, general counsels, and other persons performing the secretary function, working mainly at listed international companies in Europe and the United States. A majority of the interviews were conducted face-to-face but some were conducted over the telephone and two were completed via a detailed questionnaire based upon the interview guideline. The interview write-ups were done both manually and with automatic coding. We employed the software Nvivo to produce coding reports by section, thus ensuring both a structured and quick approach to content analysis.

Self-completion questionnaires

The questionnaires (see Appendix) were distributed and collected by mail, largely sent out in June 2006. The following sets of addresses were bought from commercial providers and sent to the individual regions (see Table 2.1):

Table 2.1 Distribution of geographical regions targeted

Geographical region	Number of questionnaires sent
Europe	3,000
United States	3,000
Asia	2,000
Rest of the world	500
Total	8,500

We received a total of 334 completed questionnaires that corresponds to a response rate of roughly 4 percent. A comprehensive outlier analysis revealed that only few variables had outliers (with a standard score of more than four); for those variables outliers were not implausible, for example, job duration, number of supporting staff, and company size (number of employees, market capitalization, and total assets). We also carried out a missing value analysis and concluded that missing values occurred at random.

For two reasons, we dropped several cases from the sample:

- Small company size: Small companies are unlikely to employ an individual who is involved in corporate governance at a reasonable level. We removed 24 observations in which the company size reported by the respondents was below 500 employees.
- High number of missing values: We also dropped an additional three observations since their share of missing values exceeded 20 percent of the total number of variables which cast doubt on respondents' willingness and/or ability to respond to the questionnaire.

We tested the interval variables for non-normality through a combined skewness and kurtosis test. Out of 41 variables, 24 were significantly non-normal in skewness and kurtosis. Non-normal distribution can be resolved through the transformation of variables. We refrained, however, from doing so since (1) statistical techniques applied (t-tests and regression) are rather robust against violation of the normal distribution requirement and (2) variable transformation also has several weaknesses.

We employed several techniques to analyze the observations retained.

- One-way ANOVAs to compare interval variables across the contingencies, that is, whether there were any statistically significant differences across industries, company sizes, and so on.
- Chi-square tests to compare categorical variables (again across the contingencies).
- Multiple linear regression to analyze potential causal relationships between variables.

In general, we report results that are statistically significant at a 0.05 level or higher.

2.3 Samples

In this section, we provide more detail on the samples (interviews and self-completion questionnaire) of our survey.

2.3.1 Interviews

Company or corporate secretaries, assistant secretaries, general counsel, chief governance officers, and heads of the CEO's or chairman's office at the companies shown in Table 2.2 in Western Europe and the United States agreed to provide an in-depth look into their activities. The interviews were primarily held in face-to-face meetings; some of them were conducted over the telephone. Two respondents filled in a special questionnaire (designed after the interview guide). We greatly acknowledge the contribution of all the participants to this study.

The characteristics of the interview sample are described in the following paragraphs.

Industry

The industries covered by our interviews are shown in Table 2.3.

Location of headquarters

The number of countries covered was restricted due, in part, to practical considerations/convenience (see Table 2.4). However, the seven countries where interviews were conducted are host to an extraordinarily big number of large, international companies. The countries included – United States of America, Germany, France, United Kingdom, Netherlands, Switzerland, and Italy – make up for 87 percent of the top 30, 77 percent of the top 100, and 70 percent of the "Global Fortune 500" companies (published in *Fortune*, Europe Edition, Vol. 156, Iss. 2, July 23, 2007). The only other countries hosting a significant number of large companies, but not included in our interviews, would have been Japan (12 percent), China (4 percent), and South Korea (2 percent).

Our interviews covered 14 of the top 30, 31 of the top 100, and 53 of the Fortune 500 companies.

Size

The smallest company covered reported 3,900 employees, the largest one 460,000. Of the companies interviewed, 7 percent have less than 10,000 employees, 20 percent between 20,000 and 50,000, 35 percent between 50,000 and 100,000, 26 percent between 100,000 and 200,000, 6 percent between 200,000 and 300,000, and 6 percent more than 300,000.

Table 2.2 Interview sample – companies represented

Country	Companies that contributed through personal interviews with their company secretaries
France	– Alcatel – Assurance Générale de France (AGF) – Bouygues – Compagnie Générale de Géophysique – France Télécom – Groupe Danone – Renault SA – Société Générale – Total SA – Veolia Environment
Germany	– Allianz SE – BASF Aktiengesellschaft – Bayerische Motoren Werke AG (BMW) – Commerzbank AG – DaimlerChrysler AG – Deutsche Bank AG – Deutsche Telekom AG – Dresdner Bank AG – E.On AG – SAP AG – Siemens AG – Volkswagen AG
Italy	– Eni SpA – Fiat SpA – Intesa Sanpaolo SpA
Netherlands	– ABN AMRO Holding NV – Aegon NV – ING Groep NV – Rabobank Nederland – Royal DSM NV – Unilever NV
Switzerland	– Credit Suisse Group – Firmenich SA – Holcim AG – Nestlé SA – Novartis AG – Roche Holding AG – Schindler Holding Ltd. – Swiss Life Holding – Swiss Re – Tetra Laval International SA – UBS AG – Zurich Financial Services

Continued

Table 2.2 Continued

UK	– Anglo American plc – AstraZeneca plc – Barclays plc – BP plc – British American Tobacco plc – BT Group plc – Cadbury Schwepps plc – GlaxoSmithKline – HSBC Holdings plc – Prudential plc – Royal Dutch Shell plc – Smiths Group plc – Vodafone Group plc
USA	– Altria Group, Inc. – American Express Company – Avon Products, Inc. – Bank of America Corporation – Chevron Corporation – Ensco International Incorporated – General Electric Company – Johnson & Johnson – Microsoft Corporation – Pfizer Inc. – The Procter & Gamble Co. – Unisys Corporation

Table 2.3 Sample distribution (interviews) – industries

Industry	Number and percentage share of companies	
	Number	**%**
Industrial products	3	4.4
Energy/oil and gas	7	10.3
Pharmaceutical/healthcare	6	8.8
Automotive	5	7.5
Technology/telecommunication	10	14.7
Financial services	20	29.4
Food & beverage	3	4.4
Chemical	2	2.9
Multiple industries/diversified holdings	3	4.4
Others	9	13.2

Table 2.4 Sample distribution (interviews) – location of headquarters

Country	Number and percentage share of companies	
	Number	%
France	10	14.7
Germany	12	17.7
Italy	3	4.4
Netherlands	6	8.8
Switzerland	12	17.6
United Kingdom	13	19.1
United States	12	17.7

As to market capitalization, the companies covered by our personal interviews are on the upper end of the scale: 82 percent are among the FT Global 500 (data as of March 30, 2007). The largest company interviewed had a market value of USD 363.6 billion, the smallest one, USD 3.2 billion. Of the companies, 13 percent are valued at less than USD 25 billion, 25 percent between 25 and 50 billion, 33 percent between 50 and 100 billion, 20 percent between 100 and 200 billion, 8 percent between 200 and 300 billion, and one company at more than USD 300 billion; only two companies worldwide are above USD 300 billion, both are American. Four companies interviewed are not listed.

Looking at revenues and profits, 31 of the companies interviewed are among the top 100 of the "Fortune 500," and 22 are among the top 100 as to assets.

Listings

Only four of the companies interviewed (6 percent) are not listed (two are family-owned, one is a 100 percent subsidiary, and one is organized in the form of a cooperative). London and Frankfurt are the primary listing for 19 percent of the companies, the New York Stock Exchange (NYSE) for 16 percent, Paris for 15 percent, and Zurich for 13 percent. Twelve percent have other primary listings (Amsterdam, Milan). Half of the companies have a secondary listing in New York (often for their American Depositary Receipts – ADRs), about one-third are additionally listed in London, and many companies are listed on a large number of stock exchanges including Tokyo, various national (mostly European) exchanges, and regional exchanges in the companies' domestic markets.

Ownership structure

Given the chosen sample for the personal interviews, a huge majority of the companies have a dispersed ownership, some of them with hundreds of thousands of shareholders. Only a few companies report significant/dominant private shareholders or an important government stake in their capital; two companies are family-owned and two are strongly or fully dominated by their parent.

2.3.2 Self-completion questionnaires

In this section we will describe our questionnaire sample in greater detail.

Industry

Overall, our respondents are scattered across a large variety of industries as the substantial share of other industries (29 percent) illustrates. Financial services (23 percent) lead the sample. Roughly 7 percent of our respondents are active in multiple industries (see Chart 2.1).

Headquarters and listings

As Chart 2.2 illustrates, the companies that responded are primarily headquartered in Western Europe – accounting for almost 50 percent of all responding companies if the UK respondents are included. The sample is dominated (in terms of countries) by UK- and US-headquartered

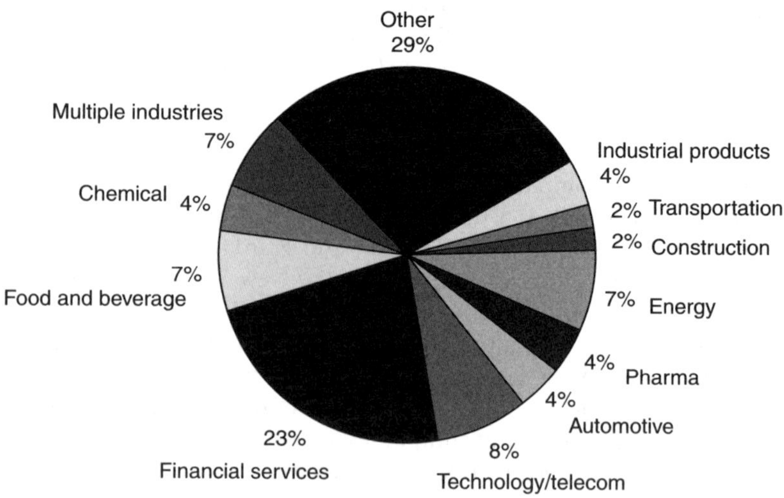

Chart 2.1 Sample distribution (questionnaires) – industries

firms; 7 percent report a secondary listing at the London Stock Exchange (LSE), 12 percent at National Association of Securities Dealers Automated Quotations system (NASDAQ)/NYSE.

Eighty percent of our study sample are publicly listed companies. It is plausible that, as illustrated by Chart 2.3, the distribution of listings is largely congruent with that of the location of headquarters.

We also discovered a higher share of publicly listed companies among larger corporations, nonsubsidiaries, and companies with dispersed ownership. Finally, we noticed a statistically significant association between headquarters and listings: Companies headquartered in Asia were most frequently listed, followed by those headquartered in the

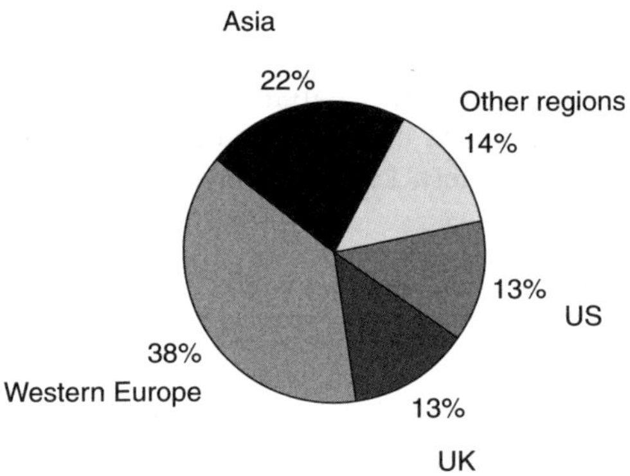

Chart 2.2 Sample distribution (questionnaires) – location of headquarters

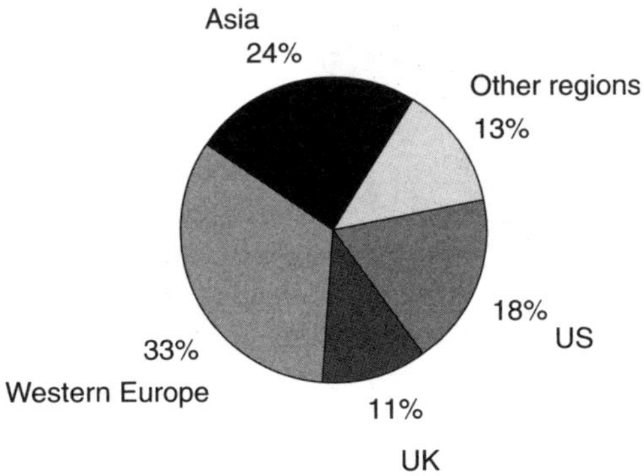

Chart 2.3 Sample distribution (questionnaires) – location of listings

United States, United Kingdom, Western Europe, and Other Regions. This may be due in part to sampling bias. The lower share of listed companies headquartered in Other Regions – mostly emerging economies and developing countries – seems to be plausible.

Size

As Table 2.5 shows, we have an average company size with roughly 18,000 employees. The largest companies belong to the automotive, pharmaceutical, and other industries, the smallest to chemical, energy, and financial industries.

As one would expect, we found that listed companies are larger then nonlisted ones and family businesses smaller than nonfamily ones.

Ownership structure

The majority of our companies have dispersed ownership, roughly one-third have a few, dominant shareholders (see Chart 2.4). Dispersed ownership is most frequent in the United Kingdom and United States and less frequent in Western Europe and Asia. It is also more common

Table 2.5 Sample distribution (questionnaire) – company size

Company size	Mean	Minimum	Maximum
Number of employees	18,000	500	340,000
Market capitalization in USD	43 billion	16,000	49 billion
Total assets in USD	149 billion	186,000	1,7 trillion

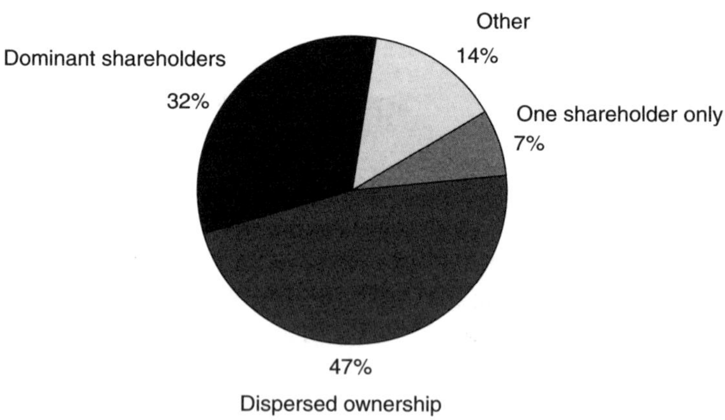

Chart 2.4 Sample distribution (questionnaires) – ownership structure

in listed and larger companies as well as nonsubsidiaries; it is less frequent in family businesses.

Expectedly, the share of companies with few dominant shareholders is higher in family businesses and subsidiaries. It also varies across the listings – more specifically it is highest in Asia, Other Regions, and Western Europe and by far the lowest in the United Kingdom.

Other sample characteristics

Eighteen percent of our respondents come from family-owned companies. Their share is highest in companies listed in Asia, Other Regions, and Western Europe and lowest in companies listed in the United States and United Kingdom.

Seventeen percent of our respondents are associated with a subsidiary. Their share is lower in listed and larger companies and it also varies across listings. It is highest in Asia and Other Regions and lowest in the United Kingdom. The mean of subsidiaries per company/respondent amounts to 88, and 8 percent of our sample report zero subsidiaries; the maximum number of subsidiaries is 4,200 (again, these numbers are self-reported). As one would expect, the number of subsidiaries increases with company size and tends to be lower if the company itself is a subsidiary.

Finally, the majority of our respondents are between 40 and 50 years (42 percent) and 51 and 60 years (37 percent).

3
Descriptive Evidence

3.1 Drivers for corporate governance

One of the assumptions regarding our research on the role of company secretaries was that internal and external factors are increasingly shaping the structure of companies and their boards: There are many direct and indirect impacts on the positioning, as well as the tasks and responsibilities of company secretaries. Therefore, in our self-completion questionnaire we asked the respondents to indicate how strongly certain factors influence their company's approach to corporate governance. As is illustrated in Chart 3.1, corporate governance is driven by regulation and listing standards rather than public pressure and competition.

In the following section we report on the individual significance of the drivers.

3.1.1 Regulation

Domestic regulation is by far the strongest driver for a company's approach to corporate governance. More than half of the respondents to our questionnaire (54 percent) said that "domestic regulation" very strongly influenced their company's approach to corporate governance. As a consequence of corporate scandals in the United States, and in some European countries, special governance frameworks were recently introduced, at least for listed companies: Whether by legal provisions or by the establishment of mandatory corporate governance requirements, these governance frameworks are an important issue for listed companies. This may explain our finding that large and listed companies indicate domestic regulation much more frequently as a main driver than do smaller and family-owned businesses. Interestingly, secretaries in companies domiciled in the United States are not among those with the

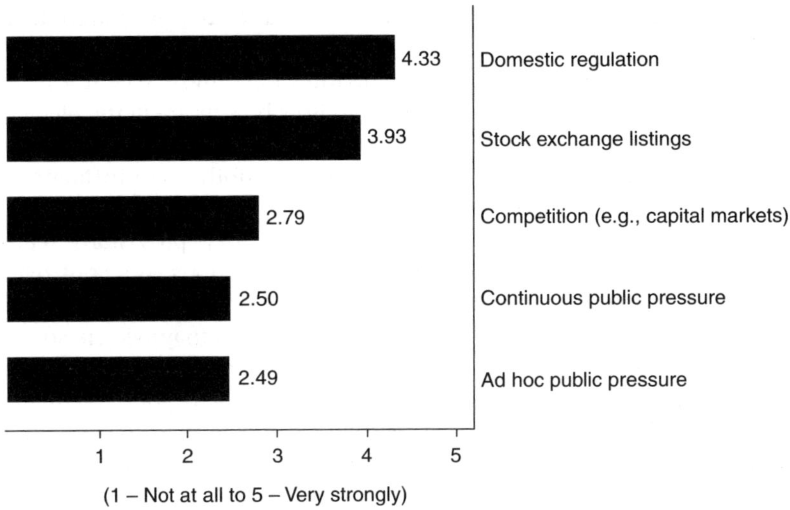

Chart 3.1 Corporate governance drivers (strength of effect)

highest rankings for regulation as a main driver; this despite the fact that corporate governance has been a strong focus in the United States for the last few years and US rules are among the most stringent. As a result, US secretaries have been familiar with corporate governance standards and requirements for a long time already and they might consider this as "normal standard" rather than a result of domestic regulation. On the other hand, regulation is, not surprisingly, seen as a most important driver by larger corporations which are also more frequently listed.

In addition to legal and stock exchange provisions, corporate governance codes have been issued in most countries over the last few years. Many of the respondents to the questionnaire may have also included these in the "domestic regulation" driver.

The fact that public pressure (also see Section 3.1.3) is perceived as a less important driver by the questionnaire respondents may be explained by the mechanisms of legislation – public pressure, which was and still is strong in the field of corporate governance, often leads to legal changes over time, increased regulatory attention, and new self-regulating industry standards. The companies normally respond to such "regulations" rather than respond directly to public pressure. The personal interviews confirm, however, that pressure from shareholders and shareholder activist groups significantly influences the behavior of many companies in regard to enhancing corporate governance structures.

Combined chairman-CEO mandates are challenged by shareholders and increasingly discussed within boards, although legal provisions may allow for this structure. US companies have most recently faced growing pressure from shareholders as to how boards are being elected. During the 2007 AGM season many companies were confronted with shareholders calling for improved/extended possibilities of influencing board composition (topic: "majority voting").

Whether or not increased legal and regulatory provisions really improve corporate governance is being discussed and is very controversial. There is no doubt that some fundamental rules have to be followed and that a lack of corporate governance structures may be one source for bad management, poor performance, and even corporate scandals. But it is also true that rules alone do not make a good company. Unfortunately, today's efforts of legislators and regulators very often reflect a tendency to put form over substance in the hope that formalized corporate governance standards impede corporate scandals. Many of the company secretaries interviewed voiced their concerns about this development that is unlikely to prevent future criminal acts completely but does impose heavy bureaucratic burdens on all companies.

The very detailed and formalized independence requirements for directors as stipulated in the NYSE listing standards are probably the most obvious example of this tendency. As one of the American secretaries interviewed comments:

> Unfortunately there is a tendency to "formalize" independence definitions which does not take into account the most important aspect – the mindset of the directors: real independence is a result of strong personality.

This view is supported by a colleague who says:

> Requiring independence, as such, is asking the wrong question: Board members must add value to the company. And this is not something that can be answered by checking boxes.

One French secretary even challenges the concept of "independence" as a strong means for enhanced governance:

> In very complex businesses, directors without in-depth knowledge of the company's activities, although being independent in theory, will never be independent in fact. They will strongly depend on the information provided by management (which is often and quite normally somewhat biased) and not be able to really take independent decisions.

Other secretaries refer to the importance for the board to have directors with in-depth knowledge of the business and even of the individual company as well: former executives, long-standing outside directors – neither of which are considered independent under various governance codes.

Many company secretaries interviewed also mention the increasing burden caused by never-ending changes in domestic and international rules. Boards are increasingly busy, primarily with adapting internal rules to new requirements and trying not to make mistakes. They are losing their focus on dealing with their first responsibility, making the company successful. One British secretary states the point:

> Board members are getting more and more anxious, concerned about formal issues and, as a consequence, use too much time for continually monitoring compliance of their activities with all the new rules and regulations. I hope that corporate governance is going to "calm down" a bit over the next years, with less new rules and regulations. I am, however, not really confident that this will happen.

A colleague, also British but working in a different industry, seems to confirm this sentiment:

> Additional directives will come from Europe, which are, unfortunately, often not practice-relevant. More business people and less bureaucrats and academics should be involved when such rules are designed.

These critical remarks, however, must in no way be seen as a fundamentally skeptical approach of a majority of company secretaries to corporate governance. A huge number of the interviewees confirm the positive impact of the recent developments on board work which has become much more intensive with board members being fully aware of their responsibilities. In past times many directors considered their board mandate as a social event rather than as performance-oriented work and a crucial success factor for the company.

In our interviews we also asked whether special regulators had a significant impact on the companies' corporate governance. Although many industries (banks, insurance, pharmaceutical industry, etc.) are subject to special supervision of their business activities, only very few special regulators exercise some influence in the field of corporate governance. Financial services companies, foremost the banks in many countries, must comply with enhanced governance requirements. This is mainly to protect the market against bad corporate management in this sector since it plays a crucial role for the economy as a whole. For the large companies surveyed, these special regulatory requirements do not, however, lead to significant differences in corporate governance structures. One exception should be mentioned: Swiss banks, contrary to all other companies under Swiss company law, are required to have two completely separate boards and no member of the supervisory board (Verwaltungsrat) is allowed to also be a member of the executive management.

3.1.2 Stock markets

Listings

It is obvious that listing standards have a strong influence on companies' corporate governance. Stock exchanges increasingly define minimum standards for all issuers – domestic and foreign. Forced delisting can be the ultimate consequence of poor governance standards. Certainly, most companies will take all necessary efforts to avoid being publicly reprimanded by stock exchange authorities, or even being sentenced by a regulator as a result of noncompliance with corporate governance requirements. The New York Stock Exchange (NYSE) Listing Standards are considered by many to be the most stringent; quite a number of non-American companies listed on the NYSE had to adapt their governance structures well beyond the legal requirements of their home markets. Therefore, it comes as no surprise that in our survey the influence of stock exchange listings on the respondents' corporate governance ranks second, only a little behind domestic regulation. If we take into consideration that listings are less frequent among family-owned and small companies we can say definitively that listing regulations have a significant impact on corporate governance at large companies and are of similar importance to that of legal frameworks. The impact may even be stronger for companies with domestic regulations leaving room for various governance structures on the one hand and a listing on an exchange with more clearly defined and strict governance rules on the other. Our self-completion survey also shows that respondents from Asian countries consider stock listings a strong driver for their company's corporate governance. Whether this is a result of a secondary listing on the NYSE or is driven by rather weak domestic stock exchange regulations remains an open question. For respondents from the United States and the United Kingdom it is obvious that their exchange listing standards are seen as very strong drivers.

Competition

Respondents to our self-completion questionnaire rated competition as a driver of medium importance for their companies' corporate governance. This allows for several interpretations: Respondents might judge their corporate governance as significant for the credit rating of the company, leading to lower interest rates and therefore serving as a factor which improves their competitive position on the capital markets. Possibly they believe that positive corporate governance ratings, by specialized governance rating agencies or by the media, help create a competitive advantage as they do to their companies' reputation. Some might value the impact of such competitive advantages on the company's share price. It will be difficult to really quantify such effects but it does seem clear that company secretaries do not underestimate the importance of corporate governance – even in the field of competition. Some of them will certainly remember discussions within the boardroom about published ratings: Why did competitor X get much better marks? And what should we do to catch up with the best companies? Such discussions may lead to changes in the corporate governance of companies or, at least, make board members aware of existing deficiencies. Discussions are likely to intensify if better corporate governance rankings of competitors run parallel to their better financial performance.

3.1.3 Public pressure

Public pressure, whether ad hoc or continuous, was ranked by the respondents to our questionnaire of medium importance in terms of affecting their company's corporate governance approach. Companies in Western Europe and the United Kingdom feel a stronger pressure than those in the United States. This is most likely because the United States has introduced strict corporate governance rules, mainly the Sarbanes-Oxley Act of 2002, after the corporate scandals of recent years, thus reducing public pressure for additional changes.

Nevertheless, public pressure continues all over the corporate world (and in the United States as well) – from shareholder activists, corporate governance rating agencies, and the media. The primary focus today is on executive compensation and the manner in which it is structured. Increasingly, shareholders are claiming to have a say on that topic and the US Congress recently took a first step toward strengthening shareholders' rights in regard to establishing the compensation for top management.

The combined chairman-CEO function, allowed in many countries, is another issue of increased attention in the public opinion. Splitting the two highest responsibilities within a company is being called for by an increasing number of governance specialists. They argue that the most critical function of each board – namely the supervision and control of the executive management – cannot be really guaranteed if the chairman, in practice, supervises his own management team and ultimately himself.

Confirming the existence of public pressure, one American secretary summarizes the situation in the United States as follows:

> The separation of the chairman and CEO functions is still not really accepted in US companies. Where they were split over the past years, this happened mostly because of shareholder pressure.

Controversies about the dual mandate at the head of companies are not addressed with equal frequencies and commitment in various countries. As it is illegal in Germany and the Netherlands for the CEO to also assume the role of chairman, dual mandates are not an issue in those countries. In Switzerland, only banks are prohibited from merging the two functions into one, while all the other companies are free to do so. Most other countries do not have legal provisions prohibiting the combined chairman-CEO role but a majority of national corporate governance codes propose establishing a separation (for more details see Section 3.2.2). This tendency is clearly confirmed by the respondents to our questionnaire. While 262 respondents report that legislation would allow executives on the board, only 98 of the companies have an executive chairman of which 67 also assume the CEO role.

Our interviews show, however, that quite a number of secretaries working in such structures perceive the combined chairman-CEO function as an absolute positive. With a rather humorous tone, one French secretary draws a parallel to the country's government system:

> French companies are still mostly governed like "monarchies" as is France as a state. There is nothing wrong with this. All depends on the people involved.

Another French secretary even goes further stating:

> The French PDG (Président-Directeur Général) system – roles of chairman and CEO combined – supports a cohesive management

and is less expensive than an organization with split functions where often the former CEO becomes chairman and keeps his high salary. The concentration of powers in the hands of the PDG, however, necessitates strong control standards to ensure checks and balances.

Debates about the separation of powers, however, remain animated among shareholders and in the media. If the company is performing well, criticism normally weakens but if things go wrong, or if performance falls behind competitors' results, the combined role also becomes a topic at shareholders meetings: Did the checks and balances work? Was the board independent enough to take the necessary measures, challenging and even opposing opinions of the chairman-CEO?

3.2 Organization of the board

How companies organize their board – composition, authorities, working methods – is often one of the focal points in corporate governance discussions. Are there structures in place that support the company's success? Or, looking at it in reverse: Is corporate failure mostly a result of poor corporate governance? And, ultimately: What is good corporate governance?

We asked for information about board characteristics in the self-completion questionnaires. Through our personal interviews we collected additional information about how, in practice, boards work.

There is one quick answer and one that is perhaps disappointing for all those who hope that corporate governance excellence leads to better performance: There is no empirical evidence at all (neither in this study nor in any other studies we have examined) that boards fully applying the highest of corporate governance standards achieve a better financial performance. We cannot even say that complying with best practice governance standards avoids corporate failure. It is the people who matter, not the structures. We firmly argue, however, that having people in charge who perform poorly is very likely worse if a company's governance structures are not state of the art!

3.2.1 Board characteristics and composition

There are two fundamentally different "philosophies" regarding national laws which define a company's basic organizational setup: The one-tier (or unitary) boards which combine executive and nonexecutive directors in one corporate body with no legal separation of duties, and the two-tier boards which legally separate the supervisory role from the management function. Some countries require a general manager, or managing director, with defined responsibilities who is separate from the board. In Italy, companies opting for the unitary board structure are required to have a special "board of statutory auditors" – a corporate body with mainly control functions – appointed by shareholders.

Very roughly, we can say that Austria, Germany, and the Netherlands have two-tier boards and the Anglo-Saxon countries, the United Kingdom and United States, have unitary boards. Although they have mostly unitary boards, the Nordic countries – Finland and Sweden – ask for a clearly separated managerial leadership. France, Italy, and Spain have a priority for unitary boards although they offer other structures in their company laws. Switzerland imposes a strict two-tier structure to banks but leaves the choice to all other companies.

Of the companies interviewed, 56 percent have a one-tier and 44 percent a two-tier board structure. In our self-completion questionnaires, 86 percent of the respondents say that, according to their domestic legal system, executives are allowed on the board. Not surprisingly, the quorum is lower in Western Europe where there are a number of countries with legally required two-tier structures. Asian respondents report an above-average quorum suggesting that many Asian countries follow Anglo-Saxon corporate structures where having executives on the board is the corporate organizational norm.

If we look more closely at the composition of the boards, we now find a huge variety of structures: executive and nonexecutive chairmen, CEOs as chairmen, independent chairmen, strong position of executives on the board, little or strong majority of independent board members, employee representatives, and government representatives (Table 3.1). We also find differences regarding the size of the boards depending partly on the size

Table 3.1 Board characteristics

Board characteristics	% of respondents
Chairman is an executive	33.9
Chairman is the CEO	23.4
One or more executive members who are neither chairman nor CEO	46.7
Majority of board members are nonexecutive	81.6
Majority of board members are independent	58.9
Board includes employee representatives	15.8
Board includes government representatives	13.5

of the company and also, to some extent, on legal provisions. Large German companies are required to have 20 board members with 10 of them representing shareholders and 10 of them representing the domestic workforce. The majority of the companies interviewed excluding those in Germany, have 10 to 15 board members.

Only 16 percent of the questionnaire respondents reported having employee representatives on their boards. Not surprisingly, the quorum is higher in Western Europe given the German legal requirement explained above. Legislation in France gives employee shareholders a right to be represented on the board if staff accounts for more than 3 percent of all shareholdings. Some French companies also have ordinary employee representatives on their boards, with or without voting rights. The rather strong representation of German and French companies in our personal interviews explains why 28 percent reported having an employee representation on their boards. Employee representatives are least frequent in Other Regions and Asia, and they are not common in the United States.

As to government representatives on the boards, there is a significant difference between the self-completion questionnaires and the personal interviews. While 13 percent of the companies covered by the questionnaire have government representatives on their boards, this is a clear exception in the companies personally interviewed. The sample of our personal interviews – mostly large, listed companies, all in Western Europe, the United Kingdom, and the United States – explains this difference. The result from the questionnaires indicates that government representatives on the boards are most frequent in Asia – partly certainly due to former or still existing political structures of the domestic economy – and Other Regions, and least frequent, even 0 percent, in the United States and the United Kingdom. Listed companies also have government representatives on their boards much less frequently.

3.2.2 Executive and nonexecutive chairmen

The questions of whether the chairman is an executive or a nonexecutive, whether he/she is independent or not, and whether he/she also assumes the CEO function play a key role in current corporate governance discussions. Of course, the legal environment is a clear factor shaping this topic. Where two-tier boards are mandatory executive chairmen, and even more so chairman-CEOs, are just not possible. In countries with unitary boards, companies normally have a choice: 34 percent of the respondents to the questionnaire report having an executive chairman and for 23 percent he/she is also the CEO. We can conclude that in about two-thirds of the companies the chairman is not an executive. Having an executive chairman is by far most frequent in the United States (67 percent of all respondents) and in Asia, least frequent in Western Europe, Other Regions, and the United Kingdom. The situation in the United Kingdom is interesting – today most companies, although they have unitary boards, go for a nonexecutive chairman, a solution strongly supported by the Combined Code on Corporate Governance. This model is based on the conviction that, especially with unitary boards, a nonexecutive chairman is better able to ensure checks and balances as he/she is not dependent upon management and is less attached to the company as such. The survey also showed that executive chairmen are more common in family-owned companies, most probably demonstrating a stronger involvement of family members in both management and supervision. In the companies we targeted with personal interviews, 54 percent have nonexecutive chairmen.

There remains, however, some room for interpretation: It is not crystal clear what companies mean when they refer to the "executive chairman." Some qualify their chairman as "executive" because he uses 100 percent of his time for the mandate; others only do it if he/she is a member of executive management. And we found that Italian companies sometimes use the term "executive" exclusively for someone being vested with individual management power such as the CEO. These nuances of interpretation do not, however, change the overall picture.

The chairman-CEO is by far most popular in the United States (62 percent) and least frequent in the United Kingdom (with 5 percent) and Western Europe. Within Western Europe, the situation differs from country to country. Of course, Germany does not have any chairman-CEOs because of the legal provisions prohibiting executives on the board. Our personal interviews showed, however, that in France and in Italy a significant number of large companies still have chairman-CEO structures in place although developments are tending toward the split solution. Only 9 percent of the interviewees' companies have an executive chairman who is not also the CEO.

3.2.3 Executive and independent board members

Slightly less than half of the companies interviewed have executive members on their boards who are neither chairman nor CEO. The self-completion questionnaires provide a very similar picture (with a 47 percent share of executive members who are neither chairman nor CEO). In some countries, mainly in Western Europe, where two-tier boards prevail, this is not legally possible or at least not at all popular as discussed before. In the United Kingdom and in Asian countries the key functions of the executive management (CEO, CFO, sometimes COO, general counsel, etc.) are also mostly members of the board of directors. In France both solutions are known to occur. The same applies to the United States where there is a development toward having the chairman-CEO as the only executive on the board, thus reducing the influence of executives on the board. Yet, one British secretary is convinced:

> The CEO should not be the only executive on the board because that makes him too strong compared to the other executives.

Almost all corporate governance codes today propose that boards have a majority of independent members. By generally used definition, executives are not independent but it is no trivial matter to determine "independence" of external board members. The situation regarding independent board members is quite special in Germany: The requirement that half of the supervisory board members be employee representatives makes it almost impossible to have a majority of really independent members. Some say, however, that employee representatives although being fully dependent on the company (since it pays them their salary) are "independent" of management because labor laws guarantee that they cannot be fired as a result of their activities on the board. This may be the case in theory but it shows how difficult it is to find clear definitions of "independence."

British companies have an interesting rule: most require that the chairman be independent upon appointment but they do not consider him independent as soon as he/she assumes the chairman function. Quite a number of companies, and also some corporate governance codes, qualify directors having served on the board for an extended period of time as nonindependent. The limit is normally between 8 and 12 years. And what about the independence of large, even dominating, shareholders if they are board members? Answers to this question are controversial and may be strongly influenced by the definition of "independence." A large shareholder on the board is normally clearly independent of management and in many cases also independent of the company as a whole but he/she might have strong personal interests and therefore lack independence when taking certain strategic decisions.

Eighty-two percent of the companies that responded to our questionnaire have a majority of nonexecutive board members and 59 percent a majority of independent directors. The number of nonexecutives on boards is higher in listed companies than in others. Listed and large companies more often have a majority of independent directors. And in terms of countries these majorities are by far the most common in the United States; they are also more widespread in Western Europe than in Other Regions. The majority of independent board members is contingent on ownership structure as well: Family-owned companies and companies with few dominant shareholders still often do not have a majority of independent board members. Not surprisingly, boards of subsidiaries more frequently fail to meet the independence criteria because directors are primarily members of the parent company's senior management and therefore cannot be considered independent of the company.

We excluded the German boards in our interview analysis because of the country's mandate of having 50 percent employee representation – independence becomes too difficult to define. Generally, however, a significant majority of shareholder representatives on German boards are independent. Of the other companies interviewed, 4 percent, all of them French, have one-third or less independent members, another 13 percent have less than 50 percent (France, United Kingdom). In 30 percent of the companies the quorum is between 51 and 70 percent (mostly in the United Kingdom), whereas 32 percent of the companies have between 71 and 90 percent independent directors (mostly United States, Switzerland, Italy). Finally, in 21 percent of the companies the board is composed of more than 91 percent independent directors (Switzerland, Netherlands, United States).

We would like, however, to caution the reader to take these percentages at face value. Definitions of independence are difficult and vary from country to country and, in part, also from company to company. Of course, some national regulations and a number of stock exchange listing standards propose criteria for directors' independence that are certainly helpful. Yet, they will never provide a comprehensive picture of what is really important:

- On one hand, is a director truly independent who has no business relationship with the company although he/she maintains having a mandate on the board because it is crucial for his/her ego and/or the position within society?
- On the other hand, is a director nonindependent because he/she has business relationships with the company, although he/she is financially completely independent, has a very strong personality, and regularly voices dissenting views against the chairman-CEO?

And there is yet another important question: Is independence defined primarily by being independent of the company or by being independent of management? Whichever criteria we use, it is the personalities who are crucial not the formalities.

3.2.4 Internal organization

Because our self-completion questionnaire was primarily focused on the collection of information concerning the roles and responsibilities of company secretaries, we only collected data about the secretary's involvement in the various board committees (this information is dealt with later in Section 3.2.4.1). The primary sources of information about how boards are functioning in practice are the personal interviews.

Of course, the companies we targeted for personal interviews do not provide an "average" picture. Smaller and nonlisted companies are likely to have fewer special committees and family-owned companies might often be differently organized. It is also possible that companies in Asia and Other Regions have different structures. Nevertheless, the information from the large, listed companies in Western Europe and the United States is interesting – it shows how strongly board work is professionalized today. It also illustrates that increasingly boards care about the role of independent directors to provide the checks and balances necessary in the running of these firms. In the following sections, we report on the internal organization of board processes in more detail.

3.2.4.1 Board committees

Today almost all corporate governance codes propose, or even request, that boards create specialized committees. Many codes also request that these committees are composed exclusively of independent directors or at least have a clear majority of independent members. The most common committees are the audit, the compensation or remuneration, and the nominating and/or corporate governance committees.

Ninety-seven percent of our personal interviewees' firms have a special audit committee. One of the company secretaries mentioned a combined audit and corporate governance committee. As described before, Italian companies with unitary boards have to appoint a special "board of statutory auditors" which assumes most of the functions audit committees fulfill in other companies.

Next in board committee frequency are the compensation committees, established in 63 percent of the companies interviewed. Nominating/corporate governance committees are in place in 50 percent of the companies. An additional 24 percent have a committee that combines the roles of the compensation and the nominating committees. The variety of organizational setups is, however, even much broader: Seven companies assign personnel issues (normally including appointments and compensation) to a chairman's/presidential committee. In seven companies, this chairman's committee has responsibility for corporate governance and nominating issues and in two companies for corporate governance and compensation. Another five companies have a chairman's/presidential committee which primarily prepares board meetings and/or has the authority to take urgent decisions between official board meetings – one such committee has been delegated the responsibility for supervising internal audit and risk issues.

Whereas a large majority of audit, compensation, and nominating/corporate governance committees are composed exclusively of independent board members, the chairman's/presidential committees by definition usually have, with varying degrees, a strong complement of executive directors. This might be an issue if these committees have the final authority in areas where "good corporate governance" requires independent decisions. Delegating compensation decisions to a chairman's committee, therefore, is certainly not "best practice" in a company with a CEO assuming the chairman role. Only one of the companies interviewed, however, has such a structure and not surprisingly it is a company with a chairman representing the majority family shareholder. Whether or not a chairman's committee should be responsible for nominating decisions also depends upon the people involved. There is nothing wrong with a nonexecutive chairman playing a strong role when new board members are being evaluated – be it in his function as head of the chairman's committee or in an advisory capacity on an independent nominating committee. However, the times when the CEO selected board members from among his friends are definitely over as well they should have been.

Companies are increasingly aware of their roles beyond financial performance. This is made clear by the fact that 12 of the company secretaries interviewed work in firms that have established a special corporate responsibility committee at the board level and 2 others have an ethics and/or environment committee. Addressing the more traditional responsibilities of boards are the 12 finance and investment committees, the 8 strategy committees and the 6 special risk committees. Companies in the pharmaceutical and technology sectors also often have board-level science/technology committees. Some companies, mostly in the United States, have established so-called executive committees; their primary mandate is to act on behalf of the full board in between formal meetings if urgent decisions are required. Most of these committees, however, never meet. As mentioned above, a special legal requirement exists for German companies based on the Co-Determination Act requiring that companies of a certain size must have an equal number of shareholders' and employees' representatives on their supervisory boards. These companies have to establish a "mediation committee" (Vermittlungsausschuss) that would be called upon if the appointment of a new member of the management board (Vorstand) did not receive the required quorum from the full board. None of the companies interviewed, however, ever had to call a meeting of this committee over the past years.

In light of this wide range of committees we collected additional data on the total number of committees per company: 70 percent of the companies interviewed have three or four committees (24 companies each having three and four), 9 companies have only two, and 11 firms have five or more committees at the board level. If we consider the fact that independent directors assume the majority of committee membership, it becomes evident that accepting an election to the board of a large, listed company not only means taking responsibility for important decisions but also means devoting a lot of time to the mandate.

3.2.4.2 Board and board committee meetings

The intense time commitment required for a board mandate becomes even clearer when we look at the meeting frequency of these companies. On average, the full boards of the companies interviewed met 7.8 times during the last financial year, audit committees 6.7 times, compensation committees 4.8 times, nominating/corporate governance committees 3.8 times, chairman's/presidential committees 7 times, and "other" committees about 5 times.

The frequency of meetings differs significantly, however, from company to company. This may also be strongly influenced by extraordinary corporate events in specific years such as large mergers or acquisitions, financial, or personnel problems. Only five companies (9 percent) reported less than five full-board meetings, 79 percent of the boards met between five and ten times (16 percent five times, 15 percent six times, 12 percent seven times, 19 percent eight times, 13 percent nine times, 4 percent ten times). Twelve percent of the boards met between 11 and 16 times and one board had to gather 21 times.

In addition to the full-board meetings, a majority of the companies regularly hold so-called executive meetings. The understanding of these executive meetings differs somewhat depending upon the company and the country. The meetings can be gatherings of all the independent directors, as stipulated for companies listed at the NYSE or they can consist of the nonmanagement board members whether independent or not. Companies with two-tier structures sometimes refer to their supervisory board's meetings as "executive" if no representatives of management attend. Irrespective of how such meetings are defined, they all have a similar goal – providing external, independent board members with the possibility of discussing certain topics among themselves without any direct influence from management and with the aim to strengthen checks and balances.

Meeting frequency for the audit committees is slightly lower than that for full-board meetings. A strong majority of the audit committees reported four to six meetings (14 percent four meetings, 25 percent five meetings, 13 percent six meetings); another 30 percent had between seven and ten meetings and there are one or two companies each reporting between 11 and 15 meetings. At the other end of the spectrum, we find one audit committee that only met once, one that met twice, and three committees that met on three occasions.

Forty-four percent of the compensation committees met four or five times last year, 20 percent two or three times, and three committees met only once. For 12 percent of the compensation committees six meetings were necessary, seven meetings occurred for another 12 percent, and two compensation committees held eight meetings. One compensation committee had to schedule 11 meetings, another one even 16 – clear signs of extraordinary situations in the given year.

The nominating/corporate governance committees normally meet less frequently, two-thirds of them between two and four times per year, 21 percent five or six times, two committees seven and eight times respectively and one company reported ten corporate governance committee meetings in one year, obviously because of significant boardroom shuffles.

In companies where a chairman's/presidential committee has been established, primarily in Germany and Switzerland, meetings are called quite often. In Germany they are called, on average, five times and in Switzerland more than ten times. It is not surprising that these companies have two-tier boards. Separate supervisory boards have a stronger need for "managing" the board and the chairman's committees assume a large part of this function.

When we take a closer look at meeting frequency focusing on the various countries we see that companies with unitary boards normally meet more often than two-tier boards. The most frequent full-board meetings are reported in the United States, the United Kingdom, and then in France and Italy; the lowest meeting frequency is found in Germany. Committee meetings are held more frequently, by far, in the United States and are the least frequent in Germany. The United Kingdom, France, and Italy take an average position between the two and in Switzerland we saw a clear tendency toward more committee meetings than they held previously. The strong involvement of committees in the United States – very likely – is a result of the stringent corporate governance rules for listed companies and the severe sanctions that have been established there for failing to comply with legal requirements in this area. In this respect, Italy also has a special situation with the "boards of statutory auditors" appointed directly by shareholders which normally meet quite frequently, more than 20 times per year in the companies interviewed.

The high number of committee meetings, combined with the increasing trend of having exclusively independent directors on the three main committees, creates a heavy burden on these members. As stated before, board mandates are no longer easily facilitated; board members must be in a position to spend the time necessary to fulfill their duties. Having to go to up to 20 meetings per year is no longer unusual and if the company is active on a global level the necessary travel can be an additional challenge. This is particularly true for those external board members who are running firms either as CEOs or serving in another leadership capacity as their primary professional activity. It is not a major surprise that many company secretaries report that it is increasingly difficult to find the right people for such mandates.

3.3 The company secretary

Before we take a closer look at the roles and challenges of the company secretary we want to reach a clearer understanding of what the function is all about. Every company needs someone to take care of all the necessary administrative issues that fall under the board's responsibility. In the past, many companies did have a "company secretary" who was mainly in charge of ensuring smooth board processes. With the increased requirements resulting from legal and regulatory changes over recent years, some companies strongly enhanced the function of their secretary. They assigned the position a significant number of new responsibilities, placed it higher in the internal hierarchy, and named the function holder a "corporate governance officer."

When we look at various countries we find all kinds of legal frameworks on which the function of the company secretary is based. The earliest codification of the position is the UK Companies Act of 1948. It required all companies to appoint a secretary with some clearly defined responsibilities, mainly in the field of regulatory reporting and record keeping. Detailed task descriptions, however, remained an authority of the individual companies and their boards. Other Anglo-Saxon countries – primarily the United States under various state laws – also have some legal provisions about the appointment of a secretary but they do not define the function in detail. Some of the national corporate governance codes mention the secretary function, often in connection with the requirement for boards to provide external board members with full access to information or with the support of the nonexecutive chairman (see also Section 1.2). A detailed job description of the secretary to the board is contained in the Code of Good Practice for Boards and Directors, published by the Spanish Institute of Directors–Administrators that goes so far as defining the rules for appointing such a secretary. The Dutch Corporate Governance Code also looks at the appointment of a company secretary and roughly defines the function:

> The company secretary shall see to it that correct procedures are followed and that the supervisory board acts in accordance with its statutory obligations and its obligations under the articles of association. He shall assist the chairman of the supervisory board in the actual organization of the affairs of the supervisory board (information, agenda, evaluation, training program, etc.).

The Swiss Company Act requests that the board of directors appoint its chairman and a secretary who does not need to be a member of the board. The legal provision says nothing, however, about the responsibilities and the function of the secretary. In Germany, the company secretary function is widely unknown; when we planned to interview German companies about the secretary function it was not easy to find the right person with whom to speak. In general, we had to talk to the general counsel or to the head of the CEO's staff department. Some French companies have a "secrétaire général" (general secretary) who assumes parts of the company secretary role but is often in charge of public affairs and corporate protocol while a specialized lawyer takes care of most secretary and corporate governance responsibilities. Italian companies normally assign the official title of "secretary" to one of the board members, often a lawyer or a chartered accountant or auditor.

The role of these secretaries is to make sure that official documents are compliant with laws and regulations; for the most part, they sign such documents on behalf of the board. Italian companies, of course, also have in-house staff responsible for handling traditional company secretary duties – administrative as well as legal and regulatory.

Through our personal interviews we gained a broad picture of what "company secretaries," or whatever their official title might be, are doing. We also learned where these secretaries are coming from both professionally and personality-wise, how they are positioned within the organization, and what the main influencing factors are on their positions. With our self-completion questionnaire, we collected complementary quantitative information on a broader sample of companies, most notably about educational background, prior roles and positions, job duration, reporting lines, and working relationships.

3.3.1 Career

We first wanted to know who the company secretaries are. What is their educational background, what are their professional track records, how long have they been in their current job function, and what are their future career opportunities?

3.3.1.1 Educational background

The self-completion questionnaires and the personal interviews show that boards most frequently choose lawyers when appointing their secretary (see Table 3.2).

Sixty-eight percent of the questionnaire respondents indicated "legal" as their educational background and 85 percent of the secretaries interviewed said they have legal backgrounds. This finding is enforced when we analyze the questionnaire responses – 92 percent of the respondents

Table 3.2 Educational background

What is your educational background? (Mark all that apply)	**% of respondents**
Business	27.1
Finance/accounting	9.0
Company secretary	2.6
Legal	68.4
Economics	18.4
Communications/journalism	3.2
Engineering	3.2
Other	6.5

in the United States and 79 percent and 71 percent of those in the United Kingdom and Western Europe, respectively, are lawyers by education. The percentage of secretaries with legal backgrounds is also significantly higher in both large and listed companies. Owing to the fact that our personal interviews covered large companies in the United States, the United Kingdom, and Western Europe, almost all of them listed, the high percentage of lawyers is in line with the broad survey.

Interestingly enough, we learned from our self-completion questionnaire that secretaries in the pharmaceutical, chemical, and energy industries are more frequently lawyers than those in the financial services, food and beverage, and technology industries. Our personal interviews do not confirm these differences by industry. Also it is not quite obvious why, for example, financial services firms should have less need for a secretary with a legal background working with their board, given the particularly tough regulatory environment in this industry. One possible reason may be that more financial services firms assign highly challenging compliance issues to specialized lawyers rather than to the company secretary.

In our interviews only 13 percent mentioned having studied economics/business administration (some of them hold an MBA in addition to their law studies) and 10 percent studied political sciences/external affairs (also mostly in addition to law). Each of the following disciplines were cited by one interviewee as their educational background: engineering, communication, accounting, and sociology. Another respondent cited the basic education of a chartered secretary; another worked his way up the ladder "on the job" in various businesses.

In the next section we deal with the professional history of today's company secretaries and describe a number of different paths that have led respondents to becoming the secretary of a large international company.

There is no doubt that the growing importance of legal, regulatory, and compliance issues that must be dealt with encourages companies to appoint lawyers to their company secretary positions. There are, of course, other ways to define the role of the secretary – there is no solution that fits all situations. One secretary explains:

> My predecessor was a lawyer whereas I clearly have a strong business background with various assignments within our firm. The reason why the board chose me is simply that our company wants the board to have strong strategic influence and more involvement in the day-to-day business. And if the board needs legal support they get it from the legal department.

In many companies the title of company secretary is still assigned to the general counsel/head of legal affairs. This person officially assumes the secretary functions but is increasingly forced to delegate part of those responsibilities to members of his staff, mostly to a formally appointed assistant secretary or to someone with the title of corporate governance officer. Not surprisingly, these function holders have, almost exclusively, a legal background. One French secretary voices a clear opinion:

> I cannot imagine how someone who is neither a lawyer nor, at least, a financial expert would be able to fulfill the many crucial tasks of a company secretary.

A German general counsel who acts as secretary to the supervisory board takes a down-to-earth view:

> The general counsel function has always assumed controlling activities and was therefore well prepared to take on the new challenges resulting from increasing board responsibilities, including all corporate governance requirements. If a special secretary without legal background were appointed, he or she would simply have to rely on our legal department for most of the corporate governance tasks.

3.3.1.2 Prior role and positions – professional background

Looking at the professional history of the company secretaries who answered our self-completion questionnaire we first learn that the numbers are almost equal for those having assumed another function within the current company and those having joined from outside the firm:

- Forty-six percent were with another company in different industries and functions (many of them with a private law firm, some of them with central banks and governments and a few having joined directly after university).
- Forty-four percent moved to the secretary position from another assignment within the company.

Another 5 percent of questionnaire respondents were assigned to a subsidiary of the current employer, to its holding or parent company, or to an associated company prior to becoming secretary (see Table 3.3).

It is clear that making a career change within a group occurs more frequently in bigger companies. Larger firms usually have more subsidiaries and there are more possibilities to provide a candidate for the secretary function, as well as for exposure within the organization.

On the other end of the spectrum, secretaries are more frequently hired from the outside in family-owned companies – probably because many of these firms are smaller, have less internal resources and are, as a result, looking for external expertise. Large companies tend to appoint "insiders." In-depth knowledge of the company may be more important in large organizations due to their complex businesses; hiring a secretary from a competitor in the same industry is rarely an alternative.

Large majorities of the respondents in the United States, and a great number of those in Western Europe and in the United Kingdom, assumed legal functions before becoming company secretary. This career background is more common in bigger companies because they may have larger legal departments, allowing for in-house recruiting of a specialist for the secretary job. In Asia and Other Regions financial positions lead to the secretary role much more often. Family-owned companies also appoint secretaries with financial backgrounds more frequently (see Table 3.4).

Table 3.3 Prior engagement

In what company did you work immediately prior to your current role as company secretary?	**% of respondents**
Subsidiary of current company	4.9
My current company	44.3
Another company	45.6
Other	6.5

Table 3.4 Prior positions

Which position did you hold prior to your current role as company secretary? (Mark all that apply)	**% of respondents**
Legal	56.9
Finance	20.6
Company secretary	6.2
Public affairs/communications	11.1
Strategy	10.1
Operations	7.5
Other	20.3

We were able to obtain a detailed look at the personalities assuming the secretary role in large international companies from our personal interviews. A wide variety of backgrounds are represented in their professional histories, but again legal backgrounds dominate the field. We see that about half of the interviewees were part of a corporate legal department prior to becoming secretary; about 25 percent were in private practice (for either shorter or longer periods of their professional careers). Interestingly more than 10 percent have had experience with governmental or public administration assignments. In addition, four individuals (accounting for approximately 6 percent) started academic careers early in their lives – two of them continued as part-time professors when they were appointed as company secretary. Almost 25 percent of the interviewees had many different kinds of business assignments including finance; 7 percent were in human resources and another approximately 5 percent had positions in accounting and controlling. Last but not least, there are some current function holders who assumed the secretary job at the onset of their careers.

Is there an ideal professional history for a company secretary? Our interviews showed that people with a wide variety of different backgrounds can be successful in the company secretary role. This is true especially if they have a broad track record, ideally a strong character, and are willing and able to "manage" this challenging job.

When we asked the interviewees to define their positioning in the internal hierarchy we wanted to find out how companies value the function of the secretary. In the past, company secretaries were often in the middle or lower management ranks. Today, however, many confirm that the position has been upgraded over the past years. This has happened either by promoting the current function holder or by granting a higher rank to a new secretary when he/she was appointed. Titles and rank structures, of course, vary from company to company. Irrespective of titles (corporate officer, senior vice president, vice president, and others) we can say that a broad majority of our interview partners (about 60 percent) are positioned at the first level below top management – only 15 percent on the second level. Nine percent of the interviewees do not have a formal ranking within the company hierarchy but do have a direct reporting line to the chairman. We found a dearth of formal titles primarily with young function holders – their youth probably making it difficult for companies to give him/her the usual top-level rank within the official hierarchy. On the other end of the spectrum, we met one secretary who, in his capacity as general counsel, is a member of the unitary board himself. We also encountered six secretaries who are members of the executive board/executive committee – all of them working in companies with a unitary board. We found another 15 percent of the company secretary function holders who have senior executive positions as members of an "extended management board," a "group management committee," or a "group managing board" – all various names for the level of management positions directly below the executive board.

Overall, we can say that the increasing responsibilities of company secretaries, added to the necessity of hiring highly qualified people, has led to a higher positioning of the function in organizational hierarchies.

3.3.1.3 *Job duration*

Our examination now brings us to the next important aspect of a company secretaries' career: How long do they stay in the job?

From the field of questionnaire respondents, the shortest amount of time a company secretary has been in the function is half a year, the longest 36 years. We learned that job duration is longest in Asia and the United States, shortest in Western Europe and the United Kingdom. Furthermore, company secretaries stay longer on the job in family-owned companies and shorter in large corporations.

These are averages and somewhat random numbers since job duration obviously is a reflection of the situation in any given moment: Whether the respondent's predecessor has just stepped down or has recently retired, or the respondent plans to retire shortly after a long career results in completely different answers. Hence, our data do not allow for any interpretation of shorter or longer job duration. The average tenure of those responding to the questionnaire is 7.9 years on the job.

Our personal interviews also suggest that secretaries in large companies tend to have somewhat shorter terms in office. Seventy-six percent of the interviewees have been in their positions for less than ten years, 50 percent for a period of four to eight years. Many secretaries confirmed that the function should not be assumed for too long a period of time. Some added that the increasing workload and resulting pressure on the function holder might require a quicker job rotation. One young secretary even expressed the view that she would stay in this job for only two to three years and then move on to a management role, possibly in a smaller unit within the organization. Another secretary who has been with the company for more than 25 years and in charge of the secretary function for 17 years has a very different view:

> After such a long time in service I have a strong influence on the decision making process. This makes the secretary function increasingly

> more attractive although I do not make decisions myself. And the role has changed so much since my appointment. I do not have the impression of having done the job for a long time – there have been a broad variety of different jobs.

Another interviewee, having been with his company for more than 30 years and in charge as company secretary for over 10 years, defines his position today as that of "éminence grise" – having significant influence behind the scenes.

Job duration is also likely to be a result of the definition of the role. If it has a rather strong focus on administrative, legal, and regulatory processes, short tenures are certainly preferable. However, if the secretary is assuming the role of the corporate governance professional – responsible not only for monitoring but also for designing and shaping the company's governance – serving a longer time in the job becomes a necessity. A secretary who meets this description is often the chairman's confidant and the main source of information for external board members.

We also asked the respondents their age in our self-completion questionnaire. The overwhelming majority of respondents are between the age of 40 and 60 years, 42 percent are between 40 and 50, and 37 percent are between 50 and 60. Only 13 percent are younger than 40 years of age.

In our personal interviews some secretaries voiced the opinion that being young in this job is difficult for a variety of reasons – a more senior person with a strong professional track record might command more respect from the board and also have better contacts with senior management.

3.3.1.4 Future career opportunities

Our discussion about age also includes how company secretaries view their future career opportunities; one of the statements that they ranked in the questionnaire (see Chart 3.2).

The result is rather surprising at first glance. The mean level of agreement with the statement about future career opportunities is quite low at 2.99, indicating a slightly below medium level of satisfaction. Only 15 percent of the questionnaire respondents agree with the statement about significant career opportunities to a great extent; 14 percent do not agree at all.

Whereas career opportunities within the respondents' companies are best in Asia and Other Regions, they seem to be the worst in the

Chart 3.2 Career opportunities (level of agreement)

United States and United Kingdom. The reasons for these differences are not clear. There may be a difference in perception of what career opportunities really are but it may also be true that US and UK company secretaries are often quite highly ranked executives and therefore do not see much room for further advancement in the company hierarchy. We also found that secretaries in family-owned companies rank their career opportunities higher presumably because the secretary, through his/her personal contacts with the owners in a family-owned company, is well positioned to get other, interesting assignments within the firm.

In our personal interviews, we had the opportunity to further discuss the career perspectives in much greater detail. One very common opinion expressed was that the rather unique position of the secretary can be an obstacle when it comes to looking for the next assignment within a company: The secretary is seen as an extremely high-ranking person with close and strong contacts with the chairman, the CEO, and top management.

Also, others may view the company secretary as a kind of bureaucrat without very much business experience. It is possible that he/she is not a welcome colleague in a business unit within the firm. These questions help illustrate a variety of concerns: Will he/she be a team player? Will he/she exhibit a certain kind of arrogance, an attribute often assigned to people working in the "center of power"? Will he/she really add value in the new function? Will the former secretary be a sort of a "spy" for the chairman or the CEO?

The secretary of a British company discusses the harsh realities of the subject:

> The company secretary is often hated by many people in the firm because of this role which forces him to repeatedly put pressure on others to ensure good board functioning. Documents have to be delivered on time and in a form adequate for the board which often means redoing papers. And last but not least, the secretary knows too much but is – due to confidentiality constraints – not sharing his knowledge with those who would also like to be involved!

Although a number of the secretaries interviewed were not this straightforward about the topic, quite a number share this outlook, at least in part. Many of them also conclude that company secretaries should not be too young when they start the job, making them less dependent of career considerations. A Dutch secretary who has had a very successful business career and only recently assumed the role of company secretary says:

> I am happy that this is my last assignment in the company as I am retiring in a few years. I am well respected within the board and in my contacts with top management. I am also much more independent in expressing my views. Younger secretaries might be tempted to be overly accommodating, trying to please everyone for career considerations.

And a British counterpart even goes a step further:

> Career should not be a main focus when accepting the secretary role and one should not be too ambitious about one's personal future because that might cause unnecessary tensions. However, as the function of the secretary is extremely interesting and provides an enormous variety of insight into all the important activities of the company – probably more than any other position within the company – you don't need to look for further career opportunities.

Some younger secretaries see their future in a more relaxed way but they all confirm that they would not stay in the function for more than a few years; they know that it becomes more difficult to find a new position within the organization if they have been "in the middle of the power center" for too long. For them the secretary role is simply an interesting step in building a career – one that might lead to a management position within the company whether it be at a subsidiary or in a staff department, or by becoming a country manager for the firm, if they have the necessary business background. Those who now report to the general counsel consider becoming a successor in that function a promising and challenging opportunity.

Two British secretaries outlined an interesting perspective – both are considering an early retirement from their current secretary job and have an interest in becoming a nonexecutive director in another company. As one of them says:

> I would like to build a small portfolio of nonexecutive directorships after an early retirement. With the experience as secretary and compliance officer I would be able to add value to other companies, perhaps rather middle-sized ones that do not have the necessary resources in-house to ensure good governance and the smooth run of all these issues.

His colleague, active in another industry, envisions the same type of future activity but also sees its limitations:

> This career path has not really been followed so far. Probably the "charisma" of the secretary function is still not high enough and many boards are looking for well-known names when proposing new external directors.

Nevertheless, the idea of bringing the broad knowledge of an experienced secretary to the board of smaller companies that may not have a specialized secretary should probably be given a closer look, particularly as more and more companies are facing difficulties with (1) finding external independent directors and (2) maintaining the necessary corporate governance expertise on the board.

3.3.2 Reporting lines and discretion

In the following sections we outline our findings regarding the reporting lines of company secretaries. We also address the support they get from their chairman, as well as the discretion they are given to decide what they do and how they do it.

3.3.2.1 Reporting line

An interesting piece of evidence regarding the role that companies attribute to their secretary is his/her reporting line. Are the company secretaries reporting primarily to the chairman of the board – executive or nonexecutive – or to the CEO? Do they have a reporting line to someone positioned lower down in the hierarchy? What does it mean if the secretary is working for the chairman and the board to a large extent but reporting to the CEO? Do the company secretary's reporting lines have an impact on the board's independence from management?

Both our self-completion questionnaires and our personal interviews provide a comprehensive picture of the significant variety of reporting lines (see Table 3.5). Many of the secretaries have dual reporting lines. This is best shown by the fact that the 307 respondents to our questionnaire said they had a total of 471 reporting lines.

Of the respondents, 67 percent are reporting to the CEO and 60 percent to the chairman of the board. Company secretaries reporting to the chairman do so most frequently in Western Europe and the United Kingdom and least frequently in the United States. The lower percentage of secretaries reporting to the chairman in the United States may be a result of interpretation. Most secretaries in their role as corporate officers consider their formal reporting line to be with the CEO, even when the CEO assumes the dual role of chairman and CEO (which is still very popular in US companies). Also the general counsel often assumes the secretary role in US companies or has the secretary reporting to him/her. The general counsel, of course, reports primarily to the CEO and not to the chairman.

However, the higher percentage of a reporting line to the chairman in Western Europe and the United Kingdom is not confirmed by our personal interviews. In Germany, for instance, many secretaries do not have any reporting line to the chairman and a formal reporting would,

Table 3.5 Reporting line

Who do you as company secretary report to? (Mark all that apply)	**% of respondents**
Chairman of the board	60.3
CEO	66.8
Head of investor relations	1.0
Head of finance/chief financial officer	12.7
Head of legal affairs	7.2
Other	5.5

in most cases, not even be possible. The chairman of the supervisory board, who has to be external and independent, has almost no personnel resources and is in some cases not even allowed to appoint personal staff. Of the UK company secretaries we interviewed, only 4 out of the 13 have a primary reporting line to the chairman; 6 report primarily to the CEO, 2 to the CFO, and 1 to the chairman and the CEO jointly. In many UK companies the secretary has to be appointed by the board which may include a sort of "reporting," although it is not formally referred to as such.

Overall in our personal interviews, we found 28 percent of secretaries reporting to the chairman and 36 percent reporting to the CEO. Of the interviewees, 15 percent have a formal dual reporting, mostly to the chairman and the CEO; 12 percent are reporting to the general counsel (mainly in the United States) and 4 percent to the CFO or the deputy CEO. One of the interviewees reports to the head of corporate communication and one to the chief of staff. In fact, it is clear that the 40 percent of the secretaries interviewed who assume both the general counsel and the secretary role very often have a dual reporting line – to the chairman for their secretary role and to the CEO in their capacity as general counsel.

The results of the self-completion questionnaires show that reporting lines to the chairman are more common in bigger companies, which makes sense: The bigger the company, the higher the possibility that the secretary is working more or less exclusively for the board, allowing for a reporting line to the chairman. In smaller companies, the secretary often has a number of other responsibilities that call for other reporting lines.

If we look at the less frequent reporting lines indicated in the questionnaires, we find 13 percent of the respondents reporting to the finance director and 1 percent to the head of investor relations. Such reporting lines are more frequent in Other Regions, Asia, and the United Kingdom and are by far less frequent in the United States. As we learn from our personal interviews this sort of reporting is quite often the result of the secretary's professional background. If he/she was active in the finance department before becoming company secretary it may well be that their previous reporting line continues. In our interviews we found only two secretaries in the United Kingdom who have a primary or secondary reporting line with the finance director; there was none in the United States. Finally, 7 percent of the respondents to the questionnaire are reporting to the head of legal affairs/general counsel. Whether these are primary reporting lines or not cannot be concluded from our data. The rather low number, however, is not surprising – quite a significant number of secretaries are assuming the dual role of general counsel and secretary and are, therefore, themselves "head of legal affairs." Our finding that the secretary reports to the head of legal affairs more frequently in bigger companies can most certainly be explained by the fact that in bigger companies the general counsel is often not in a position to assume the role of secretary himself/herself – he/she instead "delegates" a specialist from among his staff to handle the secretary function.

3.3.2.2 Support from the chairman of the board

Our respondents appear reasonably satisfied with the support they get from the chairman (see Chart 3.3).

Forty-one percent of all respondents agree to a great extent with the statement, "I typically get enough support from the chairman." This is the highest share across all 11 statements. It is definitely good news in light of the increasing importance of the secretary function. Chairmen seem to be aware of the importance of having a company secretary who is satisfied with his/her job and they therefore provide the necessary support. Only 1 percent of the respondents confessed that they did not agree with the statement at all. Of course, one can wonder how self-critical our respondents allowed themselves to be in such a survey,

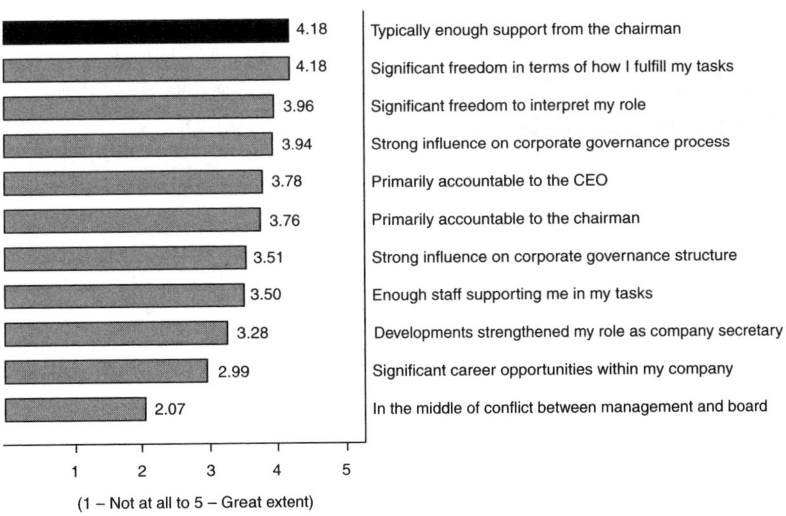

Chart 3.3 Support from the chairman (level of agreement)

particularly with respect to one of the more sensitive questions. Even taking this possible bias into consideration, the results are interesting; especially when one takes into account that only 60 percent of the company secretaries have a reporting line with the chairman (see Section 3.3.2.1). It seems that chairmen, irrespective of reporting lines, support the company secretaries in their performance of such a crucial function for the company.

3.3.2.3 Discretion

Chart 3.4 illustrates that overall our respondents are pretty happy with the level of freedom they have in terms of how to interpret their role and slightly happier with the operational discretion, that is, how they do fulfill their tasks (rather than what they do).

The difference between these two responses, or levels of agreement, although rather small is understandable. It is clearly the primary responsibility of the board to define the role of the secretary ("strategic" freedom) but it makes sense to leave it to the person in charge to define the ways in which they fulfill the tasks ("operational" freedom). Interestingly, however, 25 percent of respondents indicate that the statement, "I have significant freedom in terms of how I interpret my role as company secretary," matches their own situation to a great extent. This is certainly a sign that an impressive number of secretaries seem to play a

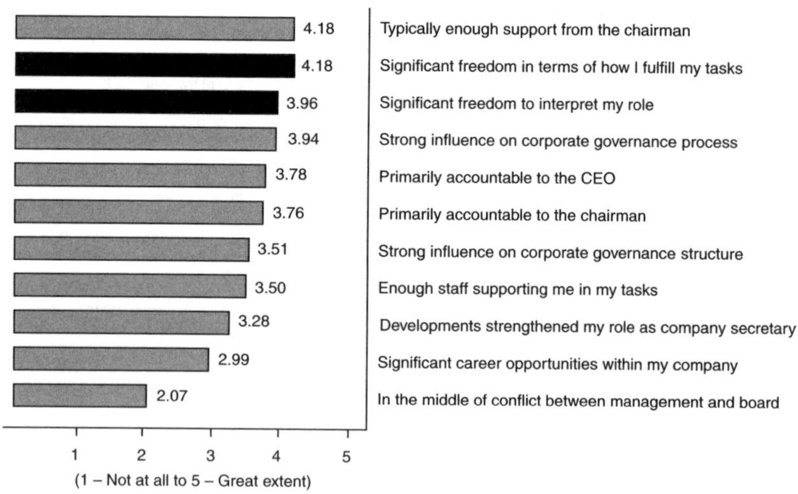

Chart 3.4 Strategic and operational discretion (level of agreement)

strong role in their company. On the other end of the scale, none of the respondents reported that they had absolutely no freedom at all in terms of interpreting their own role; only one respondent expressed the feeling that he/she had no room to exercise any type of operational freedom.

Our personal interviews confirm this overview. Many of the secretaries interviewed are strong personalities who are willing and able to shape their own function. Or, as one interviewee summarizes:

> Strong personalities have their own ideas and take initiatives. Weak ones do what they are told to do.

Legal and organizational structures and constraints, of course, have their impact and the personalities of the chairman and/or the CEO also play a role. One Swiss secretary working in a company that has experienced a number of organizational changes over the past years discusses the situation:

> With the increasing challenges our company was facing because of its global development I grew into a new role and I was given the opportunity to develop a new corporate governance design of the firm, partly necessary because of our listing at the NYSE. Based on my growing experience, I also gained the full support of the chairman. The secretary function was upgraded in the internal hierarchy.

A French secretary demonstrates passion and confidence in initiating significant changes:

> I am continually fostering the introduction of further improvements in our board performance. The chairman is sometimes hesitating a bit when I want to go forward too quickly. But I try hard to convince him and the board of the importance of strong governance standards. As a next step we are now planning, upon my proposal, to have the chairman of the audit committee present the activity of his committee directly to shareholders at the AGM. This will make our AGM a more active, more interesting event.

Such personal comments may be somewhat biased. In fact, the respective secretaries may not normally make such comments in public, knowing that the secretary is not the person "running" the board but is a person who is able to influence a lot "behind the scenes." These statements do show that it is not always necessary to really be in the public focus to exert influence. Another Swiss secretary encapsulates this sentiment:

> The secretary should be omnipresent but invisible.

3.3.3 Working relationship and allegiance

3.3.3.1 For whom are the secretaries primarily working?

The person to whom a company secretary reports directly is not automatically the person for whom he/she primarily works. The reasons for this are manifold. It is possible that a previous reporting structure continues despite changing working relationships; it may also be that there are organizational reasons that do not allow for congruent structures. German companies, for instance, normally do not have their secretary report to the chairman due to the fact that the chairman is not an employee of the company and, therefore, cannot have managerial responsibilities.

Of the questionnaire respondents, 60 percent indicated that they reported to the chairman (see Table 3.5) but 60 percent also said their primary working relationship was not with the chairman. We see an even more contradictory picture with those reporting to the CEO, 67 percent, while only 47 percent have their primary working relationship with the CEO. One reason for this lack of congruence may lie in the definition given by the respondents to what the primary working relationship is in practice. Many might have put their focus on the respective corporate bodies rather than on the individual people, indicating that they were primarily working "for the chairman and the board in general" or "for the CEO and management in general." Of all respondents, 40 percent reported that they are primarily working for the chairman, 56 percent for the chairman and the board in general, 47 percent mentioned that they are primarily working for the CEO, and 47 percent for the CEO and management in general (Table 3.6). A significant number of secretaries have strong working relationships with both board and management, or with the chairman and the CEO.

Primary working relationships with the CEO are most frequently reported by secretaries in the United States (by a large margin) and by secretaries in Western Europe – results that are in line with the structures of the respective boards. In the United States, most secretaries working with a chairman-CEO are likely to consider the CEO's role as the key function and would therefore not make a clear distinction between work done for the CEO and work done for the chairman.

Table 3.6 Working relationship

As company secretary for whom are you primarily working? (Mark all that apply)	**% of respondents**
CEO	46.7
CEO and also management in general	47.1
Chairman of the board	39.9
Chairman of the board and also the board in general	55.9
Investor relations	10.8
Finance	11.8
Legal affairs	27.5
Other	3.6

In some Western European countries, mostly those with two-tier boards and nonexecutive chairmen, it is standard practice that the secretary works primarily for the CEO because the chairman holds an external position and often does not even have a permanent office at the headquarters. Our personal interviews also confirm that those secretaries who are in charge primarily as general counsel have a much more intense working relationship with the CEO; they often delegate part of the secretary duties to a staff member while concentrating themselves on legal affairs.

The least number of secretaries who say that their primary working relationships are with the CEO come from the United Kingdom and Asia. The increasing number of UK companies with a strict separation of chairman and CEO functions, despite the unitary board structure, certainly supports a more intensive direct working relationship of the secretary with the chairman.

Overall, we also see that secretaries in listed companies are more frequently working primarily for the chairman and the board in general than secretaries in nonlisted companies. These findings are underpinned by our personal interviews and are easily explainable. Secretaries in large organizations (more numerous among listed and publicly owned companies) are often much more exclusively active on the board side of the organization and therefore are not working for the CEO at all. Furthermore, a primary working relationship with the chairman is more common in family-owned companies than in companies without family ownership.

Aside from the two primary working relationships – chairman/board and CEO/management – we find 28 percent of the respondents having a strong working relationship with legal, although only 7 percent are also reporting to the head of legal affairs. Presumably, a number of secretaries need help from the legal department when working on complex legal and regulatory issues and they would, therefore, have a strong working relationship with legal. The outcome that this working relationship is more frequent in bigger companies, however, is in line with the higher percentage of secretaries reporting into legal, which was identified in bigger companies.

Twelve percent of our respondents to the questionnaire indicated primarily working for the finance department; this may be a bit surprising, although about the same percentage of respondents is also reporting into the financial area. The role of the company secretary is only rarely a financial function and it may be that the working relationship with finance is strongly based on financial reporting. The fact that an additional 11 percent of respondents reported that they are working primarily for investor relations may confirm this assumption.

3.3.3.2 To whom are the secretaries primarily accountable?

Having analyzed the reporting lines and the primary working relationships, we wanted to know to whom the secretaries are primarily accountable: We felt that this would provide us with a more comprehensive picture of secretaries' position within the corporate governance structure. Is the reporting line more important than the main line of accountability or does the primary working relationship prevail? And what if the various people and organizational units do not always follow the main goals?

Again, we first look at the question whether secretaries are rather accountable to the chairman or to the CEO. While for reporting lines and primary working relationship we used multiple-choice questions (see Table 3.5 and Table 3.6), we measured respondents' accountability through Likert scales ranging from 1 to 5 (see Chart 3.5).

The statements "I am primarily accountable to the chairman of the board" and "I am primarily accountable to the CEO" match the respondents' situation at almost identical levels: 3.76 and 3.78, respectively. Of all respondents, 33 percent used the top ranking (five) for their primary accountability to the chairman, 40 percent for their primary accountability to the CEO. On the other end of the scale, 4 percent have no primary accountability to the chairman and 9 percent have no primary accountability to the CEO.

Whereas the 9 percent that have no primary accountability to the CEO can be explained – structures with a two-tier board, an independent

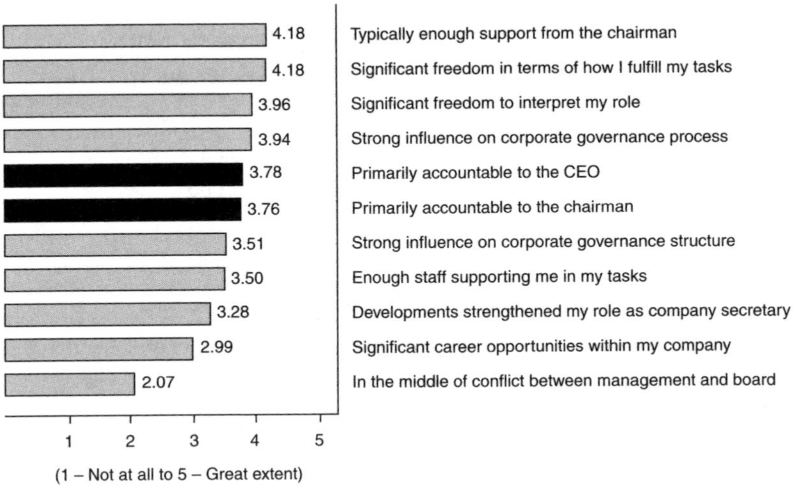

Chart 3.5 The secretary's primary accountability (level of agreement)

chairman, and a secretary exclusively reporting to the chairman – it is difficult to understand how someone can act as the secretary to the board without being accountable to the chairman, even if we only asked for primary accountability.

Secretaries in listed and larger companies reported a stronger accountability to the chairman of the board while overall accountability to the CEO is weaker in bigger companies. This is plausible for the following reasons: Larger companies more often have company secretaries working exclusively with the board (likely even more so if the companies are listed). Nevertheless, the split between reporting and accountability may lead to problems, tensions, and even conflicts of loyalty.

3.3.3.3 Allegiance and loyalty conflicts

Having dual reporting lines to the chairman and the CEO, or reporting exclusively to the CEO and primarily working for the board, is not a big issue if the two individuals (and in the case of two-tier boards, the two corporate bodies) work well together. As Chart 3.6 suggests, conflicts occur with minor intensity and/or frequency. This is good news (although responses to this rather sensitive question should not be taken lightly at face value). Hopefully, most boards work well and in the interests of all stakeholders, putting personal conflicts aside. But we all know that conflicts occur. CEOs are fired for myriad reasons and chairmen are forced to step down. Leaking strategy disputes between the

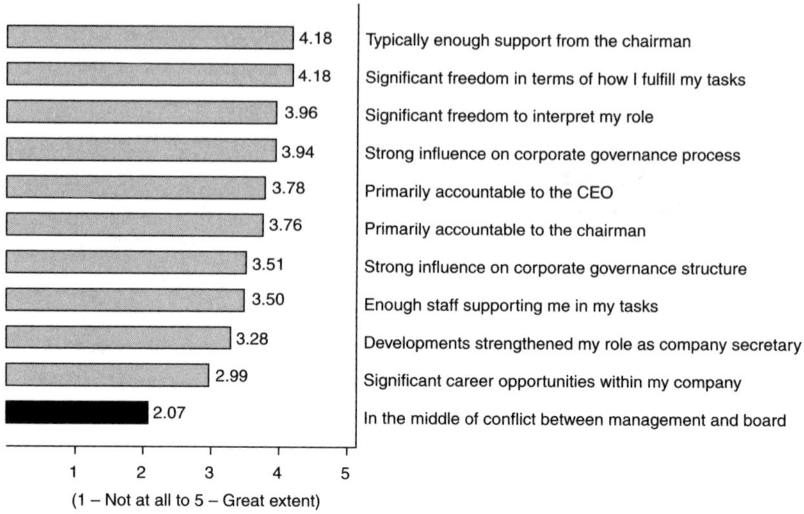

Chart 3.6 Conflicts between management and board (level of agreement)

board and management to the public is no longer an extraordinary event but it can be a clear sign of deep-seated conflicts among a company's top leadership. For the secretary who finds himself/herself stuck between the two sides such a dispute can be enormously difficult. Secretaries might be somewhat hesitant to officially confirm these types of conflicts – a social-desirability bias. If, however, we look at the response details to our question we see that almost 30 percent of respondents rated their agreement with the statement about occasional conflicts between board and managements between three and five (five means agreement to a great extent). This clearly suggests that frictions can – by no means – be ruled out.

The results of our questionnaire show that conflicts between board and management are more frequent in Western Europe and Asia and less frequent in the United States and Other Regions. This is not surprising; in the United States the combined chairman-CEO role is still very popular and conflicts between chairman and CEO are, therefore, not possible. Differences between board and management do, however, also happen but the problem solving might take a different form. In some Western European countries, mainly those with two-tier boards, tensions between chairman and CEO are understandable to some extent, particularly if both are strong personalities and if the definition of the two roles is not crystal clear.

To better understand the role of the company secretary in the broader context of corporate governance, we placed an emphasis in our personal interviews on the question of how secretaries are handling potential conflicts of loyalty in the case of severe differences between chairman and CEO. Quite a few interviewees responded like a true Solomon:

> My loyalty is neither with the chairman nor the CEO; it is with the company.

However, we all know that this might be true in theory but probably not really work in practice.

The clearest and easiest position is for secretaries working in two-tier systems who have an exclusive reporting line to the chairman. The board discusses highly sensitive personnel issues without participation of management and the secretary does not feel embarrassed, because of not having an allegiance with the CEO. One secretary whose company went through a tough discussion about firing the CEO looks back:

> Our board had extremely unpleasant discussions because of intense tensions between the chairman and the CEO and it came to the conclusion that only by separating from the CEO could there be an acceptable solution. As the secretary to the board I was involved in all these discussions, and confidentiality was a top priority, at least in the first phase of the process. I don't know how I would have handled the situation if I also had a reporting line with the CEO.

Generally, in companies with unitary boards the situation is less critical, mainly in those firms with a combined chairman-CEO role. If there are extreme tensions between the board and management, the chairman-CEO remains the key person and to some extent is "sitting on both sides" of the conflict. In this situation the secretary will automatically be seen to be on the chairman-CEO's side of the issue. The only question is whether he/she might be involved in discussions of the (nonmanagement) board members regarding the possible steps that might be taken against the chairman-CEO. A French secretary is quite relaxed about that:

> Severe conflicts between the chairman-CEO and the rest of the board would have to be resolved in a reasonable and flexible way, with "common sense." There would not be additional problems for me as the secretary because it is clear for the board that I am part of management, as is the chairman.

An American secretary working closely with the chairman-CEO but formally reporting to the general counsel points to a different potential loyalty conflict: In the case of really critical personnel issues discussed within the board he might feel some "loyalty conflicts" with his boss, the general counsel. Owing to confidentiality requirements he would not be able to keep him adequately informed.

For the most part, secretaries in both unitary and two-tier board structures who simultaneously assume the secretary and general counsel function do not have problems with defining their position in theory; they "act in the interests of the company," "concentrate on pure legal considerations," "make an independent judgment," and so on. But they also quite openly admit that in practice this could be much more difficult.

A pragmatic "solution" – namely, the board holding a special meeting without the secretary present – is described by a number of secretaries who work primarily in two-tier structures where the secretaries report to the CEO (although this is also applicable to some working in companies with unitary boards). Extremely delicate issues, mainly personnel decisions with conflict potential, may be best dealt with in this manner.

In one of the most striking examples of how delicate these situations can be we interviewed the secretary of a German company on the topic of how he would handle a potential conflict if his CEO, who he reports to, found himself in a clash with the supervisory board. Rumors about tensions between his company's supervisory board and his CEO had been rampant in the media over the last weeks prior to our discussion. Our interview partner, who had already experienced the forced departure of a CEO some time earlier in his career, said that he expected the supervisory board to discuss such delicate issues in an executive meeting without the secretary present. This would prevent him from running the risk of finding himself in the middle of a loyalty conflict. The weekend following our interview confirmed his perspective: The CEO stepped down upon "mutual agreement," without a formal board meeting and without the secretary being involved.

An American secretary defines the situation as "divided loyalty" but underlines that his primary loyalty in a severe conflict between board and chairman would definitely have to be with the board, despite his close association with the chairman.

> In such a situation it is crucial that the board has full trust in the secretary knowing that he would never break his confidentiality

> commitment, regardless of personal and working relationships with the chairman.

A Swiss secretary reported his experience with a difficult situation that involved his company going through a process of separating from more than one member of the executive board, including the CEO, after the discovery that there had been an inappropriate use of compensation vehicles. Despite his reporting line to the CEO, the secretary, who also serves as the general counsel, worked closely with the external chairman in an attempt to provide optimal support, mainly on the legal side of the issue, and with the aim to solve the problem. He comments:

> Such a situation requires that you completely avoid playing politics. You have to contribute to finding solutions in the interests of the company, giving first priority to legal considerations although you should always be aware that nobody is able to be completely neutral and to fully abstain from making own judgments.

This assessment is certainly correct but it shows the potential problems inherent in dual reporting or split accountability. The view expressed by a British secretary, primarily reporting to the finance director and with a second reporting line to the external chairman, confirms this dilemma. He hoped that he would be able to take an independent judgment but was aware of the difficulty given the personal relationships. He openly expressed his relief about potentially being excluded from such critical meetings:

> The board would solve problems resulting from a severe clash between chairman and CEO outside the meetings and I would therefore not be directly involved.

An American secretary, who in a previous assignment with another company experienced the firing of the chairman-CEO by the board, confirmed this handling of the awkward matter:

> I was not invited to act as secretary for the critical meetings. The chairman of the corporate governance committee assumed the secretary function and I was only later informed, of course before the decisions were made public because I had to take care of some organizational issues, mainly in communication.

It seems that this way of handling difficult personnel decisions is quite common. Almost all the German secretaries, who usually have no primary reporting line with the chairman but are reporting to the CEO, and often also assuming the general counsel role, told us that the supervisory board would probably deal with such issues in meetings without the secretary. The same was confirmed by some of the British and French secretaries.

When we asked, however, how formality issues would be handled in such a situation, we found that many of the secretaries were somewhat hesitant to answer, possibly knowing that formalities could really be a delicate issue. Who would make sure that all board members were informed properly before the meeting, including timely convocation, that the decisions were recorded properly, that confidentiality and ad hoc publication requirements were respected? One secretary even confirmed that the board would not take formal minutes of such "executive meetings." In today's legal environment, where any type of small formal mistake might lead to litigation and missed ad hoc publication to regulatory reprimands and/or fines, companies would be well advised to prepare for the formal side of extraordinary events. Of course, the firing of the CEO is certainly not what boards are dealing with most frequently, but today it is also no longer an absolute exception. For an American secretary whose company would also deal with such difficult situations in executive sessions, without the secretary present, there is no real reason for concern, however:

> Our lead director fortunately is fully aware of all legal and regulatory requirements and would therefore inform me in due course and in a legally perfect way of what has to be formally minuted.

One French secretary, reporting to the CEO in his role as general counsel and to the chairman as secretary, hinted at a rather drastic solution:

> In case of a real clash I might have to submit my resignation as secretary to the board.

Obviously, the option presented may not be an easy one, either for the secretary or for the board. A Dutch secretary believes that in a situation of a severe conflict between board and management his supervisory board would decide where the secretary's loyalty in the specific case would have to be and he would accept that decision.

There are a few companies where the potential problem of separating from the CEO seems to be less burdensome: If some very large shareholders are strongly represented on the board and those shareholders want to separate from the CEO, they may take very informal decisions without involving the secretary, sometimes only formally "informing" the other board members after the fact. A dominating shareholder on the board may even just "talk" to the CEO.

One of our American interview partners referred to potential loyalty conflicts, even in rather "normal" situations. External directors sometimes ask him for details on pending issues and transactions that for regulatory reasons cannot yet be provided, not even to the members of the board because this would trigger ad hoc publication obligations. He also reported on a situation in which he was confronted with a loyalty conflict toward his chairman-CEO, whose ordinary succession was handled by the corporate governance committee without the outgoing chairman being involved. The secretary had taken himself out of the process, acting only as facilitator for strictly administrative support but was nevertheless better informed than his boss. A US interviewee is very tough about all such situations:

> A person holding the secretary title must be in a position to deal with potential loyalty conflicts without taking any personal positions. This is part of the required profile.

Overall, we conclude that split accountabilities pose a significant challenge and should be avoided where possible.

3.3.4 Resources

Having enough staff supporting the secretary's work came out at a rather low 3.50 rating, eighth among the 11 proposed statements (see Chart 3.7). Apparently, there remains room for improvement be it on the organizational side within the secretary unit, through changed or adapted job descriptions, or by allocating additional resources to the existing structures.

Not surprisingly, secretaries in listed companies reported higher satisfaction with staff support, most probably because listed companies are facing stronger challenges in their effort to fully comply with a lot of highly complicated and always increasing requirements in the field of corporate governance and reporting. In order for companies to cope with these responsibilities, often falling within the aegis of the company secretary, more adequate support staff is provided.

In our personal interviews we did not find widespread problems with the staffing of the secretary offices. There are several explanations for

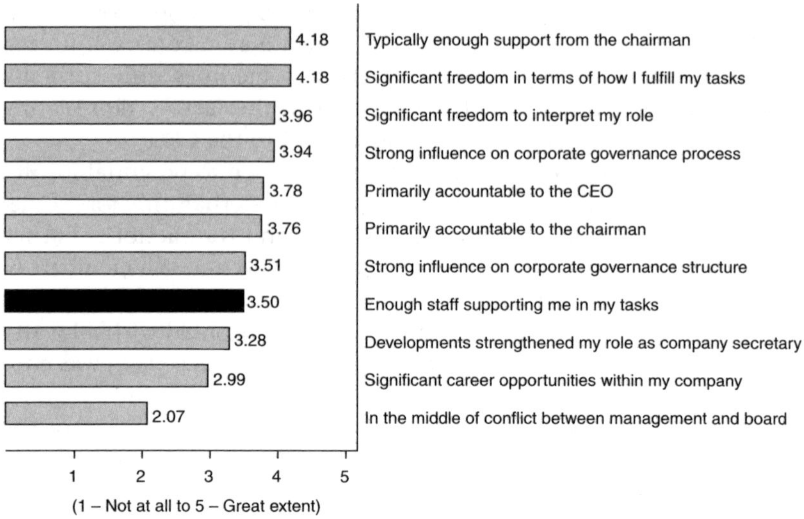

Chart 3.7 Staff support (level of agreement)

this: The fact that most of the secretaries interviewed are with large and listed companies confirms the findings of the survey. Efficient working organization and methods, good lobbying for enough staff within the firm, or, hopefully, the boards' recognition of the importance of well-functioning secretary units may be further reasons.

In addition to judging whether staffing was sufficient, secretaries were also asked how many people there were providing this support. The answer is anywhere between 0 and 200. Here, the job description makes the difference: Whether the secretary just has to handle board meetings and some additional administrative and regulatory issues, has overall responsibility for corporate governance, shareholders contacts, and administration, or has been assigned legal and regulatory reporting, ghost writing, or all sorts of other tasks clearly determines the staffing requirements. Furthermore, when answering our question, some secretaries might have focused simply on the actual "secretary" job, others on all their responsibilities; 200 people just for "secretary" responsibilities would clearly be difficult to legitimize. We also have to take into consideration that for smaller companies the company secretary is often not a full-time job and his/her support staff is most likely also engaged in a number of other activities.

In our personal interviews we found a wide variety of organizational setups in the secretary offices, partly a reflection of the significant range in the number of support staff. Most of them, although active in rather large companies, are quite modestly staffed. Those having more than ten people working in the secretary's area have specific additional responsibilities:

- In Swiss companies, it is quite common that the secretary's office is responsible for keeping the shareholders register in-house, which may necessitate five to ten employees.
- In British and American companies, secretaries largely have responsibility for keeping corporate records and/or for managing subsidiary functions.
- Other secretaries are assigned to administrating compensation benefit plans, handling dividend schemes, and even managing corporate events.

We discuss the various tasks and responsibilities of the company secretary in Section 3.3.5 and present their huge variety, which explains the widespread answers regarding staffing.

If we look at all the respondents to our self-completion questionnaire, we find that they have an average of six people supporting them in their secretary function; 18 percent of them have zero to one supporting staff, another 18 percent only two staffers. Overall, 77 percent have five staff members or less whereas 91 percent have ten and less.

3.3.5 Tasks and responsibilities

In our self-completion questionnaires we listed 15 different tasks asking the respondents, in their role as company secretary, to rank them in terms of their importance (see Chart 3.8).

The results are very much in line with what we expected and they provide a good overall picture of the company secretaries' role, as well as the priorities within their various tasks and responsibilities. Before discussing our proposed tasks and responsibilities, we take a short look at the broader picture that we gathered through personal interviews. What are company secretaries doing in addition to the 15 jobs listed? How do they see their function overall?

One Swiss secretary with an exclusive reporting line to the chairman of the board said:

> The company secretary is the "nerve center" with the responsibility to proactively manage all board affairs which includes providing ideas and acting as the sounding board for the chairman.

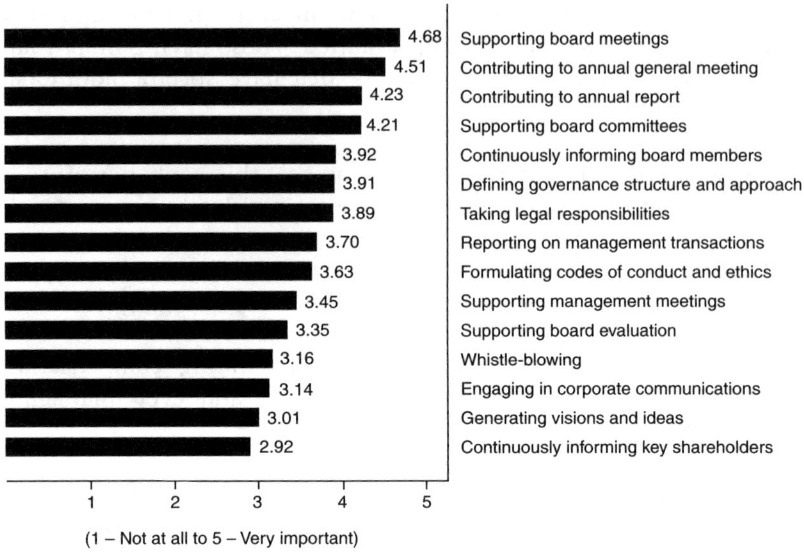

Chart 3.8 Importance of tasks and responsibilities

A French secretary who is head of legal affairs on Group level, summarizes:

> My role is that of being the "legal conscience" of the company and, therefore, I keep a lot of the key tasks of the company secretary in my own hands, without much delegation.

Another French secretary views his role in a much more narrow way when he explains:

> The main function of the secretary is to certify board decisions.

Or, as an American colleague formulates it:

> My mandate is to ensure that all corporate actions taken are properly prepared, reviewed, authorized and documented and that all processes related to the board and executive committee run smoothly and efficiently.

We found a somewhat special situation in many German companies that have a strict two-tier board system with the rule that the supervisory board, in general, does not have its own personnel resources. In most of the companies, the "company secretary" function does not exist. The tasks and responsibilities mentioned in our questionnaire are sometimes taken on in a rather ad hoc way; they are often assumed by the general counsel or the head of the CEO's office (Vorstandssekretariat) who, in English, might be called a "corporate secretary." Not surprisingly, these "secretaries" normally have more responsibilities with the management than with the supervisory board, resulting in the following often heard statement:

> Most of my time is taken by the responsibilities I assume on behalf of the "Vorstand."

In one of the German companies surveyed, the general counsel supports the supervisory board, while the "Vorstand" relies on the support of the head of the chairman's office (Vorstandssekretariat).

Most of our interviewees have a broad variety of responsibilities – a large portfolio of different tasks. One British secretary reported that there are six different departments within his unit – corporate governance, board secretariat, group risk, corporate social responsibility, security, and business ethics. The business portfolio of a French "secrétaire général" looks even more diverse – legal affairs for the Group, compliance monitoring, taxes, internal audit, regulatory reporting, ethics, and sustainable development. Another French general secretary is responsible for the following tasks for the Group – legal department, corporate governance (including governance of all the subsidiaries), functions such as corporate responsibility, security, insurance management, the relationship with institutional shareholders, government relations, group real estate worldwide, general support for the head office, competition and regulatory affairs and last, but not least, a number of specific tasks which he assumes on behalf of the chairman-CEO (e.g. communication and group organizational issues). One British general counsel/secretary has the overall responsibility for remuneration issues at the highest level of the company. Another British secretary manages the employee share schemes, while a third assumes significant functions with the preparation of acquisitions whenever shares of the company are involved.

In the United States, one of the secretaries referred to his responsibility for a widespread list of topics involving the company's stock, such as long-term incentive plans and senior executive compensation. The corporate secretary's responsibility of keeping the share register is quite popular in Switzerland, while in some other countries the secretary simply oversees the external transfer agent's (external firm running the company's share register) activities. A Dutch secretary who also assumes responsibility for the share register is additionally responsible for the company's hospitality services, the company drivers, and the chairman's and the CEO's personal assistants. Another Dutch secretary mentioned public affairs, sustainability, and donations as his special assignments.

If we take into consideration the significantly large variety of interviewees' tasks and responsibilities, it may be correct to suppose that the respondents to the self-completion questionnaire also assume a number of other responsibilities than those proposed in our list. Some respondents made explicit mention of their additional tasks. From these citations, we quote the following rather than citing specific individual answers: supervision of internal control soundness, quality management systems, litigation management, board remuneration, corporate planning, and the insurance portfolio.

The relative importance of the different tasks may well depend, in part, on whether the respondents really examined the list with their "secretary hat" on as we had asked them to do in our questionnaire. This might have an influence on the ranking of the various tasks. We are, however, confident regarding the overall picture provided.

In Sections 3.3.5.1–3.3.5.7, we report in detail about individual tasks and responsibilities.

3.3.5.1 Board support

Almost by definition, board support is the most important element in the job of any company secretary. This understanding also makes it clear that the secretary role, as important as it might be, remains a support function. The secretary is not a separate and independent "corporate body" and it would be wrong to look at the secretary as the person making corporate governance or even corporate strategy decisions by himself/herself. The boards are responsible for running the company and they are accountable to shareholders. They are legally liable if anything goes wrong. But the fact that company secretaries do not ultimately make the decisions does not mean that they do not play an important and crucial role in preparing them.

Through our personal interviews we learned a bit more about support of the board in a general sense, beyond just supporting board meetings (which we will cover in a separate section below).

In many firms, the company secretary is the person who becomes the chairman's first point of reference, whether the secretary has a direct reporting line to him/her or not. Some respondents explain that they are the "person of confidence," the "person of trust," some others act as "sounding board" for the chairman. We found a number of secretaries supporting the chairman as ghost-writers by answering letters from shareholders, clients, and the general public. They also organize the chairman's business trips and meetings with clients and government officials.

Most secretaries are also in charge of planning board activities, in part based on their own initiative and in part following the chairman's instructions. By establishing the annual activity program of the board, the secretaries assume the burden of making sure that all legal and regulatory requirements can be met – meetings have to be scheduled in a way that allows the board to make its decisions in a timely manner, that committee meetings preparing the board's decisions take place in a reasonable timeframe prior to the full-board meeting, and that the necessary documents for the meetings are available on time.

As one of his important responsibilities, an American secretary cites, "helping the chairman and the directors to properly perform all legal and regulatory duties and requirements." A French colleague formulates his mission in this respect as "making sure that decisions are taken in the correct way by the competent bodies, avoiding conflicts of interests." Most company secretaries have the overall monitoring responsibility in the field of corporate governance compliance that is highlighted by a British secretary who says that his role is to ensure that board activities are in full compliance with listing standards. Serving as liaison-officer between the board and the management, a job that differs in one-tier and two-tier structures, is a role mentioned by many of the secretaries interviewed. In companies with supervisory and management boards which are strictly separated, it is quite often the secretary who has to make sure that the information flow is functioning properly – which is not always an easy task. If the company secretary is placed on the management side of the company (reporting to the CEO), there might be some hesitation on the board's side as to whether the information provided is really neutral or just "management's view." If, however, the secretary is firmly on the board's side (reporting exclusively to the chairman), it is possible that getting the necessary information from management is more difficult. We conclude that being successful in this part of the job really depends upon the personality of that secretary; he/she is well advised not to play politics and not to use the position of his/her boss when asking the "other" side for support. It should be the secretary's persuasiveness that leads to the results.

Acting as intermediary between nonexecutive board members and the company is another important responsibility that most secretaries have in the field of general board support. With the increasing importance given to the independence of boards, mainly vis-à-vis management, there is a growing need for a confidant to assist the external board members in performing their duties. In most companies, the secretary assumes that role and many companies state explicitly in their corporate governance guidelines that all directors have full access to the secretary. Some national Codes of Best Practice even consider this free accessibility of the secretary for external directors as a "must" for good governance.

Many of the secretaries interviewed qualify their intermediary and support role vis-à-vis the external directors as crucial; some of them confirmed that this might lead to tensions between the secretary and the chairman and/or the CEO. It appears that some chairmen and CEOs still have to be convinced that "independence" of the external directors means being in a position to take independent decisions, not just having no business relationships with the company. The following quote from a Swiss secretary illustrates the point:

> At the beginning my chairman was not really happy when I had direct contacts with the external directors and even more so, if I helped them with collecting independent information. I had to convince him that this was in no way an unfriendly act against either chairman or management but that I tried to contribute to a better understanding of the issues to be dealt with by our directors. Of course, I inform the chairman of important requests but I think it would be wrong to always have to ask for his permission as I am completely aware of what is in the overall interests of the company.

We discuss the challenging relationship that sometimes occurs between the secretary and the independent directors, as well as the relevance of the support given to those directors in Sections 3.3.5.1.1 and 3.3.5.1.2.

When we asked our interviewees how they would summarize their overall role with supporting the board there were almost as many definitions as there were interviews. One company secretary may, however, be summing up the concept of board support in a short, broadly acceptable formula:

> To guarantee the legally correct, and smooth, running of the board.

3.3.5.1.1 Board meetings

Among the 15 tasks and responsibilities listed in our questionnaire, "supporting board meetings" received the highest average importance rating (see Chart 3.9).

Of all respondents, 76 percent chose the top rating of five, another 19 percent the second highest rating. Supporting board meetings has no

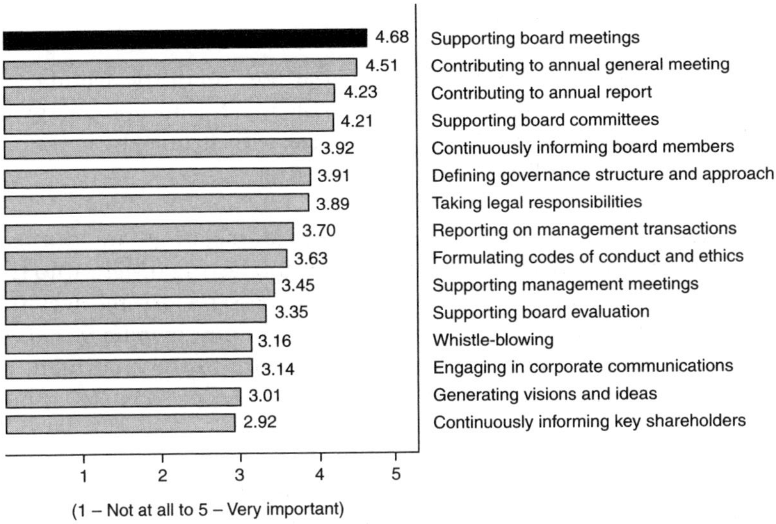

Chart 3.9 Supporting board meetings (task importance)

importance at all for only four out of 306 respondents. There is no significant variation between countries, different industries, small and bigger companies, or ownership structures. The only statistically significant difference we detected occurs between listed and nonlisted companies: Supporting board meetings is more important in listed companies. We attribute this to the fact that, on average, listed companies have larger boards and tend to hold meetings more frequently.

Our personal interviews allowed for a more in-depth look at what "supporting board meetings" means in practice. Of the interviewees, 94 percent are drafting agendas and are responsible for document distribution, 91 percent participate in the board meetings, 77 percent of those participating also write the minutes whereas 23 percent review the minutes which are drafted by someone else. Only four (accounting for roughly 6 percent) of our interview partners do not have any function regarding board meetings. In the following paragraphs, we will describe the tasks associated with supporting board meetings in more detail.

Agenda and supporting documents

When we talk about drafting the agenda, this also means quite different things to different people. Some company secretaries report that they simply put the standard agenda items together, others provide a lot of personal input as to the content and structure of the agenda.

As one secretary comments:

> Whether I put a topic on top or rather at the end of the agenda can make a difference: Directors might devote much time and energy to the item or they might be happy to deal with it quickly, if time is running out towards the end of the meeting.

The manner in which agendas for board meetings are drafted, discussed, and finally approved provides an interesting insight into the internal "power play." In some companies the secretary receives the input for the agenda exclusively from the CEO and/or members of executive management and submits the agenda only to the chairman for information. We also found some country-specific approaches to agenda setting:

- In German companies the agenda is discussed and agreed upon primarily with the CEO and sometimes even with the whole Vorstand before being submitted to the chairman for formal approval. This is primarily a result of the lack of a formal secretary function in that country and the lack of a reporting line to the chairman of the person supporting the board.
- There are similar procedures in French companies, especially when the chairman also assumes the CEO role.
- Although British companies generally split the roles of chairman and CEO they employ different approaches: In some companies the secretary discusses the agenda with both chairman and CEO. In others the secretary deals primarily with the chairman who makes the final decision about what should be included into the agenda.
- In American companies it is becoming common practice to have the presiding independent director give his final approval to the agenda. If the role of the presiding director is really to ensure checks and balances he must be the one to have final approval authority.

In all companies with a chairman independent from management, whether they have unitary or two-tier boards, it should go without saying that the chairman approves the agenda of board meetings.

Many secretaries reported having numerous contacts with various people in the organization when preparing the agenda. The secretaries collect input from the CEO, the CFO, the business division heads, the general counsel, the strategic planning or the investor relations department and others, and, last but not least, from the board committee chairmen. Of course, there are a number of items to be dealt with on a regular, even mandatory, basis and some companies seem to deal mainly with those topics. Other companies use board meetings to better familiarize the external directors with the company's business, therefore bringing the heads of various business units to board meetings so they can make presentations. It is often the responsibility of the secretary to make sure that these presentations receive the appropriate amount of time and adequate positioning on the agenda.

The collection and distribution of supporting documents to the members of the board is the next important step in terms of preparing board meetings. Almost all secretaries interviewed have this responsibility in their job description but the way they carry it out varies significantly from company to company. While a few of our interview partners simply distribute the documents they receive from management, the majority of them play a more or less significant role in preparing what goes out to the board members. They must approach the respective people within the company who have to prepare the documents, tell them what information should be provided, and explain the needs of the external directors. The company secretaries check the papers coming in and, if necessary, go back to the issuer with proposals for changes or amendments. Quite a number of secretaries are preparing some of the documents to be delivered themselves, mainly regarding the topics of corporate governance and legal issues, share transactions, and statistics. This also applies to other selective areas where the respective secretary has special knowledge or expertise. For example, one interviewee prepares most of the strategy papers himself; another has in-depth knowledge on compensation systems and programs.

One British secretary reviews all the documents before submission to the board. He is convinced that he is in a better position to provide the information necessary for external directors. Members of executive management and their high-level staff are often too closely involved with the topics and have too much detailed knowledge to understand what the external directors need. Documents tend to be too detailed and not close enough to the point. An Italian secretary confirms this issue: He "sees" all the documents before they are finalized and often takes action to make them more suitable for board members. He adds, however, that he is just advising the authors of the papers, not deciding to change documents. This is what he understands as "seeing" rather than "checking" the documents. One American secretary interviewed stresses the importance of reviewing all documents for legal compliance before their distribution.

Almost all our interview partners are confronted with one huge challenge when preparing document distribution for the meetings and that is time constraint. Ever-increasing legal and regulatory requirements necessitate more time for the preparation of documents. As a consequence of growing complexity, more and more explanations and comments are needed, requiring an increased amount of time for the external directors to familiarize themselves with the documents. And last but not least, financial markets expect quick and efficient board decisions and their immediate publication thereafter.

The technical handling of document distribution is usually a responsibility of the secretary's office. This is part of taking care of all of the logistics around board meetings including, in most cases, travel and hotel arrangements for external board members. A few companies have a special administrative assistant for the handling of logistics. In some companies this person is integrated in the staff department of the CEO, or is part of the general secretariat, and in others can even be the chairman's personal assistant.

The electronic distribution of board documents is still not very popular. One Swiss secretary talks about a special board tool set up for the distribution of meeting and other board documents but he reports that it is not widely used. Not surprisingly, the only company where documents have been distributed to board members exclusively via encrypted e-mail for more than two years now is a business software firm. Most secretaries informed us of their attempts to better use technology but such initiatives seem to meet significant obstacles. The main hurdle remains the issue of confidentiality despite the fact that encrypted systems are readily available. And as soon as documents have to be transmitted cross-border the hesitation increases. Companies seem to have more trust in the physical delivery of highly sensitive documents; many external board members also prefer receiving board material in a paper format. Those who study financial reports or complex strategy papers on the computer are still in a small minority. And board members who have to undertake long-distance travel to attend the meetings prefer printed documents so they can use their flight time for studying the material.

Our discussions with the secretaries confirmed an almost identical approach to the timing of document distribution. The agenda and supporting documents should be in the hands of the directors at least one week prior to the meeting. One secretary says:

> I always try to make sure that directors have at least one weekend between the delivery of the documents and the meeting. Many of our independent directors have busy schedules which may not allow for serious review of the papers during the week. I know that I have

> to put some pressure on all those in charge of preparing the documents but it is certainly not "good corporate governance" if our external directors are not in a position to build their own views and then to take informed decisions.

Security in general is a growing concern for many companies and not just regarding document distribution. Some secretaries, therefore, have responsibility for all necessary security arrangements in conjunction with board meetings (including personal protection). Others are only responsible for properly informing the internal security department of upcoming board events.

The board meeting itself

For some secretaries the preparation work for board meetings is completed when the documents that have been prepared by others are on their way to the board members. Most of our interview partners, however, are in charge of many additional preparatory responsibilities. One German secretary reports that he is drafting possible decisions on important agenda items for submission to board members unable to attend the meeting, allowing them to submit a written vote. In most companies, casting votes in writing for board meetings is not legal but if law and company statutes permit, it can be a way to avoid random outcome of important votes. In Germany it may be crucial to have all board members casting their vote because of the legal requirement of equal representation of shareholders and employees on the supervisory board. In the United States, where formalities have a much higher priority than in other countries, corporate secretaries often prepare formal resolutions to be voted on at the meeting. These proposals for resolutions are either distributed to board members ahead of time or are submitted to them during the meeting.

There seems to be some hesitation on the part of secretaries to mention that they can have a significant influence on how the chairman is running the meeting. One Dutch secretary is more relaxed, openly confirming that he writes a detailed speaking note for the chairman, a kind of "script" for the whole meeting. He sees nothing unusual with this since the chairman is nonexecutive and is not a lawyer himself. The responsibility falls on the secretary to make sure that nothing goes wrong legally during the meeting. A Swiss secretary confirms this outlook on the issue:

> My chairman asks me to provide every possible support for the smooth running of the meeting that includes giving him the comfort

> that all legal and regulatory requirements are carefully respected and that he has all legal background at hand, if needed. Of course, he knows best what to do on the strategy and/or business side. But it is my responsibility to guarantee compliance.

It is possible that more secretaries assist their chairman in a similar way but did not mention it to us because they consider it to be "normal" support or because they did not want to overstate their role. Some confirmed that they do sit down with the chairman before the meeting to review all of the meeting topics, discuss potential critical points, and decide how to handle them.

During the meeting

Support from the company secretary often goes further than meeting preparation; this is confirmed by a British secretary who said that he was "whispering into the ear of the chairman" during board meetings. Of course, this only occurs when the chairman has an explicit request to concentrate on business issues and not on meeting formalities. The primary aim is to make sure that all rules are followed correctly.

The role that the secretaries play during board meetings differs significantly from company to company. Some 90 percent of the secretaries interviewed personally participate in all board meetings, many of them alone and others together with an assistant secretary or someone else from the secretary's office. Generally, participation during the meetings is rather passive. Secretaries take a proactive role only rarely by intervening in board debates. One of our interviewees, a British secretary, is an obvious exception because he is an elected member of the board. A few others – members of the executive committee, mainly in their role as general counsel – may also take a more active part during the meetings; not primarily as "secretary" but in their management role. But when it comes to discussing corporate governance issues, it is likely that the secretary takes the lead, preparing the documents and contributing input during the deliberations. One British secretary reports that he has been preparing a corporate governance report for each board meeting, always the first topic on the agenda. In addition, he presents agenda items in greater detail and occasionally lays out "real-life cases" from the field of compliance and governance for board discussion. Another British secretary makes regular presentations to the board on changes of legal and governance provisions. He also shows updated statistics about how the board utilizes its time on a variety of issues. This provides the board with the ability to set future priorities. A German interviewee, who assumes the role of chief compliance officer, informs the supervisory board of important developments in the corporate governance field; he also makes presentations about compliance issues facing the company. An American secretary, while confirming her rather "quiet" role during the meetings, says:

> I am only active if governance issues have to be dealt with. But I know what my role is, namely to make sure the board members understand the issues and the resulting requirements. It is not my role to run the company.

Other secretaries prepare regular updates on share ownership and significant respective changes. Secretaries who also assume the position of general counsel generally play a more active role during board meetings. Their presentations and/or contributions to board discussions are overwhelmingly legal and sometimes of a regulatory or governance nature. Most of these secretaries, however, do not see these activities as part of their "secretary" role.

Minutes

Our interviewees have different views about the relative importance of taking board meeting minutes. Whereas for some of them this is just a burdensome responsibility, others see it as a crucial part of their job. As mentioned before, about three-quarters of the secretaries participating in board meetings take the minutes; one-quarter of them only review the minutes that are taken by a deputy. There are different reasons for this function split: In some cases, the secretary may not have the necessary time to assume the rather time consuming job of writing minutes, mainly if he/she is also the general counsel. Others assign the task primarily to a younger staff member giving him/her a challenge as well as potential career exposure. And there may be others who, to put it bluntly, just do not like taking minutes. As one British secretary openly confesses:

> Taking minutes is a strenuous, rather boring and bureaucratic job. I hate it but I know that I have to do it. Our chairman would not accept that someone else did it.

This, however, is a rather singular opinion. Many of our interview partners voiced a completely different view, rating the taking of minutes very highly:

> I would never delegate the taking of minutes to someone else. Correctly editing the minutes is highly challenging and interesting

> as one has to find the right way to finally have everything on record what is necessary.

One French secretary adds that in today's world taking minutes must be a lawyer's job. This view is confirmed by a colleague from another French company who refers to the legal responsibilities of board members and the importance of having complete and correct records in case of litigation.

This leads us to the question: What should be recorded in the minutes of board meetings? There are different philosophies about this and there may, of course, also be legal requirements as to what must be recorded. On one end of the spectrum specialists claim that minutes should be as short as possible, containing nothing more than the facts and figures leaving no room for interpretation. On the other end, there are those who feel it necessary to reflect all of the important opinions voiced during a meeting. They are convinced that these details might serve as clarification for individual board members in the advent of later disputes or even litigation. If minutes include information about the way the directors exercised their business judgment, they can be helpful in a court case where judgment is questioned. Detailed minutes may, in such cases, provide evidence of the directors' thoroughness when dealing with an issue. Too many details, however, can also be harmful. Taken out of context, the single statement of a director during a meeting can lead to wrong interpretation. Some of our interviewees add that directors can, of course, request to have their dissenting views recorded. But most of them also say how delicate this might be in really controversial situations. Therefore, it is not an exaggeration to say that taking the appropriate minutes is an art. Many of our interviewees confirm this point. One American secretary is very clear on the issue:

> This is the most important function of the corporate secretary. I therefore always take the minutes myself.

Other interviewees, in all countries, agree completely:

> Intelligent minuting of board debates is one of the most important tasks of the secretary.

The manner in which minutes are edited and finally approved by boards also vary from company to company. We found a few secretaries who just write the minutes and submit them to the chairman for approval and signing. There are, however, a substantial number of secretaries who have the draft reviewed by all board members and sometimes by attending executives as well. In some companies the secretary has to submit the draft to the CEO for review and later to the chairman for approval. Others have them reviewed by the general counsel for legal compliance. In most companies the board must approve the minutes at its next meeting so that they become legally binding.

There still seem to be some discussion about whether or not copies of the minutes should be sent to all directors; broad distribution includes the risk that confidential information can be leaked to the outside world. A number of companies may have found a feasible compromise: Minutes are sent to all directors prior to the next meeting. After the approval, copies are recollected and destroyed, avoiding having too many copies in circulation. This also avoids any discrepancy that might ensue when minutes are approved but not all of the changes are recorded in each of the existing documents. Despite one's approach it is the secretary's responsibility to make sure that corporate records are kept correctly; this also means having only one version of the final document.

Follow-up

When the board meeting is over, secretaries usually have to follow-up on the decisions taken. The most obvious follow-through is that he/she maintains a pending items list. The list is a means of monitoring what subsequent actions have to be taken and what issues have to be dealt with by the board again and therefore need to be put on the next board agenda. Many secretaries are in charge of providing excerpts from the minutes, informing a broad variety of people and organizational units within the company of decisions taken. Excerpts have to be delivered to all kinds of public authorities. One Dutch secretary reports that he passes all relevant information from board meetings to the communication department, which is then responsible for organizing the release of news if necessary. This may be a rather unique solution; important company information normally has to be prepared well in advance of the board meeting and communication staff should be involved with the early drafting of important internal and external releases. One of the American companies surveyed has a formal process for the appropriate distribution of information after the board meetings. The secretary and the chairman have an official debriefing with senior executives to ensure that everyone is properly updated and that the required follow-up is executed.

Executive sessions

A consequence of the increasing importance of outside independent directors and the aim of corporate governance to guarantee checks and balances between supervision and management is that most large companies (primarily those with unitary boards) now hold regular "executive sessions," that is, meetings exclusively including the nonmanagement or the independent directors. There are even some boards in two-tier structures utilizing the instrument of executive sessions, which in these cases usually refers to meetings without any management representatives present.

With the exception of companies where the secretary reports exclusively to an independent chairman, therefore not being part of management, the question of who "handles" executive sessions is not easily answered. Should the secretary, given his/her special accountability to the board, prepare such meetings, participate in them, and take the minutes? Or should the nonmanagement directors meet among themselves without any assistance from a management representative? From our interviews we learned that companies take different approaches. For many of them it seems not to be an issue if the secretary participates in these meetings, even if top-level personnel issues are discussed. Others have the secretary prepare the meetings, participate in them and take minutes but only for "ordinary" businesses. As we discussed earlier (Section 3.3.3), a frequent solution seems to be that executive sessions dealing with top-level personnel issues take place without the secretary, some with one of the board members taking the minutes and others without any record taking.

In companies with unitary boards it is generally the lead or presiding director who chairs the executive sessions; he/she is also in charge of informing the chairman and other members of senior management regarding the outcome of the meetings. If the relationship between nonmanagement directors and the secretary is based on complete trust, it is possible that the secretary participates in the meetings despite his/her reporting to the chairman. The board, however, must feel comfortable that the secretary will not leak any information to the chairman and/or other members of management unless he/she is formally authorized to do so. As one of the American secretaries says:

> Acting as secretary at executive sessions requires that you are extremely discrete, not disclosing any confidential discussions neither to your boss – the CEO – nor to anyone else. Sometimes you need some stomaching.

But even with the best understanding between secretary and external board members there may be some individual cases where the directors want to restrict the meeting to themselves. We had the impression during our interviews that strong secretaries, those who are self-confident in their role, will not have a problem with accepting such a decision. However, there is one thing that secretaries should not let go of under any circumstances: Making sure that decisions taken during executive sessions are properly recorded.

3.3.5.1.2 Board information

As outside independent directors play an increasingly important role in company oversight – including the definition of its strategy – and in the supervision of management, the more crucial it is to keep these directors informed. Only informed board members can make independent decisions. But who has to take care of this continuous flow of information?

It is generally the CEO or chairman who decides how external board members are informed between meetings. Many companies include board members in their distribution list for media releases; others distribute regular press clippings or put directors on the list of financial analysts' reports. In some companies, management provides a regular written report on financial and business developments. A Dutch secretary mentions explicitly that the chief internal auditor might also distribute information directly to external board members in very specific situations – very likely delicate ones. An American secretary specifies the rule in his company that is clearly the opposite:

> All information to be sent to external directors has to go through my office. This is the only source.

In another American company it is the presiding director who ultimately has the right to decide what information is being distributed to the directors.

The number of companies offering a special electronic information tool to their external board members is still quite small. One British secretary reports that his company has an electronic "team room," a password protected special information system for all board members. This system is frequently used by the external directors and contains all-important public releases, as well as information for internal use only. Other interviewees are rather disappointed that their systems do not really receive a lot of attention.

Some secretaries mention the organization of ad hoc telephone conferences, led by the chairman, for communicating important information to the outside directors. All this information, however, generally comes exclusively from the management side.

Given the importance normally attributed to directors' independence, it makes sense to raise the question of whether or not it is sometimes necessary to present the other side of the coin. One British secretary voices an interesting view when he explains that in special cases he tries to add a somewhat "external" view to some issues presented by the management:

> It is normal – and, in fact, the key responsibility of management – to look at things primarily from a business point of view. Things must be done in an efficient way. But it could well be that there were other aspects to be considered by the board when making decisions, e.g. the impact on the company's reputation, possible reactions of employees or clients, etc. It happens that I propose to the chairman that we add some "soft factor" considerations to the papers prepared by the people responsible for the business.

At first glance, a secretary's proactive approach to his/her role in informing board members may be rather unique. Yet in our interviews quite a large number of secretaries confirm that they always keep the needs of the external board members in mind when anything of interest happens in the company. Whether or not items are relevant to the external board members is sometimes a question of judgment. A Dutch secretary discusses this dilemma:

> Sometimes the importance of an event is questioned by members of the management who, due to their in-depth knowledge of all the circumstances, consider it more routine. I then try to take the view of the outside directors and see my role in best informing them – eventually even against the predominant view of management.

Many of our interview partners mention that they use their direct contacts with external board members as the primary way of providing them with important information. For most of the interviewees this seems to be so obvious that they do not even talk about it.

There are a few interviewees who are not allowed to provide information to external board members without the explicit approval of the CEO or chairman. Fortunately, this restrictive approach to communication seems to be fading away. Instead, general thought is moving toward the idea that board members have an explicit right to contact the secretary directly if they wish to gather information from company executives or other specialists. This grows out of burgeoning corporate governance guidelines, internal board regulations, and even a company's articles of association. In one of the American companies interviewed, we found an extremely open information policy: All board members have full access to about 100 senior executives throughout the company. A list including the executives' names, functions, business, and private contact information is distributed to all directors who then have access to these managers. There is no formality in this approach and communication is free and open without permission from the CEO or the secretary.

When we talk about supporting board members in this manner, we think that there might well be a special role for the secretary – intelligently gathering a selection of information, adding relevant internal facts and comments and distributing these materials. One French secretary voiced his conviction:

> I consider informing our external board members of important developments as one of my key tasks. This information must be timely, documents informative and self-explaining, not too comprehensive and focused on board members' needs.

In our self-completion questionnaire, "continuously informing board members" features as the fifth most important task (see Chart 3.10).

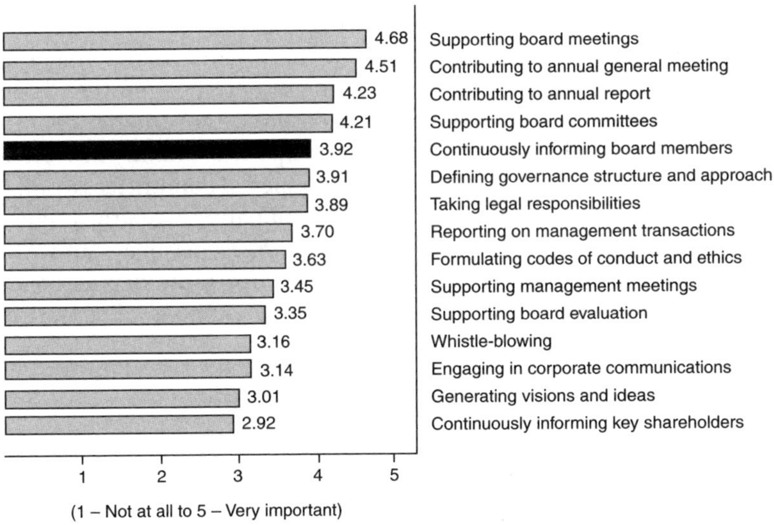

Chart 3.10 Continuously informing board members (task importance)

Respondents in Asia and the United Kingdom placed this task higher in their priorities than those in Western Europe and the United States; it is also given more weight by secretaries of listed and large companies. This latter significance is easily understandable because information needs in large and listed companies are generally higher and listed companies tend to be more strongly exposed to public scrutiny, making it even more important for board members to be well informed on a continuous basis. Why secretaries in Western Europe and the United States gave somewhat lower marks to this task is difficult to interpret. Because US companies have more board meetings in general, it is possible that there is less need for interim information. And regarding some Western European countries which do not have formal "secretary functions," it may well be that external board members are directly informed by management, if needed, without any secretary involvement.

It is obvious that supporting board meetings, rated at 4.68, is the top priority of most company secretaries. But owing to the increasing significance of corporate governance and the call for greater board independence, the need to keep board members better informed may well assume greater importance in the years to come. It may, in fact, be the company secretary who takes this responsibility even further than it is today.

3.3.5.2 Committee work

In Section 3.2.4 we discussed the growing emphasis on board committees, the way in which such committees are organized and how they work. It is a matter of fact that the creation of board committees is one of the key factors in the development of corporate governance over the past few years. Until only recently, many companies – mainly in Western Europe – had just an audit committee or no special committees at all. In the following sections we report on how company secretaries support the work of these board committees, what role they play, and with which committees they are primarily active (for more details on the number of committees per company and the number of committee meetings please refer to Section 3.2.4).

3.3.5.2.1 General board committee support

"Supporting board committees" ranks fourth among the tasks listed in our self-completion questionnaire (see Chart 3.11).

Only 4 percent of our respondents said that supporting board committees had no importance to them at all. Interestingly, however, 13 percent have no secretarial functions in any board committees (see Table 3.7).

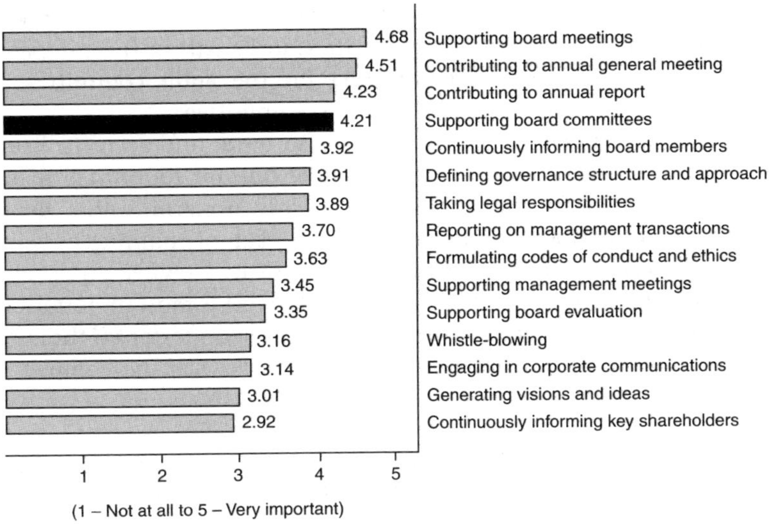

Chart 3.11 Supporting board committees (task importance)

It may be that some secretaries, while not acting as secretary to any of the board committees, still have some supporting responsibilities for board committees, possibly on the administrative and organizational side.

Our questionnaire data show that the importance of board committee support is contingent on a variety of factors:

- Location of headquarters. Board committee support is most important for secretaries in Asia and the United States and least important for those in Western Europe (by a wide margin). Furthermore, having no secretarial role on any committee is much more frequent in Western Europe and Other Regions and the least frequent in the United Kingdom and United States. It is plausible that committee support is an essential part of US company secretaries' work, particularly in light of stringent corporate governance rules that make the establishment of at least three independent board committees mandatory. Most Asian countries have similar legal structures to the United States and, therefore, the position of the secretary in the committees may also be similar. There is a far weaker involvement of the secretary in Western Europe. This is certainly the result of the lack of a defined secretary function in some Western European countries as well as some different structural board setups with less committee work. Committee support in these structures comes much more often from the respective business units within the company, for example, accounting/controlling for the audit committee or human resources for the compensation committee.

- Listing. Board committee support is also more important in listed companies; the lack of a secretarial role on any committee is less frequent in listed companies. This clearly underpins that board committees play a much bigger role (as a result of committees being mandatory) in listed companies than in privately owned ones.
- Ownership structure. Board committee support is most important in companies with dispersed ownership and least important if the company only has one shareholder; they may, in fact, be completely obsolete if there is only one shareholder.

In our personal interviews we wanted to get some more information on what secretaries are doing in practice. Interestingly, 18 percent of our interviewees do not assume any function with board committees – a higher percentage than what came out from our survey (13 percent) despite the fact that in the interviews the share of listed companies is much higher than in the survey. Yet, the share of Western European companies is also much higher among our interviewees than it is in the survey. Of our interviewees, five of those who have no role with board committees work for German companies where the secretary function broadly does not really exist and tasks are, therefore, often split among various specialists; three of the secretaries without committee responsibility are with Swiss firms, three with Italian, and two with French companies. One interviewee is with a Dutch firm where the secretary does not have administrative responsibilities; these duties being vested with special assignees from different areas. Governance issues, however, remain within the secretary's domain in this Dutch company.

The secretaries who assume committee responsibilities normally provide almost all of the same support as they do for the full board – drafting the agenda (primarily with the committee chairman), collecting supporting documents for the agenda items, distributing the documents, participating in committee meetings, taking minutes, and providing follow-up.

During the personal interview process we gathered additional information about the involvement of the secretaries regarding board committee work: Whereas 18 percent of interviewees are not participating in any board committee meetings, 14 percent participate in the meetings of one committee, 33 percent in two committees, 25 percent in three committees, and 10 percent in four or more committees. Almost all of those interviewees participating in committee meetings are also taking the minutes, mostly by themselves (85 percent) or partly assisted by a deputy or a specialist drafting the minutes that are subsequently reviewed by the secretary. Fifteen of the secretaries or their deputies are taking minutes in only one committee, twenty-four secretaries assume this role in two committees, seven secretaries perform this task in three committees. Finally, seven secretaries take the minutes themselves in four different board committees – obviously quite a heavy burden.

The responses to our self-completion questionnaire show that in terms of their work with board committees about 34 percent of the respondents assume secretarial functions in one committee, 28 percent in two committees, 23 percent in three committees, and 15 percent in four or more committees.

Through our personal interviews we learn that the level of secretary involvement in preparing board committee meetings differs significantly from company to company. The preparatory work for the committee meetings is likely to be in line with that of full-board meetings. Secretaries who simply collect documents from the internal specialists for distribution when preparing board meetings will normally do the same for the committees. Those who actively contribute to defining what to distribute to board members will often also exercise their influence on what is provided to directors for committee meeting preparation. All secretaries, of course, need more or less support from specialists depending upon the committee meetings' agenda topics. Some specific details will be discussed later when we describe the activities of the secretaries in the various committees.

3.3.5.2.2 The various board committees and the secretaries' involvement

While in our self-completion questionnaire we just asked in which committees the respondents were acting as secretary – with the logical possibility of multiple responses – we discussed the details of the role with our interviewees. The results are, therefore, not completely comparable. The survey shows that 43 percent of all respondents are acting as secretary to the nominating committee, 69 percent to the audit committee, 56 percent to the remuneration committee, 26 percent to the corporate governance committee, 31 percent to any other committees (e.g. investment or finance committee, risk management committee, corporate responsibility committee, investor's grievance committee, environment, health, and safety committee). Thirteen percent of respondents have no secretarial role in any committee (see Table 3.7).

Table 3.7 Secretaries' involvement in board committees

In which of the following board committees do you act as secretary? (Mark all that apply)	% of respondents
No secretarial role in any committee	12.9
Remuneration/compensation committee	56.3
Nomination committee	43.0
Corporate governance committee	26.2
Audit/compliance committee	68.5
Other	30.8

It should be noted that committees are not referred to by the same name in all companies. Firms may only have one or two committees assuming different responsibilities (see also discussion of committee work in Section 3.2.4), hence we have to take the results of the survey "cum grano salis." For example, the nominating committee is called corporate governance committee in many companies or it simply assumes both functions. We might, therefore, have to add the secretaries indicating having a secretarial role in the nominating committee to those with a function in the corporate governance committee. But we also see that quite a number of secretaries indicated that they act as secretary to the nominating as well as to the corporate governance committee (although it is rather unlikely that many companies have two different committees for these issues). Overall, we learn from our survey that the responding 302 secretaries assume a total of 586 secretary functions in their company's audit, compensation, and nominating/corporate governance committees. Yet, it is also likely that a respondent being the secretary to a combined nominating/compensation committee would have indicated a secretarial role for both committees thus increasing the number of secretarial functions.

From our personal interviews we are able to report that secretaries most often have an active role in the nominating and/or corporate governance committee. This is the case in almost 90 percent of all companies that have such a committee. In terms of secretary involvement, the audit committee ranks second in frequency with 60 percent and the compensation committee follows with 53 percent.

On the basis of our questionnaire findings we are able to detect several factors determining the overall secretarial activities for board committees. Secretarial activities for board committees are the most comprehensive in the United States and United Kingdom and the least in Western Europe and Other Regions. These duties are also more extensive in listed than in nonlisted companies as well as in companies with dispersed ownership; they are less so in family-owned companies and those with only one shareholder. Overall these results are plausible: Board committees play a more important role in the United States and the United Kingdom than in Western Europe and they are more important for listed companies (which normally have a dispersed ownership) than for family-owned companies – especially those which are non-listed – and firms with only one shareholder. Listed companies, for instance, generally face more detailed and challenging reporting requirements; therefore, committee work has to be organized much more professionally. These findings are underpinned by our personal interviews.

In the following chapters we will report in detail on the secretarial activities in the individual board committees.

Nominating and corporate governance committees

For the following analysis we combine the nominating and the corporate governance committees; in many companies there is just one committee that assumes both the nominating and corporate governance responsibilities. The mandate and responsibilities of the nominating and corporate governance committees may differ from company to company and are also influenced by the domestic legal systems and the respective corporate governance standards. Most of them, however, play a strong role in designing and monitoring the company's corporate governance and in preparing the nomination of board members. Normally they also oversee the outside directors' independence and support board self-assessments.

From our total number of respondents to the questionnaire, 130 said that they have a secretary role in the nominating committee, 79 have an assignment with the corporate governance committee – a total of 209 out of 302 respondents or 69 percent. But, as explained before, there may be some double counts in our survey. The characteristics of our respondents' engagement in the two committees do not differ significantly. For both committee types, secretaries are more involved if their companies are headquartered in the United States and the United Kingdom; they are less involved if their firms are based in Western Europe, presumably because companies in the United States and United Kingdom tend to have more of these committees. Secretaries are more often engaged in listed companies and large corporations. In addition, the responses to the question about nominating committees show that the secretaries seem to be assuming secretary roles less frequently in family-owned companies and companies with only one shareholder.

Both results are plausible because companies with few shareholders, often the case with family-owned firms, tend to have less need for special nominating committees – the nomination of board members and also of most senior executives typically falls under the responsibility of the family or the single shareholder. The secretary role is also less frequent in subsidiaries; confirming again that there is less need for nominating committees if ownership is concentrated, which is frequently the case for subsidiary companies. In most cases, decisions regarding the composition of the board and management of a subsidiary would be made at the parent company.

We get a more in-depth perspective of this topic through our interviews. Thirty-four companies have a nominating/corporate governance committee, some of which are called an appointing, selection, or succession committee; 16 companies combine the nominating and compensation functions into one committee. Within 11 companies the chairman's/presidential committee assumes the role of nominating and/or corporate governance committee and in another 4 companies this presidential committee has responsibility for personnel issues (usually covering nominating decisions/proposals but also top management compensation). In one company the full board takes care of nominating and corporate governance issues. Finally, three companies do not have any committee for nominating purposes – all of them have a special shareholder structure, either from being a subsidiary company with a 100 percent parent control or having a dominant government shareholder strongly influencing most of the personnel decisions.

Let us look at the secretaries' tasks in supporting those committees: 80 percent play an active role in preparing the meetings and participating – some of them participating alone and some together with a deputy. About 80 percent of those secretaries participating also take the minutes, while some 20 percent review the drafts made by their deputies. Thirteen of our interview partners do not play any role with the nominating/corporate governance committee and, as mentioned above, in three of the companies there is no nominating committee at all.

It is not surprising that a number of secretaries told us that they were playing a significant role in the nominating/corporate governance committee. As corporate governance is increasingly becoming one of the core responsibilities of the company secretary, it makes absolute sense that the secretary also takes a leading position in supporting and preparing the respective committee activities. Contrary to what may be typical of the secretary's work (having a rather passive role and not participating in discussions) during full-board and most other committee meetings, some of our interview partners are quite active during corporate governance committee meetings; they make presentations on corporate governance developments, propose changes in the corporate governance guidelines or committee charters (normally after consultation with the committee chairman), and may even be involved in the nominating process for new board members. One French secretary says:

> Our chairman strongly relies on my support when it comes to preparing succession on board level. I make suggestions as to the composition of the board: The required special knowledge, mix of nationalities, gender and age etc. And I establish a long-term succession plan containing the expected retirement dates of the existing directors and target qualification for potential succession candidates. Of course, the potential candidates themselves are evaluated and later proposed by the chairman.

The responsibility of a British secretary is under review with the aim of being significantly expanded:

> The board is currently planning to give me an active role in the contact with search firms for nonexecutive directors and the board wants me to meet with potential candidates for board membership. As I know in detail what is expected from new external directors, what their activities will be and what they have to take into consideration when they consider accepting such a role, it makes sense that they have a preliminary contact with me. I think I am also in a position to judge whether the candidate would fit with the company and its board.

Most American secretaries play a strong role in corporate governance in general (see Section 3.3.5.3 for details). One of them specifically mentions her role of helping the board with selecting candidates, mainly taking care of diversity considerations. Many of our interview partners, in almost all countries, refer to their involvement with setting up and even partially running the induction programs for new directors.

Whether the secretary needs significant support from the legal department or outside legal counsel or whether he/she handles things independently (while preparing nominating/corporate governance committee meetings and providing additional support) depends upon his/her professional background. It is, however, often also a question of the secretary's personality and the relationship between the secretary and the chairman of the board and/or the chairman of the nominating/corporate governance committee. One secretary reported the difficulties he was facing at the beginning because the chairman did not like him liaising "independently" with the committee chairman, especially on personnel and succession issues. Over time, the chairman accepted that the secretary made valuable contributions to the corporate governance of the company; today he is quite happy with the secretary's active role in the committee.

Our personal interviews also confirmed that the secretaries in the Anglo-Saxon countries are traditionally more strongly involved in nominating/corporate governance committee issues. This is a result, in part, of the fact that such committees have already been in place longer than in some Western European countries where secretaries first have to establish their role.

Audit/compliance committees

The most common committee across all countries and all companies is the audit committee. In our interview sample, 97 percent of the companies have a formal audit committee. The mandate and responsibilities of the audit committees are quite similar across a variety of companies. They review the adequacy and effectiveness of the company's financial reporting and its internal controls; they also appoint the external independent auditors or propose them to shareholders for election. In most cases, the audit committee also has responsibility for approving nonaudit mandates to the independent auditors and for dealing with whistle-blowing complaints. Many audit committees have additional responsibilities for risk control and compliance oversight.

Two of the companies interviewed do not have a formal audit committee. Among the remaining companies, 60 percent of the secretaries play an active role in the audit committee, sometimes together with the assistant or deputy secretary. They prepare the meetings, collect and/or prepare documents for distribution, and also often participate in the meetings. Five secretaries report that they only participate if there are special issues on the agenda, frequently in the field of corporate governance or compliance. Among those interviewees participating in the meetings, about two-thirds also take the minutes and one-third review the minutes done by an assistant or a specialist.

Two French secretaries report a very intensive involvement in the audit committee work:

> I used to be head of accounting prior to joining my current company as a company secretary and I also assume the role of head of compliance.

> It is, therefore, normal that I play an active role, regularly providing detailed reports to the committee. And we also do fairly detailed minutes which would not be possible without in-depth knowledge of all the issues dealt with by the audit committee.
>
> I prepare a great part of the documents for the audit committee, mainly in the field of business risk assessment, where the committee plays a key role.

A Swiss secretary reports the fairly intensive work that has to be done between the meetings such as submitting requests to the audit committee, or to its chairman, for nonaudit mandates to be assigned to the independent external auditors. Such requests have to be carefully prepared in order to avoid any negative impact on the external auditors' independence – timely decisions on such requests are often of primary essence.

Who is assuming the secretary function for the audit committee, if it is not the actual company secretary? The answers to this question include internal staff from the audit, finance, accounting, and controlling departments and in some cases, the general counsel, a specialized lawyer, or a special assignee to this function.

Sixty-nine percent of the respondents to our questionnaire assume a secretary role in an audit/compliance committee. In line with our findings from the interviews, we ascertain that a secretarial role on audit/compliance committees is the most common in the United States, Asia, and the United Kingdom and less so in Western Europe. It is somewhat unclear why it is also more frequent if company ownership is dispersed. The geographic findings are confirmed by our personal interviews: Secretaries not having an active role with the audit committee come mainly from Germany, France, Italy, and Switzerland. However, we cannot confirm that such roles are more frequent in companies with dispersed ownership. Almost all companies interviewed would fall into this category. The percentage of active roles, however, is slightly lower in our interviews than what came out of the self-completion questionnaire. The difference may well lie in the different interpretation of what an active role in a committee really is, as we described at the beginning of this chapter.

Compensation and remuneration committees

In 63 percent of the companies interviewed, a special compensation or remuneration committee is dealing with management compensation issues. Another 24 percent assign this task to a combined compensation/nominating committee and in the remaining 13 percent of the companies the chairman's/presidential committee has responsibility for this matter. The involvement of the secretaries in compensation committees appears to be significantly lower than with audit and nominating/corporate governance committee work. Almost half of the secretaries interviewed do not have an active role in those committees, mostly in Western Europe but also partly in the United Kingdom and United States. In most cases, specialists from the HR department – generally the head of executive compensation or compensation and benefits – is in charge of handling compensation committee activities. Two of the interviewees' companies even have an external specialist assigned to this function. In another two cases, the committees dealing with personnel/compensation issues simply do not take any minutes of the meetings. The chairman himself, supported by specialists from the executive compensation department, prepares the meeting.

Some secretaries, however, also play a strong role on compensation issues. In the case of a Swiss and a French secretary, their important role is obvious because they both are head of Group HR in addition to serving as secretary. One German secretary who used to be the head of the Group HR department before taking over as secretary is, of course, also an expert on all compensation issues; he therefore provides a great deal of input for the committee's work.

The secretary's role in compensation committees is being impacted, however, by the increasing importance of compensation issues, as well as the growing attention it is given by shareholders and the public at large. As a result of the expanding requirements with respect to compensation reporting, two US secretaries mentioned that they were going to assume full responsibility for compensation committee support. And one British secretary has only recently taken over responsibility for the compensation committee, also because of new compensation reporting requirements. Interestingly, there is also one case with a shift in responsibility in the other direction: A Dutch secretary reports that the HR department is going to handle the compensation committee in the future due to the increasing complexity of the issues to be dealt with.

Of all of our respondents to the questionnaire, 55 percent report that they have a secretary role to the compensation/remuneration committee. This response comes most frequently from secretaries in Asia, the United Kingdom and United States and less frequently, by a wide margin, from those in Other Regions and Western Europe. These country-specific differences are in line with our interviews. We found a significantly lower involvement of secretaries in Western Europe (Germany, Italy, Switzerland,

and France) and a stronger role of secretaries in the United Kingdom. With regard to the United States, however, we see only a very recent tendency toward giving secretaries a stronger role in compensation issues. This is also reflected in the following quote from a secretary in the United States:

> The material input from HR specialists was, and is, helpful but our board often missed the overall perspective and – most importantly – corporate governance consideration was not given proper attention.

Results of the self-completion questionnaire also point to secretaries having a more active role in listed companies and a less active one in large corporations with regard to compensation committees. The latter finding may be a result of the higher complexity level of these issues in large corporations, making the assignment of compensation specialists necessary. The fact that listed companies more often assign their secretary an active role in the compensation committee may be the result of the growing reporting requirements.

Other board committees

According to the self-completion questionnaire, 31 percent of our respondents act as secretary to other than the audit, nominating/corporate governance, and compensation/remuneration committees. Those who specified their understanding of "other" listed about 25 different committees. Some of these committees exist only in one company whereas others were more commonly cited such as risk management and/or risk control committees, finance and/or investment committees, strategy, acquisition, and major projects committees, and environment, health, safety, and corporate responsibility committees. Others include an investors' grievance committee (which many companies in India have). Executive committees, chairman's/presidential committees and management committees are mentioned by numerous secretaries.

Our interviews also point to a broad variety of "other" committees that are partly described in Section 3.2.4. The most frequent ones are

- Corporate social responsibility and/or ethics committees
- Risk and compliance committees
- Strategy committees
- Finance and/or investment committees
- Science/technology committees
- Chairman's/presidential committees

Involvement of the secretary is roughly the same as for all board committees. Certain special topic committees, however, are handled by specialists from related business units instead. Company secretaries tend to be in charge of the chairman's/presidential committees. As the organization of the chairman's/presidential committees may deviate considerably across country boundaries, we will comment on a few of them shortly.

German and Swiss companies with two-tier board structures often have a special committee with sometimes fairly extended authorities; they are called presidential committee, presidium, presiding board, standing committee, chairman's office, or chairman's committee. Their common characteristic is that these committees include the chairman and are not composed exclusively of external and/or independent members. Given his strong involvement in the company's activities, the chairman, although in many cases not a corporate officer, can only rarely be considered fully independent. More than 80 percent of the German companies interviewed have a presidential/chairman's committee – one that usually prepares the supervisory board meetings and with which the secretary is therefore heavily involved. Some of these committees also have the authority to make urgent decisions between board meetings on behalf of the full board. These authorities include a certain risk if procedures are not followed precisely since there is a possibility of violating corporate governance rules or even legal provisions. The secretary should play a crucial role in making sure that the presidential committee and the full board do not run any such risks.

In two of the companies interviewed, the presidential committee has additional responsibility for corporate governance issues, in six of them for top management appointment and compensation issues and in another two for corporate governance and top management compensation. Fifty percent of the Swiss companies interviewed have a chairman's committee to which they assign preparatory functions and, in part, responsibility for dealing with nominating and corporate governance issues. One of these chairman's committees provides support to the nonexecutive chairman on strategy, corporate governance, and top management appointment issues. It also advises the board with regard to setting guidelines for top management compensation. Another Swiss chairman's committee, with a full-time nonmanagement chairman and two full-time nonmanagement vice-chairmen, acts as a risk committee on behalf of the full board and assumes responsibility for supervising internal audit. The secretary in this company is playing an important role ensuring that all corporate governance requirements are respected and that the full board is regularly notified about the comprehensive work of the chairman's committee.

Some of the US companies have established "executive committees," generally including the chairman and some independent directors with the mandate of acting on behalf of the board between board meetings. For the most part, meetings are not necessary. The secretary of one company that recently abolished its "executive committee" explains that there was no need anymore for a special body to make decisions between meetings. Electronic communication makes it possible to make urgent full-board decisions at any time. This, however, presents the secretary with new challenges – retaining confidentiality and making sure that decisions taken this way are in full compliance with all governance standards. The chairman's committee in one of the British companies is rather unique: It comprises all nonexecutive directors, of course including the chairman, who is considered to be independent.

3.3.5.3 Corporate governance

We set out to shed light on the company secretaries' role and the challenges they face with tightening of legal and regulatory requirements. Discussions with our interviewees about their responsibilities in the field of corporate governance were intense and animated. They quite clearly confirmed our assumption that company secretaries are assuming more and more responsibilities in this field. The fact that in 2005 the former "American Society of Corporate Secretaries" changed its name to "Society of Corporate Secretaries and Governance Professionals" is the most obvious sign of this development. Our discussions with both the chairman and the president of this Society, as well as our participation in one of the Society's "essentials seminars," exemplified the broad variety of responsibilities assigned to secretaries in their efforts to ensure that corporate governance standards are not only properly stated but also strictly adhered to in practice. An increasing number of secretaries are acting as their company's chief governance officer in reality, if not also in title.

In the following sections we discuss the secretaries' role in defining their company's corporate governance approach and their influence on corporate governance structure and processes. We will also outline specific responsibilities – board evaluation, certification, and reporting under SOX, formulating and monitoring codes of conduct and ethics, dealing with whistle-blower complaints and general compliance functions.

Furthermore, we will present ideas regarding how secretaries can exercise their influence in these fields and what their limits are. We note, however, that responsibility for the company's corporate governance and for its compliance with laws and regulations remains, ultimately, with the board.

3.3.5.3.1 Corporate governance structure and approach

"Defining corporate governance structure and approach" features as the sixth most important among the 15 tasks listed in our questionnaire (see Chart 3.12).

Three percent of the respondents do not give this task any importance at all. For 29 percent of all respondents, however, it is "very important." The task is of higher importance to secretaries in listed companies and those headquartered in the United Kingdom, United States, and Asia. Respondents headquartered in Western Europe and Other Regions consider it less important. These results seem plausible: Listed companies have a stronger need for fully complying with corporate governance standards and the secretary may therefore be more intensively involved. Furthermore, corporate governance requirements are more stringent in the United Kingdom and United States than in some of the Western European countries. The challenges for the companies may, therefore, be greater in the United States and United Kingdom resulting in a bigger need for a specialist in charge of defining corporate governance structures. The secretary is usually well positioned to assume this

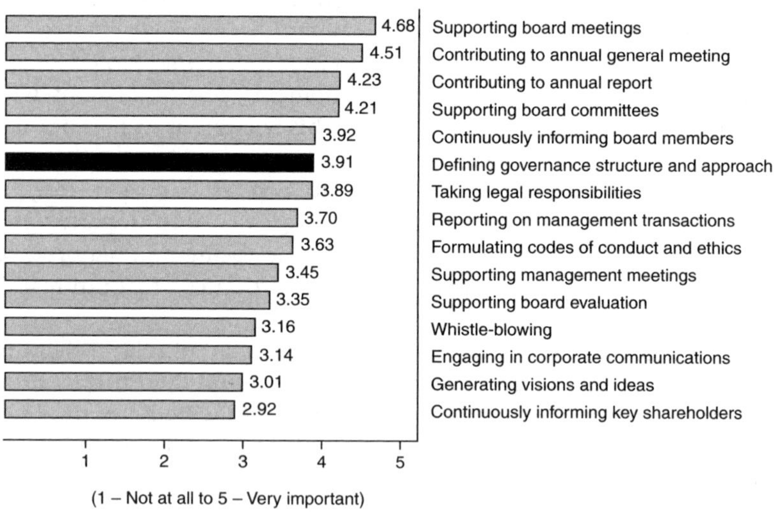

Chart 3.12 Defining corporate governance structure and approach (task importance)

responsibility. As we discussed earlier, in some Western European countries, the secretary function is not as well established and as a result companies will more often have to assign a special governance officer to monitor governance structures and approach. Again, Asia seems to have similar conditions as the Anglo-Saxon countries.

To what extent are company secretaries able to influence governance in their companies?

As Chart 3.13 illustrates, the respondents' personally perceived influence is significant. It is plausible that corporate governance processes are more strongly influenced than structure. Structure is primarily determined at the strategic level and is therefore a responsibility of the board. Processes are more operational and can be strongly influenced by the secretary. The fact that almost every fifth secretary said that he/she has a very strong influence on structure should be taken with some caution. Responses might be somewhat biased, expressing aspiration rather than actual influence.

In line with findings presented above, the secretaries' influence on structures and processes is stronger in listed companies, nonsubsidiaries, and companies with dispersed ownership; influence on structure is stronger in the United Kingdom and United States and weaker in

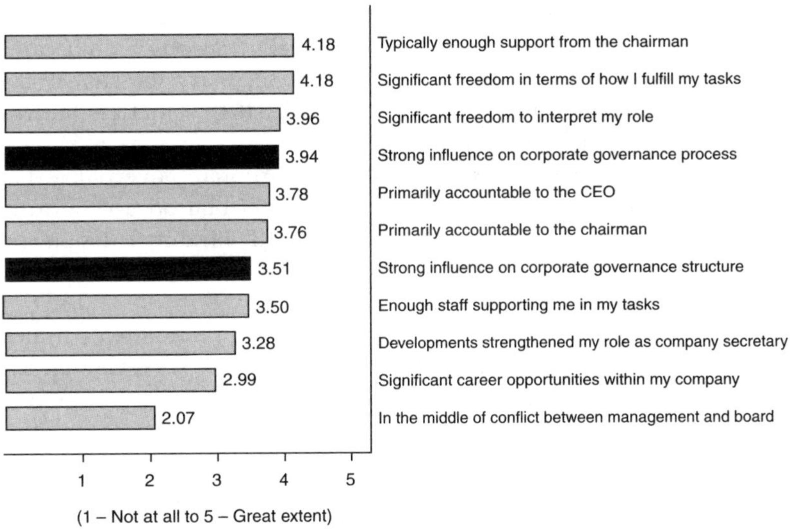

Chart 3.13 Influence on corporate governance process and structure (level of agreement)

Western Europe and Other Regions and influence on processes is weaker in family-owned companies. All these results are plausible as they reflect the corporate governance approach in the various categories of companies and in the different countries.

We see that only about 12 percent of our interviewees do not have a special function in the field of corporate governance design, monitoring, and reporting. The roles, however, vary significantly. Some of the secretaries consider these topics to be just one of their many responsibilities while others think of them as almost being a secretary's "raison d'être." One of them who established a special corporate governance department within the company secretary unit said, "This is the conscience of the company." The number of those who said that they are assuming full responsibility for corporate governance affairs is quite high. The following is one of the frequent answers to the question of what is the concrete function of the secretary concerning corporate governance:

> I am the key advisor to the chairman on all corporate governance issues. He relies fully on my advice and the board expects that I always keep them fully updated on amendments in the legal and regulatory framework, on trends and on changed best practice standards.

Of course, many of our interview partners added that they only provided all of the facts for the board to make its decisions but it became clear that there is quite some room for the secretary to "shape" the structures. Very often it is not the decision itself that matters but the ideas that lead to the proposals.

While in most Anglo-Saxon companies corporate governance has been a key topic for quite some time, some Western European countries have only recently issued self-regulatory or legally binding rules on corporate governance. The role of the secretary, therefore, has developed differently in different countries.

Although most German companies do not have a formally dedicated "company secretary," most of the companies we surveyed clearly assigned the responsibility for corporate governance design and monitoring to the person who actually assumes the "secretary" function; this is very often the general counsel. One of the secretaries reported that he was instrumental when the first corporate governance guidelines in his company were established in 2002, following the German Corporate Governance Codex. He personally informed/"educated" the members of the supervisory board and built consensus for the necessary changes in board procedures. Today he provides an annual update to the board in connection with the mandatory corporate governance reporting under the German codex. The general counsel at another German company describes his role in the field of corporate governance as that of a "coordinator." Whereas specific responsibilities are with the legal, audit, and finance departments, the secretary has to make sure that nothing gets dropped. A third German company general counsel has been formally assigned the function of corporate governance officer.

A Swiss secretary, who no longer assumes special functions in the field of corporate governance, told us that without being a lawyer by education he took an early initiative after the publication of the OECD Principles on Corporate Governance when this was not yet a real issue in Switzerland. Following the developments over the past years and the increasing importance of legal, regulatory, and reporting requirements, responsibility for monitoring and further development of corporate governance in his company was transferred to the legal department and a special head of compliance and corporate governance was appointed. Other Swiss secretaries report the existence of comprehensive responsibilities in the field of corporate governance, mainly in connection with the listing of their companies' stock at the NYSE and the reporting rules issued by the SWX Swiss Exchange in 2002. One Swiss secretary specifically mentions his mandate to regularly benchmark his company's corporate governance standards against best practice and new developments.

French companies appear to take a varying approach to corporate governance. One of our interviewees referred to his job description where corporate governance (ensuring compliance with all applicable laws and regulations) is explicitly part of his responsibilities. Another French secretary comments:

> Ultimate responsibility for corporate governance lies with the board and its committees, never with the secretary.

A Dutch secretary, who is not a lawyer himself, underlines the necessity of legal support in the field of corporate governance design and development. Nevertheless, he considers corporate governance to be an important part of his responsibilities. He may not work on details but he does monitor substance and quality.

Given the traditional legal role of the company secretary in the field of regulatory reporting, it seems quite normal for British secretaries to mention corporate governance as part of their job description. The depth and breadth of the responsibilities, however, also often differs as a result of the secretary's personality. The role of one interviewee who has overall responsibility for the company's corporate governance design and application goes far beyond ordinary monitoring:

> Among a lot of other things, it is my responsibility to help solve controversial or delicate issues in respect to the directors' independence. When we were recently confronted with shareholders challenging the independence of an individual director, because of his financial interests in the company, I talked to large shareholders explaining to them the reasons behind the board's decision. Finally most of them joined our view of the situation.

Another British secretary regularly reviews her company's governance structure and practice against UK and US regulations, as well as investors' expectations and standards issued by corporate governance organizations. She also monitors the composition of the board and advises the chairman on necessary changes. Yet another British interviewee told us about a special meeting he organized to discuss corporate governance matters between the board and representatives of institutional shareholders – possibly an indirect way of influencing the company's corporate governance. In the annual report of a British company it states:

> The Group Secretary is responsible for advising the board on all corporate governance matters, ensuring that all board procedures are followed, ensuring good information flow, facilitating induction programs for directors and assisting with directors' continuing professional development. All directors have direct access to the advice and services of the Group Secretary.

One of the American secretaries shares with us her very comprehensive, probably even exemplary job description in the field of corporate governance:

> Counsel the board of directors and senior management on corporate governance, develop recommendations regarding governance policies and practices; provide legal advice on proposed board actions, corporate transactions and securities and related matters; manage the agenda of the board and committees to ensure that each considers all relevant and necessary topics to ensure fulfillment of fiduciary

> duties; keep board, CEO and management informed about corporate governance law, listing requirements, trends, issues and best practices; conduct periodic governance reviews and provide updates for the board; provide advice concerning director education and training opportunities; coordinate new director orientation; conduct periodic reviews of corporate governance guidelines and board committee charters and recommend improvements as appropriate; orchestrate annual review of director independence; follow proposed legislation in the governance arena and make recommendations as appropriate.

It goes without saying that this secretary also has responsibility for corporate governance reporting and formalities although the company has a separate general counsel function. Finally, she is also in charge of providing training on corporate governance to the company's subsidiary directors. Another US secretary has a very special job design – she is the Senior Vice President Corporate Governance and in that function also assumes the secretary role, in addition to that of an associate general counsel. For her, corporate governance is clearly within the focus of all her activities.

Finally, we briefly discuss company secretaries' involvement in the annual reporting process with an exclusive focus on corporate-governance-related information (a more general view of their role in contributing to annual reports is provided in Section 3.3.5.5). Most companies today, at least those that are listed, have to provide separate corporate governance reports, usually as part of the regulatory reporting. Normally, these reports aim at informing shareholders and investors about the company's governance structure, board and board committee activities and performance, shareholder rights and executive compensation. Almost 80 percent of our interviewees have a significant role in the process of drafting and publishing these reports, many of them assume ultimate responsibility for the content and for full compliance with legal and regulatory requirements. Others simply provide the material input for the annual report editing team. Corporate governance is a central part of the US proxy statements that are usually prepared by the secretary. In British companies the secretary often signs the corporate governance and/or the directors' report on behalf of the board. In Germany both the supervisory board and the management board have to sign a declaration of the company's compliance with the German corporate governance codex – a very formal statement that the general counsel generally prepares for the respective boards to vote on.

In many cases corporate governance reporting is highly regulated and there is not much room for creativity. A number of secretaries may therefore consider the drafting of this report as tedious, thus questioning its value in helping shareholders make informed judgments. Does the number of meetings allow for a conclusive assessment of the board's work? Do comprehensive descriptions of board and executive compensation support shareholders' investment decisions? What do directors' résumés illustrate about the quality of their work?

A British secretary confirms that this reporting is quite time consuming and more of a formality than it is content-driven. Nevertheless, he finds that there are also positive aspects of the exercise:

> The process ensures "good discipline" for the whole organization. Once per year we all have to review whether or not we performed our duties correctly and where we can make any improvements.

3.3.5.3.2 Board evaluation

Today almost all major corporate governance codes request that the board performs regular self-evaluations to assess its performance and the performance of its committees. The degree to which the secretary is involved in these processes varies greatly from company to company but not necessarily from country to country – it is most likely a reflection of the secretary's position within the company, as well as the degree of confidence that is placed in him/her. We found a situation in a British company which may be rather unique: The secretary conducts private interviews with all of the executive and nonexecutive directors in an effort to ascertain their views on several practical, general, and personal aspects of both the board's and its committees' performance. He also collates the views of each director on the individual performance of the other board members and subsequently presents the results of his interviews to the chairman. He comments:

> At the beginning some of the directors were somewhat hesitant to openly discuss personal issues with me. Today I am fully accepted in this role and directors provide their views, even on colleagues' performance, very openly.

Another British secretary reports that initially his board had an external advisor perform the board evaluation. Today he is in charge of most of the process and he thinks that in general directors openly express their views. He also notes that this role requires a great deal of subtlety and that he must always involve the chairman if serious issues arise during contacts with individual directors. He maintains that the secretary cannot be responsible for extremely personal discussions with the directors. An external consultant recently performed an extended assessment of the board in one Dutch company and the secretary was included as one of the interviewees – clearly a sign of the importance given to the function. The aim of this particular exercise was to modernize the corporate structures. One result was that the company moved to the appointment of a fully independent chairman. In the future it will be the secretary who performs most of the evaluation process on the chairman's behalf.

In the following discussion we will provide a couple of facts and figures regarding our interviewees' involvement in board evaluation; not all interviewees are included (semistructured interviewing purposefully allows for this level of flexibility). Drafting and distributing questionnaires, collecting the directors' responses, and establishing a summary report on behalf of the chairman, the lead director, and/or the nominating/corporate governance committee constitute the majority of how the secretary supports board evaluation. Twenty-eight of our interviewees (41 percent) mention these activities as part of their participation in the process; twenty-three are not involved in the self-assessment process. About 20 percent of the company secretaries we interviewed perform the assessment with the help of an external advisor, whereas in other companies it is the chairman or the lead director who take care of it themselves. One British secretary reports that his company has been conducting the assessment with the help of an external advisor but that in the future he would assume the role, most likely including the personal interviews with the directors. A 2005 evaluation in one British company, which had traditionally performed the assessment with an external advisor, led to the conclusion that the role of the secretary should be separated from that of the general counsel. That company's current secretary comments:

> The increasing workload did not allow the general counsel to perform all the duties of the secretary himself; he had to delegate part of it to some of his staff. The board, however, wanted someone personally responsible and accountable for this job, someone who also had enough time to support the external directors.

Our discussions with the secretaries also provide interesting insight into the varying views held by different boards and their chairmen regarding the significance and value of such self-assessments. Whereas one German secretary openly acknowledges that his board does not attach high value to individual board member assessments, a French secretary points out that his chairman focuses particular attention on the personal discussions held with each director annually and takes the directors' views and opinions expressed during these assessments very seriously. A few secretaries also say that self-evaluation is not, or not yet, a real issue for their respective boards.

An interesting trend is reported by two of our American interviewees: Their board assessments today are done verbally and without questionnaires, in an executive session without the secretary and without minutes. This new practice follows lawyers' concerns that critical remarks of directors on self-assessment questionnaires might be used in an incriminating way in case of litigation against the company. The main results of the assessment are included in the minutes of the next full-board meeting, very "high level" and without any details and personal opinions.

The respondents to our self-completion questionnaire attach relatively low importance to board evaluation as can be seen from Chart 3.14.

The data also suggest that board evaluation is more important for secretaries in the United States and United Kingdom and less important for those in Western Europe. We are unable to confirm or explain this

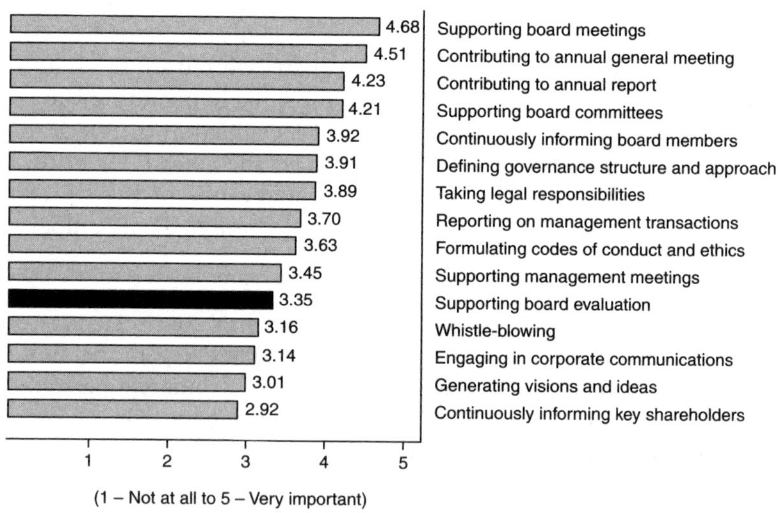

Chart 3.14 Supporting board evaluation (task importance)

through our interviews based on which we conclude that the secretary's involvement is strongly driven by his/her personality. Finally our questionnaire data show higher importance of secretary involvement in board evaluation in listed companies and large corporations and lower importance if there is only one shareholder. These results conclusively reflect mandatory self-evaluations for listed companies that also tend to be characterized by greater size and more dispersed ownership.

3.3.5.3.3 Code of business conduct and ethics

In our questionnaire, the task of "formulating codes of business conduct and ethics" ranks ninth in terms of its importance (see Chart 3.15).

The data also show that the task is more important for secretaries in the United States and Asia and less important for those in Other Regions and Western Europe. Furthermore, secretaries of listed companies consider it more important than respondents from nonlisted companies. Both results are conclusive since they reflect, respectively, the fact that such codes are mandatory for companies listed at some of the major stock exchanges.

There might be different interpretations of such codes behind the responses. Some may have only taken the codes according to the NYSE listing standards into consideration whereas others also include general codes of ethics that exist in many companies and are applicable in a

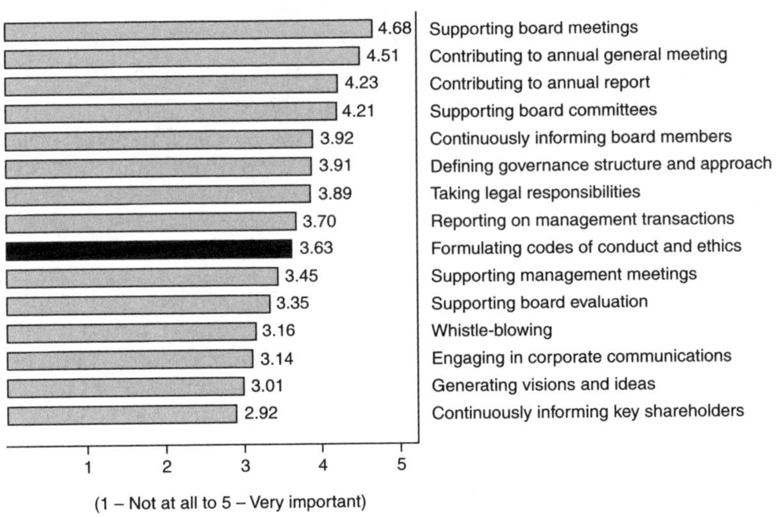

Chart 3.15 Formulating codes of conduct and ethics (task importance)

much broader range than the codes formally required under NYSE regulation. We also noticed these differences in definitions and perceptions in our personal interviews: A significant number of companies' "codes of business conduct" are a responsibility of the general counsel or the chief compliance officer. This is a clear indication that such codes are primarily compliance oriented. About one-fourth of the interviewees with whom we discussed the matter of codes do not have any role in formulating or monitoring. Codes are primarily considered a strictly legal or business issue.

Three secretaries report that there is a special unit within their organization responsible for the continuous monitoring of the adherence to the code and for dealing with violations. Secretaries who are involved – a minority of all our contacts – are primarily in charge of drafting the code and of doing some monitoring. One American secretary defines his role as significant because he has responsibility for monitoring all developments and for submitting necessary changes to the board for approval. Another American secretary assumes a strong role through his membership in the compliance committee that oversees adherence to the code. And a third secretary provides training on business conduct rules, in conjunction with the compliance department, and is in charge of making judgments on the appropriateness of behavior in individual cases.

In one British company, employees who have concerns about the correct handling of business ethics principles have the possibility to address the secretary directly if their complaints have not been given the necessary attention by management in the first place. Another British secretary has recently developed an electronic compliance program that will have to be followed by all relevant staff in the future. Finally, the published description of the secretaries' responsibilities at Unilever formally includes "code of business principles and supporting rules including arrangements for whistle-blowing facilities."

3.3.5.3.4 Whistle-blowing

Not surprisingly, yet in some contrast to the explicit provision at Unilever cited above, respondents to our questionnaire and our interviewees indicate that they do not have a significant role in their company's whistle-blowing process – this being primarily a strict legal or even business responsibility. Most companies today have some sort of institutionalized system for employees to report concerns or even make complaints anonymously. The company secretary is, however, only rarely in charge of the respective helpline and is even less involved with directly handling complaints. Some companies make a clear distinction between (1) general whistle-blowing where the line managers and ultimately the legal department or the compliance officer are normally in charge of dealing with complaints and (2) complaints about accounting matters which, in general, are a matter for the audit committee, thus ensuring an independent view. Companies listed on the NYSE are required to have a whistle-blowing policy protecting employees against retaliation for reports made in good faith. Most of our interviewees who mention a personal involvement in whistle-blowing affairs are dealing exclusively with complaints about accounting matters, mainly in their role as secretary to the audit committee. In one German company we noted a somewhat strong role of the secretary: Whistle-blower complaints are addressed to the secretary who makes a first assessment and decides where to route them. Accounting matters are automatically submitted to the audit committee without any involvement of the CEO who is not even informed in detail. The secretary explains that his company wants a strict guarantee of an independent decision by the audit committee.

The process for accounting matter complaints is similar in one of the Swiss companies surveyed: Accounting-related whistle-blowing must be addressed with the secretary, on behalf of the audit committee, without involvement of management. The secretary then does not only initiate, in adjunct with the audit committee chairman, the appropriate procedures but also controls the follow-up and has responsibility for the record keeping of such procedures. One Dutch secretary reports his rather personal and individual role – complaints that are not satisfactorily followed up by line management can be forwarded to the executive management committee through the secretary.

Overall, however, only 25 percent of the secretaries interviewed have a more or less important role in the whistle-blowing process. This is in line with the result of the self-completion questionnaire where "whistle-blowing" appears as the fourth least important task (see Chart 3.16).

Interestingly, however, 15 percent of the respondents say that this is "very important" to them. The outcome that involvement of the secretary in whistle-blowing is most important in the United States, Asia, and United Kingdom and least important in Other Regions and in Western Europe is not confirmed with our personal interviews. There might be some divergent interpretations on what the role of the secretary can be in these processes. It is also possible that some of the respondents mentioned their involvement although they assume this responsibility in their function as general counsel or as a member of the legal department. Our interviews suggest that companies with two-tier board

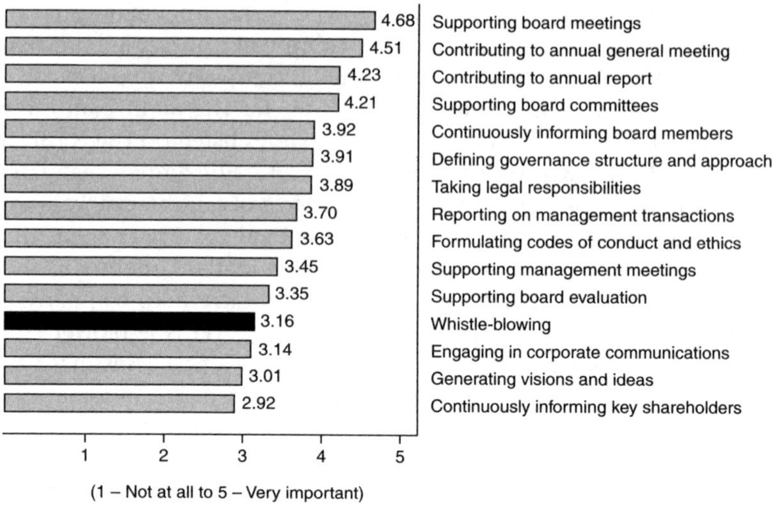

Chart 3.16 Whistle-blowing (task importance)

structures have their secretary more directly involved in whistle-blowing but, of course, only as far as accounting matters are concerned.

3.3.5.3.5 Sarbanes-Oxley Act

New reporting and control requirements following the Sarbanes-Oxley Act of 2002, mainly SOX 302 (certification of financial reports) and SOX 404 (internal control) may add responsibilities to the company secretaries' duties. Of the companies interviewed 47 (69 percent) are listed in New York and are therefore subject to the SOX legislation. Only a few of our interviewees, however, reported having a significant role with respect to SOX 302 and/or SOX 404. The most frequent role, reported by some 20 interviewees, is that of certifying specific control standards under SOX 404, mostly in connection with board processes, corporate reporting, executive compensation, and so on. Some are also in charge of monitoring or supervising the correct handling of selected control standards. Others report on their initial strong involvement when the processes for the new reporting dimensions were set up but see their current function reduced after a handover of responsibility to legal or audit. We found the strongest involvement in British companies where four of our interviewees assume the chairman role in their disclosure committees and two others are members of such committees. Some of the American secretaries also are strongly involved in SOX processes – one as the head of the disclosure committee, responsible for all SEC filings, another assuming overall responsibility for SOX compliance in the field of corporate governance.

All secretaries involved in SOX processes concurred with the view that SOX added considerable burden to their job and to that of many others within the company. But one American secretary, who has been in charge for many years and is very knowledgeable about what can go wrong in large companies, says:

> SOX 404 is a good exercise. It brings things to light that may have been known before but that nobody really wanted to talk about. This is in the interests of the company. Who could really be against it?

3.3.5.4 Management support

"Supporting management meetings" is only the tenth most important task of our respondents to the questionnaire (see Chart 3.17). This is not surprising because the questionnaire was clearly addressed to people primarily working for the board of directors, the supreme corporate body of the company.

Nevertheless, 32 percent of respondents consider this task "very important," while only 14 percent say that it is of no importance at all.

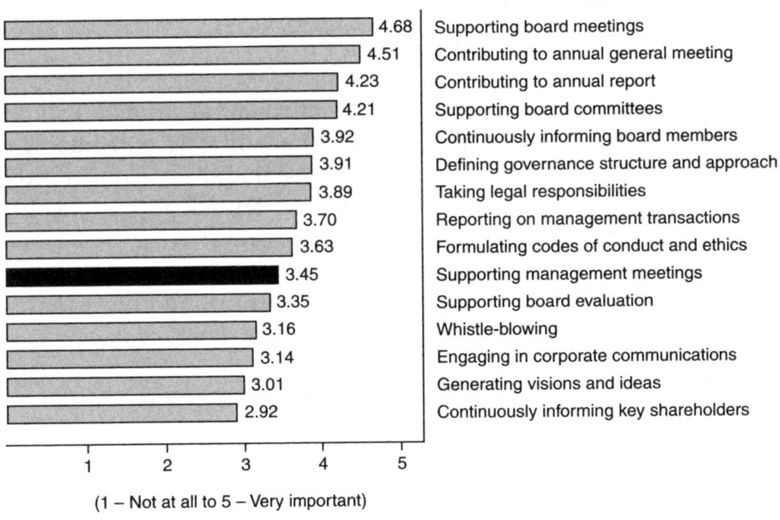

Chart 3.17 Supporting management meetings (task importance)

Quite a significant number of secretaries are obviously working for both sides – board of directors as the body supervising management on the one hand and executive management, the body to be supervised, on the other. The secretary's independence of management does not seem to be an issue in a majority of companies.

In our personal interviews we concentrated intently on the role of the secretary with the supreme corporate body and therefore only occasionally discussed the secretary's role with management meetings and support. A significant number of interviewees, however, assume both functions. Sometimes it is the general counsel who has supervisory authority for both functions and different staff members in charge for each one of the boards. We also found general counsels who exercise personal responsibility for supporting all board meetings, supervisory as well as management boards. At the opposite end of the spectrum, there is the secretary reporting exclusively to the chairman who has nothing to do with executive management.

Our questionnaire data suggest that supporting management meetings is more important for secretaries in Asia and the United Kingdom and far less important in the United States. We are unable to confirm this through our interviews; this is not unexpected since the geographical distribution of our interviews was intentionally far narrower. Among our interviewees, secretaries assuming both functions are situated in the United Kingdom, as well as in the United States, Germany, Switzerland, France, the Netherlands, and Italy.

3.3.5.5 Shareholders

The board of directors, supervisory board, or whatever it might be called in a particular company, is the corporate body directly accountable to shareholders. It therefore comes as no surprise that the two major direct contacts of the board with shareholders – the annual general meeting (AGM) and the annual report – also play a central role on the secretaries' job descriptions. Respondents to our self-completion questionnaire rank these two tasks second and third in terms of importance. In the following chapters, we will discuss them in more detail.

3.3.5.5.1 Annual general meeting of shareholders

Our questionnaire data point to the great importance of AGMs to company secretaries (see Chart 3.18). We also found that supporting the AGM is more important in listed companies and in companies with dispersed ownership. This is to be expected since the AGM becomes increasingly important and possibly also more demanding (in terms of

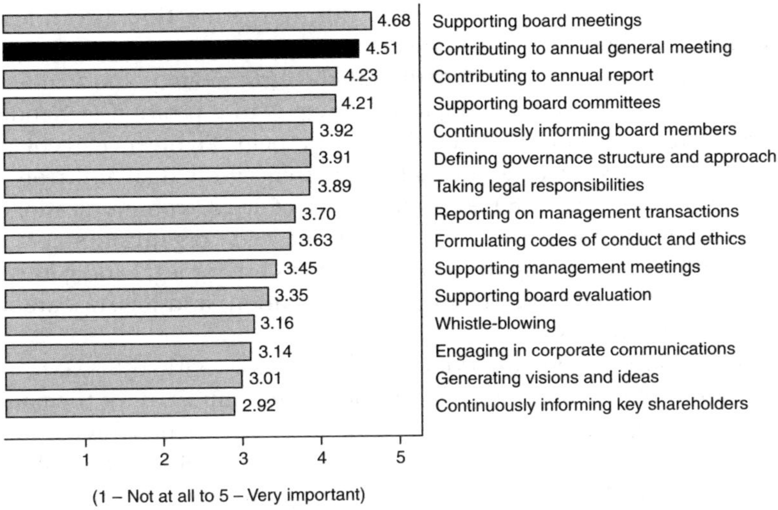

Chart 3.18 Contributing to annual general meeting (task importance)

its preparation) if the company is listed and has a greater number of shareholders and, thereby, potential attendees. The fact that there are no significant differences as to the location of the companies' headquarters is confirmation that the AGM is clearly the dominant event in all the companies – no matter where the firm is located. The board is responsible for the AGM and, accordingly, also the secretary.

The survey does not provide details about the scope of the secretary's involvement. Our personal interviews allowed for answers to a broad variety of questions: Do the secretaries have overall responsibility for the event? Are they in charge of handling legal issues, the preparation of the convocation/proxy statement? Do they write the chairman's guideline for the meeting and/or assist him/her during the event? And what is this assistance comprised of? Do the secretaries have an active role, even with answering shareholders' questions? Who is writing the minutes of the AGM? And, last but not least, who handles the logistics, visual design, "food and beverage," the distribution of gifts/take-aways, and so on?

The general picture of secretaries having a crucial role in AGMs is clearly confirmed by our personal interviews. Sixty percent of our interviewees have overall responsibility for the event. This may mean that the secretary is "handling" almost everything – from setting the date for the meeting through dealing with the legal, organizational, and logistic issues to sitting on the stage during the meeting. It can also mean that he/she oversees a more or less large team of people responsible for the various activities – definitely the most obvious and frequent solution. In a large listed company, no one is in a position to handle everything personally without third-party help. Eighteen percent of our interviewees have responsibility for some individual tasks only, while someone else – for example, head of legal, communications, finance/accounting, events – is chairing the AGM organizational task force. Fifteen percent report having responsibility for legal and governance issues only, whereas planning, organization, and logistics are in other people's hands.

With regards to our interviewees' specific role with the AGM, we ascertain that the dominant responsibilities for almost all of them are on the legal side: Preparation of agenda, proxy statement, convocation, and regulatory compliance – responsibilities that more than half of them mentioned explicitly. While some secretaries are "working behind the scenes" cooperating, in part, with the legal department when editing the various documents, others take a more visible role such as signing the convocation or proxy statement either together with the chairman or on their own, thus clearly representing the board vis-à-vis shareholders.

Our American interviewees often mention the huge workload of preparing the proxy statement, a result of the increasing number of shareholders' proposals submitted. One of them told us that more than a dozen such proposals were submitted in view of his company's 2007 AGM; they all had to be carefully considered and the secretary was in charge of proposing to the board on how to deal with them:

> I try to get SEC dispense from submission if proposals are not legally possible, which is rather frequently the case but which, nevertheless, is a quite demanding and critical procedure. When doing so I have to take the interests of the company as a whole and the individual shareholder into equal consideration. My board expects me to find the optimal solution for the handling of each of the proposals. Trying to eliminate as many proposals as possible would probably make the AGM more efficient but protecting shareholders' rights is part of good corporate governance for which I also have responsibility.

Very often, secretaries are also "visible" during the meeting, sitting on stage and normally next to the chairman. Whether or not they are also writing the minutes depends largely on legal requirements. In

Germany, for instance, having a public notary taking the notes is mandatory. With regard to the content of AGM minutes we found significant variation – from taking very formal recordings of agenda items and shareholders' decisions to a comprehensive report on all points raised by shareholders, including their arguments, factual as well as rather emotional and sometimes very personal.

A majority of our interviewees mention that they write the "guideline" for the chairman which can be a strictly formal document helping the chairman to comply with all legal requirements. It may also include explanations, comments, and positioning statements in connection with individual agenda items. Some of the secretaries are also drafting the chairman's speech which may simply be a summary of the past year's performance but which may be a kind of strategic lecture on fundamental economic or political topics, societal developments, or the long-term future perspectives of the individual company or respective industry. In most companies, however, supporting speech writing is generally a responsibility of the communications department.

Secretaries are frequently involved in preparing Q&As for the AGM – an activity that differs widely from company to company. Some secretaries are just preparing a few answers to frequent shareholders' questions, concentrating strictly on obvious shareholders' issues; others take an extremely broad view, trying to make sure that, whenever possible, no question remains unanswered no matter what it may be. In some companies the secretary, partially supported by specialists from various staff and business departments, undertakes a detailed briefing for the chairman and/or the CEO prior to the meeting. One British secretary discusses an interesting solution in his company: The briefing for the chairman and the CEO is prepared primarily by young internal lawyers, allowing them to get some personal exposure for their future career. A number of companies have huge support teams standing by during the AGM behind the scene ready to provide facts and figures if ever necessary. In some cases, the secretary acts as supervisor for such teams.

The number of secretaries who speak up during the AGM is still quite low. Some are dealing with formalities, handling the voting processes or responding to strictly formal questions. Only a very few will also answer other types of questions raised by shareholders. A British secretary (who is an executive director himself) and a Swiss secretary (who, although not a member of the board, does have responsibility for Group HR as a member of executive management) reported, not surprisingly, that they answer shareholders' questions, mainly about compensation issues, directly. They are specialists in these fields and are therefore the right people to speak on the subject. Other interviewees who mentioned their active participation in answering questions were normally doing this in the field of corporate governance – explaining processes and providing details on board and committee organization and activities.

The role of the secretary during the Q&A-sessions of the AGM is often highly important although not visible. Many of our interviewees pointed to the support they are providing to the chairman during the meeting – taking notes of shareholders' questions as a basis for the chairman's response, referring him/her to the respective Q&As prepared, providing assistance on handling formalities and sometimes even just providing a feeling of having someone at hand who has been intimately involved with the preparation of the event so that "nothing can go wrong":

> My chairman feels very relaxed during the AGM as he knows that I am in control of all processes. Because he is not a lawyer he fully relies on my support and advice. And if it comes to deciding on voting procedures or other tricky formalities he will just let me handle them.

Whether or not secretaries take an active part in designing the visual appearance of the meeting and/or the supporting program (marketing presentations, food and beverage, distribution of gifts) strongly depends on their personal preferences. If the secretary has a communications or marketing background, or just likes to be the "host" for the shareholders, he/she may well take a much more active role when it comes to organizing these "soft" factors of the event. Other companies appoint an external event manager to make sure that new ideas are brought to the table and logistics work perfectly.

In most companies the secretary oversees the voting procedure during the AGM; he/she quite often even carries out the votes personally. Large companies today normally proceed with voting by electronic devices, only a few already allow for direct internet voting during the assembly while providing proxy votes via electronic means prior to the meeting becomes increasingly popular. The role of the secretary in the premeeting proxy process varies significantly from company to company, and it is also strongly influenced by legal provisions.

3.3.5.5.2 Shareholder interface

A company secretary's direct contact with shareholders is infrequent. Their role in some aspects of shareholder interface, however, should not be disregarded. Whether the secretary has an active role with keeping or supervising the share register or not is strongly influenced by national legislation as well as practical considerations. The secretary usually has some supervisory and/or monitoring authorities no matter what the firm's organizational structure. At a minimum, he/she informs the chairman and the board of any significant changes within the shareholder base – an issue that is gaining importance in today's corporate world with the increasing number of unfriendly transactions.

Contributing to annual reporting

The secretary's contribution to annual reports ranks third among the 15 tasks listed in our questionnaire (see Chart 3.19).

Not surprisingly, secretaries in listed companies consider contributing to annual reporting more important than those in nonlisted companies. The result that this function is more important for secretaries in Asia and the United Kingdom and by far the least important for those in the United States is somewhat puzzling. American secretaries are usually strongly involved in preparing the annual proxy statements that contain what is often called "corporate governance report" in other countries. We conclude that respondents may have considered the proxy statement separately from the annual report. They may have answered the question based strictly on regulatory annual reporting (e.g. SEC filings) – generally an authority of finance and accounting.

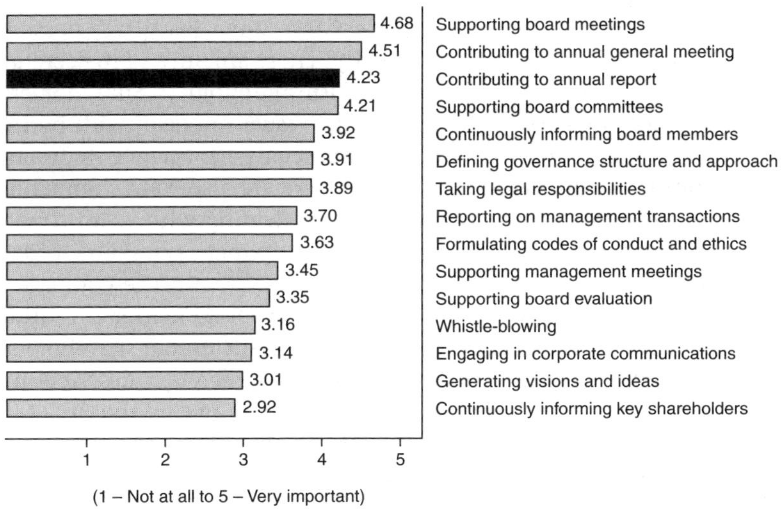

Chart 3.19 Contributing to the annual report (task importance)

Our personal interviews confirmed that secretaries play a strong role in the company's annual reporting process. When companies have to issue a special corporate governance report (e.g. under stock exchange requirements), a separate supervisory board report (e.g. under the German corporate governance codex), or a detailed remuneration report (as under the British combined code or according to SEC requirements in the United States), the secretary is almost automatically the person in charge of editing or at least reviewing these documents. As mentioned earlier, American secretaries are editing most of the corporate governance reports for their companies when preparing the proxy statement. It is likely that in the future they will also bear the main burden of drafting the extended remuneration reports.

If we look at the general annual reporting – financial report, annual review of the company – we find very different gradations of secretary involvement. Whereas about one-third of our interviewees do not have a general role in the annual reporting process – about the same number assume a reviewing and/or compliance monitoring role (without contributing to the editing of the report themselves). Some 20 percent, however, hold overall (coordinating) responsibility for at least the required regulatory documents.

Direct contacts with shareholders

As to general interfaces with shareholders, many secretaries are in charge of preparing answers to individual shareholders' letters and requests for the chairman and/or the CEO. Some just draft possible responses whereas others answer directly. There are only a few secretaries who have direct (personal) contacts with shareholders. Shareholders' requests concerning corporate governance issues are dealt with by the secretary in many companies, while financial performance issues are the responsibility of investor relations. There are also some companies where the secretary plays an active role in dealing with institutional investors who wish to discuss corporate governance issues. One of the American secretaries interviewed meets regularly with the company's major shareholders to discuss and explain corporate matters. Another one explicitly mentions having contact with institutional shareholders and shareholder activists. And a third American secretary describes his role with shareholders as that of a facilitator making sure that requests are routed to the right person within the organization. A French secretary describes his contact with shareholders as follows:

> I have direct contacts with active shareholders – asset managers, shareholder activists – and proxy solicitors before the AGM with the

aim to make sure that they have the necessary background information and for answering questions that would otherwise be brought up at the meeting.

Another secretary in France reports having regular contacts with institutional shareholders when controversial AGM topics are prediscussed to avoid, if possible, negative reactions. As large institutional shareholders in the United Kingdom usually have special corporate governance teams, some of our British interviewees mentioned their special information role vis-à-vis such groups. They emphasize that financial issues must be dealt with by the investor relations staff and by the chairman and/or CEO if the issues are critical.

On the more practical side, some of our interviewees described their role in solving shareholders' concerns or "problems." This can involve investigating lost shares, arranging for special requests on dividend payment, helping with transport arrangements for the AGM and possibly dozens of other "little" jobs – things that make the relationship between shareholders and "their" company more pleasant. Discussions with our interviewees about their direct, or indirect, contacts with shareholders show that the secretaries' roles are almost never a permanent responsibility, however, although they are sometimes quite relevant and intensive.

As a result, "Keeping key shareholders informed on an ongoing basis" not surprisingly holds the least importance to respondents to our questionnaire (see Chart 3.20).

It is plausible that secretaries in subsidiaries and family-owned companies attach higher priority to the job of permanently informing key shareholders. The shareholders in such companies are usually more clearly defined, making the direct and continuous provision of information easier and more effective. In larger, listed companies, dispensing specific information to individual key shareholders in many aspects is not even allowed for reasons of equal treatment.

Our questionnaire data also show that the secretary's continuous information distribution is more important in companies with few dominant shareholders; it is least important if there is only one shareholder. Obviously, a single shareholder owning a company does not need the information provided by the secretary – he/she will certainly know much more about everything that is going on in the firm. Finally, the higher importance of informing shareholders in companies with few shareholders is in line with our conclusion about subsidiaries and family-owned companies: Keeping a limited number of shareholders in the loop is relatively easy and effective.

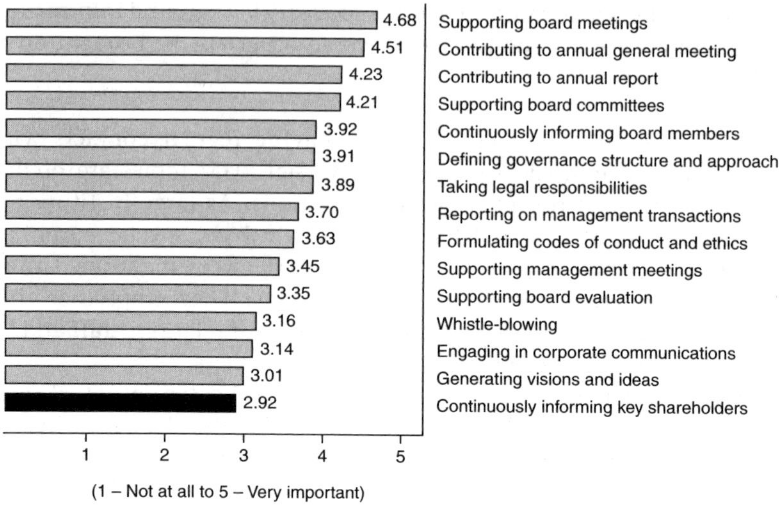

Chart 3.20 Continuously informing key shareholders (task importance)

3.3.5.6 Compliance and legal responsibilities

Compliance and legal responsibilities are, by definition, part of the secretaries' job description.

3.3.5.6.1 Legal responsibilities

When we asked the respondents to assess the importance of "taking legal responsibilities," we knew that this was not a question that could be answered in a straightforward way. Obviously, all secretaries have legal responsibilities unless they are simply holding a low-level administrative position. But rather, we wanted to know if they had additional specific legal responsibilities. In many cases, the company's general counsel assumes the secretary's role, making it evident that he/she assumes legal responsibilities. Making a clear distinction between the role as a general counsel and that of a company secretary is not always easy. This may also explain why legal responsibilities take seventh place in terms of their importance (see Chart 3.21).

US-based respondents attach a far greater importance to legal responsibilities – an obvious result of either the stringent legal requirements in the United States or the fact that in many companies there the general counsel assumes the secretary's role. Alongside respondents from Other Regions, secretaries from the United Kingdom consider legal responsibilities to be a less important task. Presumably this is because British secretaries include

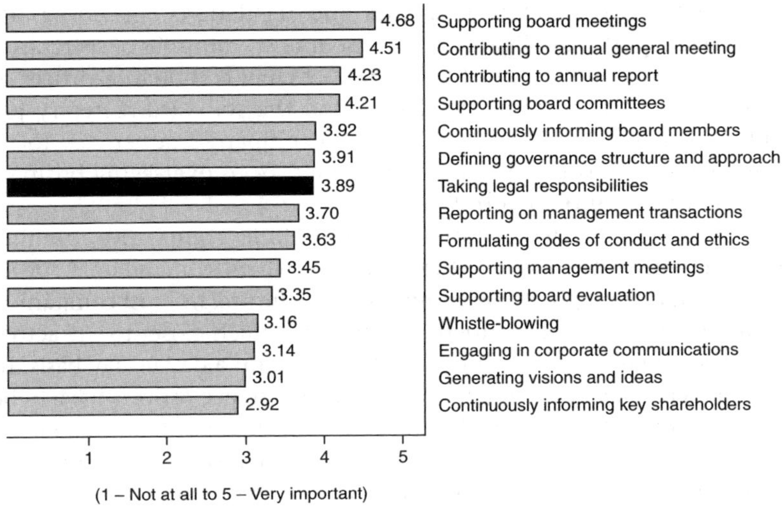

Chart 3.21 Taking legal responsibilities (task importance)

most of their legal responsibilities within their "normal" job description; they are not considered additional.

Most interviewees with whom we discussed legal responsibilities refer to their general counsel role or to their association with the legal department. Others mention their responsibility of preparing legal and regulatory reporting documents, the convocation to the AGM, the preparation of changes in the company's articles of association or board and committee charters; they did not, however, consider these tasks to be part of a special legal responsibility.

3.3.5.6.2 Regulatory and compliance responsibilities

As first officially codified in the British Companies Act, the company secretary embodies the very definition of the person who is accountable for legal and regulatory requirements compliance. Clearly, there is no question that the secretary has regulatory responsibilities in the United Kingdom. The official job description, as published by the British Institute of Chartered Company Secretaries and Administrators (ICSA) mentions the following responsibilities, among others, in this area – "monitoring company records; sending annual returns to the Company Register or the Stock Exchange; keeping records of the company's property."

In the United States, and in almost all other countries today, the secretary is the person responsible for ensuring the company's compliance with an increasing number of laws and regulations, including the respective reporting obligations. We also found a number of secretaries who are specifically assigned to the role of chief compliance officer or head of compliance. This goes far beyond the standard secretary job and may include the monitoring of the company's adherence to its ethics code, to health and safety provisions, or to overseeing business conduct rules and risk control mechanisms.

A British secretary mentioned an electronic compliance training program which she developed recently and which is mandatory for all relevant staff throughout the company in the future. In most companies, however, compliance is a function positioned much closer to the actual business to make sure that it can be monitored on a day-to-day basis. In the financial services sector, for instance, compliance officers have to be "on the trading floors" where business is done because failures must be immediately discovered and corrected. A secretary located at head-office would, in most cases, be too far removed from the action.

One British secretary adds another dimension to the question of responsibility for compliance:

> Compliance has to be done by everyone – not by a specially assigned person.

The function of keeping the insider trading list is not mentioned explicitly by many of our interviewees since it is often a regular responsibility of secretaries and therefore not worthwhile mentioning. This task includes monitoring compliance of the people on that list (who have trading restrictions) and reporting management transactions or directors' dealings (purchase and sale of shares, options and other share-related instruments on the company's stock) to the respective regulatory body – usually the stock exchange or the competent regulator.

Our questionnaire data suggest that this responsibility type is of average importance to our respondents (see Chart 3.22).

However, for 34 percent of all respondents, this task is "very important." It is particularly important for secretaries in listed companies, obviously because generally it is only listed companies which are required to report on such transactions.

3.3.5.7 Other responsibilities

In the introduction to Section 3.3.5 we described the broad variety of different responsibilities of the company secretaries – a list, however, that can never be complete. In our self-completion questionnaire we inquired about corporate communication and the creation of visions

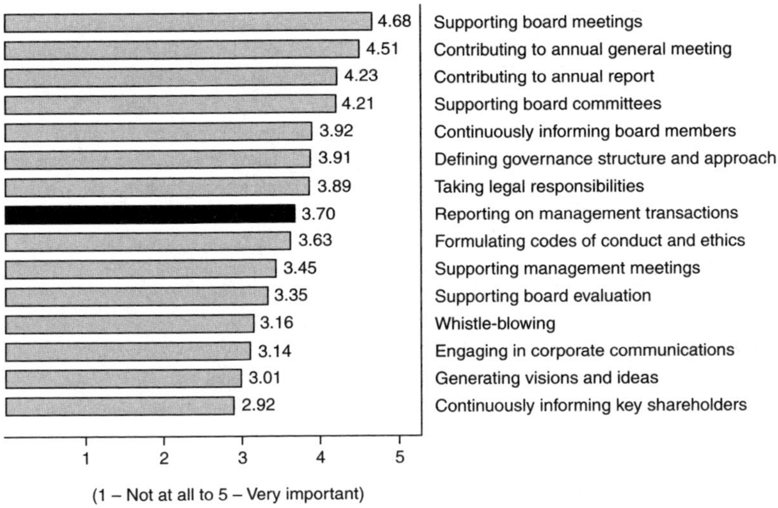

Chart 3.22 Reporting on management transactions (task importance)

and ideas. These are two tasks that play a certain role in the secretary's job description in some companies. Both functions turned out to be of low importance overall to our secretary interviewees. We will address them both briefly in the following sections.

3.3.5.7.1 Corporate communication

Only a few of our interviewees have specific responsibilities in the field of corporate communication. Some Swiss and German secretaries provide active support to the communication department in the form of drafting of media releases if board issues are concerned; they are involved with this task more frequently than secretaries in other countries. One of them even reported being responsible for all media releases relating to board issues. A US secretary who we interviewed assumes the spokesperson role when board topics, and sometimes governance topics as well, need to be dealt with. Another American secretary reported being the official company spokesperson in case of stock market rumors.

Generally, however, our interviewees found corporate communication a rather insignificant task for secretaries, as did the respondents to our questionnaire. As expected they consider it – on average – the third least important task (see Chart 3.23).

Corporate communication involvement is less important in bigger companies and in those with dispersed ownership, obviously because these companies are especially staffed for such matters. It is also of least

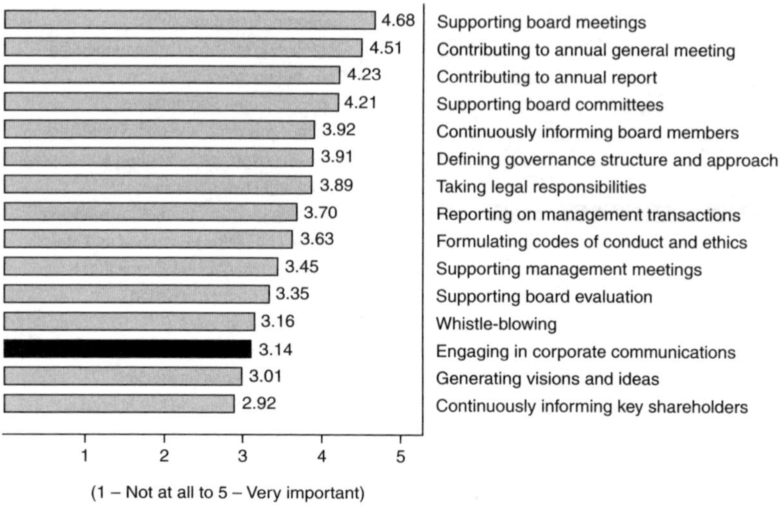

Chart 3.23 Engaging in corporate communication (task importance)

importance for secretaries in UK- and US-based companies. To comply with all of today's reporting requirements large companies in these countries require the skills of highly trained communication specialists. Finally, respondents in family-owned companies attach greater importance to corporate communication, which suggests that family businesses generally have fewer resources for corporate communications and thus the secretary steps in.

3.3.5.7.2 Vision and ideas

"Generating visions and ideas" clearly holds very little importance for company secretaries. It is overall the second least important task to our respondents to the questionnaire (see Chart 3.24).

This result makes perfect sense. Generating visions and ideas, at least with regard to discussing strategic visions and ideas, is clearly a job to be assumed by the board or by executive management. And as stated previously, the secretary is not, and cannot be, the person running the company.

3.4 A look at recent developments

In addition to providing a comprehensive view of today's corporate governance practice and the effects on the role of the company secretary

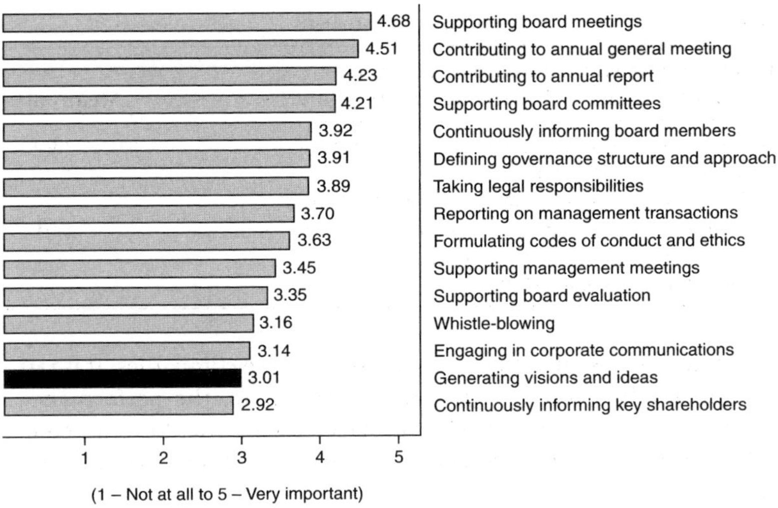

Chart 3.24 Creating visions and ideas (task importance)

(in various companies, countries, and under different legislations), we will now shed light onto significant past developments. We will also present potential further developments regarding the company secretary function in Chapter 5 and draw some conclusions as to where we might be heading.

3.4.1 Changes in companies' corporate governance

In the following two sections, we report on the data we collected on changes in corporate governance performance.

3.4.1.1 Overall governance performance

We asked the secretaries to evaluate their company's corporate governance performance in our self-completion questionnaire. The queries related first to the governance performance of peers and second to improvements that the secretaries' companies have made over the past two years (see Table 3.8).

The average respondent reports a performance superior to his/her company's peers, as well as significant improvements in his/her company's performance over the last two years.

Obviously the data should not be taken at face value due to likely bias (self-presentation, sampling). It is more interesting to compare responses across different respondents. The corporate governance performance

Table 3.8 Corporate governance performance

Please evaluate your company's corporate governance by answering the questions below	**Mean rating**
My company's corporate governance performance relative to that of its peers is (1) clearly below average – (5) clearly above average	3.99
My company's approach to corporate governance has improved over the last two years (1) not at all – (5) great extent	4.01

relative to peers is rated higher in listed and large companies. It is rather lower in family-owned companies. Furthermore, the performance is rather higher in companies with dispersed ownership, lower in companies in which a few shareholders dominate ownership. Our conclusions are given below.

Corporate governance scrutiny is higher if the company is listed, if it has a huge number of shareholders, clients, and employees and if it is an important player in the market. Often family-owned companies appear to follow somewhat divergent rules for running the business as well as for governance; further benchmarking with peers may not be as important. That companies with a few dominant shareholders rate their corporate governance weakest compared to their peers suggests that the dominant shareholders are more important than public governance standards, at least if the company is not listed.

Obviously, responses to improvements in corporate governance are also only really telling if one looks across potential contingent factors such as ownership structures, listings, and the like. The definition of what a "significant" improvement is largely depends on the company's position within the corporate governance learning curve two years ago. Interestingly, respondents based in the United Kingdom and the United States reported the least improvements, whereas those headquartered in Other Regions (i.e., emerging economies, developing countries) noted the greatest progress. This result obviously illustrates a significant variation in preexisting governance standards across the regions surveyed with the United States and United Kingdom being the forerunners.

3.4.1.2 Individual changes in corporate governance

In the following paragraphs we provide an overview of specific changes implemented in the surveyed companies in the recent past. We asked the secretaries which of six specific improvements in governance structure

Table 3.9 Improvements in corporate governance

Which of the following improvement in corporate governance structure and processes have occurred over the last two years in your company? (Mark all that apply)	**% of respondents**
CEO is no longer chairman	12.0
Majority of board members now independent	27.0
New board committees	47.6
Only independent members now on audit committee	31.5
Company secretary has become more independent	23.2
Code of conduct designed and implemented	60.0
Other	23.2

and processes (listed in the questionnaire – see Table 3.9) had occurred in their company over the last two years (multiple responses allowed).

Thirteen percent of our respondents did not answer this question – presumably for the following reasons:

- The respondent's company may not have made any changes to its corporate governance structure and processes over the past two years because it did not see any need to introduce new standards. This can be due to a company's specific ownership structure, the domestic legal and competitive environment, or because it just did not want to change anything.
- The company was already in compliance with all best practice standards and therefore did not have room for further improvement.

Results may therefore be somewhat biased, even for those responding to the question about changes. As mentioned before, changes are obviously more frequent in companies with relatively lower standards of corporate governance. Change occurs less often in countries where strict governance rules have been in place for some time already. Expectedly, secretaries from the United Kingdom and United States report fewer changes than those in Asia and Other Regions.

The most frequent change reported by the respondents to our questionnaire was the design and implementation of codes of conducts. This was followed by the creation of new board committees and, subsequently, an adjusted composition of the audit committee (independent board members only). The least frequent change reported was the move from a combined chairman-CEO function to the separation of the two leadership roles.

CEO is no longer chairman

It is not surprising that this question has the lowest percentage of positive answers. Obviously, respondents in countries where a combined chairman-CEO function is illegal are not in a position to report that their CEO was no longer chairman – he/she could simply not have assumed this role. The presence (and absence) of a combined chairman-CEO function also quite often reflects the company's long-term culture and, therefore, is not easily changeable.

Majority of board members now independent

While 27 percent of our respondents said that the majority of board members are independent today (compared to two years prior), 59 percent report having a majority of independent board members when characterizing their company's board (see Table 3.1 and Section 3.2.3). This discrepancy demonstrates that a significant number of the companies covered already had a majority of independent board members two years ago. Our questionnaire data also show that the move to a majority of independent board members occurred most frequently in Asia and Other Regions and least frequently in the United Kingdom. The change was also less frequent in bigger companies. This clearly underpins the fact that larger companies, as well as those in the United Kingdom, have obviously had a majority of independent board members for a longer period of time.

New board committees created

Almost half of our respondents (48 percent) report having had created new board committees over the past two years. This change is more common in family-owned and less so in bigger companies which, most probably, have already had the three main board committees – audit, compensation, and nomination/corporate governance – in place for a longer period of time. Family-owned companies have evidently only recently started to introduce these special committees.

In terms of newly created committees, the least frequent changes (across the different regions) are reported from secretaries headquartered in the United Kingdom, by far. This is a result of the range of different committees that have already been general practice in UK firms. Respondents from US companies are not among those reporting new board committees on the least frequent basis. This may be a result of American secretaries not having answered the question at all because this is "common practice" or a mandatory requirement, at least for the firms listed on the NYSE. Reporting the creation of new board committees on the most frequent basis came from Asia, Western Europe, and Other Regions, probably because they have had some "catching up" to do.

Only independent board members on the audit committee

Of our respondents, 32 percent reported that over the last two years their companies ensured that only independent members sit on their audit committees. This improvement is cited most frequently by secretaries in Other Regions and Asia and least frequently by those in the United States and in Western Europe. Concerning Western Europe, the mandatory employee representation on German boards makes it almost impossible to have only independent members on a committee; employees usually cannot be independent. On the other hand, there is a binding rule in the United States, at least for listed companies, which dictates that audit committee members must be exclusively independent. This makes any respective changes in this area almost impossible.

The fact that bigger companies report having only independent audit committee members less frequently and listed companies report it more frequently is similarly conclusive: Bigger companies might already have had exclusively independent members on their audit committee before and therefore do not need to change. However, listed companies, of any size, today are confronted with stock exchange requirements with regard to the full independence of audit committees.

Code of conduct designed and implemented

The design and implementation of a code of conduct is the most frequent change over the past two years; 60 percent of all respondents report this improvement. In the pharmaceutical industry, 100 percent of the companies surveyed report having implemented such a code. Implementation of a code of conduct, in general is most frequently reported by secretaries associated with the chemical and technology industry and least frequently by those associated with food and beverage, multiple, and other industries. These statistically significant differences, by industry, are not completely plausible at first glance. It is understandable that companies in the pharmaceutical, chemical, and technology industries may have felt more pressure to introduce codes of conduct, given the high public scrutiny on these industries. However, it is difficult to understand why food and beverage companies should not have been in the same position. It may be that our questionnaire respondents from that industry had already implemented such codes.

The implementation of new codes of conduct appears most frequently in Asia and Western Europe and least frequently in the United Kingdom and Other Regions. Again, results point to a leading position of UK-based companies; they also suggest that codes of conduct may still not be high on the agenda of companies headquartered in emerging economies and developing countries.

New code implementation is also more frequent in family-owned companies. If one looks at different ownership structures, our data suggest that companies with only one shareholder introduce codes most frequently and companies with dispersed ownership least frequently. The reasons for these significant differences may result from a variety of situations: Implementing new codes of conduct may have been necessary due to market and/or public pressure, new legislation, negative experience within a particular company, or a specific industry. On one hand, of course, these changes might be the result of the board's and/or management's increased sense of responsibility. On the other hand, companies that do not report having implemented such codes may not see a necessity for doing so; they may also have previously implemented such a code. The results of the survey, however, show that codes of conduct are a broadly used and accepted instrument within many companies' corporate governance structures.

Other changes

Twenty-three percent of our respondents report other improvements in corporate governance. More specifically, they most often report that today the board, and the company in general, were more aware of the importance of corporate governance. This has led to the introduction of special corporate governance codes, the issuance of guidelines and handbooks, and increased monitoring. Directors are also seen as more mindful of their roles and responsibilities. Some respondents also point to changes in the composition and the performance of their board, with the new appointment of an independent lead director, fewer executive directors, a reduction of the overall number of directors and a more careful evaluation of new members. In addition, boards claim to hold more executive sessions, perform self-assessments and give more attention to the induction and continuous education of their members. Improved and more transparent reporting on financials, as well as on governance performance, are other changes/improvements mentioned by respondents to the questionnaire.

Responses to the question of whether or not the company secretary has become more independent in recent years are discussed separately in Section 3.4.2 and in Chapter 5.

In our personal interviews we did not focus on individual or specific changes to the corporate governance of companies over the past two years; instead, we discussed the general development in this field, the influence of legal changes, regulators, and markets. The impact of all these developments on the role of the secretary is described in the subsequent section that focuses on the particular trends and issues surrounding the company secretary.

Many of our interview partners say that the structure of their board and of its procedures have not changed fundamentally over recent years. The way in which the board works, however, has undergone dramatic changes. Directors are more acutely aware of their responsibilities and of the "public eye watching them"; they also devote much more time to meeting preparation. Boards in general now have a significantly stronger focus on governance and compliance issues. Some secretaries regret that today their board spends too much of its time on formalities, as well as anxiously checking every single step of their decision making to avoid potential accountability risks. Other secretaries note that their boards are taking a more strategic approach and that their performance has increased due, in part, to the more intensive debates taking place at board meetings:

> Most of the changes over the last years were "communication-led": the board has to provide much more financial and other information to shareholders and the public at large, deadlines are getting tighter and tighter but, at the same time, board work has to be dramatically more comprehensive, more precise and more forward looking.
>
> In earlier days, our board did not really debate issues but rather approved them.

While discussing these trends with interviewees we realized that a significant aspect of the fundamental changes in a companies' approach to corporate governance approach and processes are company-specific changes. These may include an important merger, the acquisition of a strong competitor (quite often in a different market and under aegis of different legislation) or the move of the company into a new legal environment due to the relocation of headquarters. Past financial performance difficulties, partly accompanied by fundamental boardroom shuffles, were also mentioned as an important reason for shaking up a company's corporate governance approach. Obviously, globalization has had a major impact as well, illustrated by the following quote from a British secretary:

> The major changes resulted from the significant and extremely quick development of our company to a global organization. British company law has not been fundamentally changed but the environment is

different for a company active in global markets. And the size of the company really matters.

Looking ahead, many of our interviewees expect more changes to come. The introduction of new regulations will influence the board's work although, hopefully, at a somewhat lower pace. Regulations, shareholder activists, and public scrutiny may continue to put pressure on boards to reach best practice not only with business but also with corporate governance performance. We will discuss some of the expectations in Chapter 5.

3.4.2 Effects on the role of the company secretary

The effects of recent changes in companies' corporate governance structure and approach also had manifold effects on the role of the company secretary. We covered such potential effects in the questionnaire, more specifically with regard to the following:

- A strengthened role of the secretary
- Greater independence

Chart 3.25 shows that past developments have not drastically strengthened the position and role of company secretaries. The effect of past developments appears to have been stronger in Asia and the United Kingdom, as well as for listed companies; it is weaker in Other Regions, the United States, and family-owned companies. Overall, the results are conclusive: US secretaries report that they experience a strengthening of their role less frequently which is likely due to the strong position they have already had in the past.

Twenty-three percent of our respondents indicate that they are more independent of management than they were two years ago (see Table 3.9). This response is cited most frequently by secretaries from companies in Other Regions and least frequently by those in the United States and United Kingdom. We elaborate on this result in Section 3.4.2.3.

The evolving role of the company secretary, the reasons for these changes, their dimension and significance, expectations for the future, and the question of whether or not he/she should be more independent of management were the focal points of our personal interviews. As we proceed, we summarize some of the most interesting results from these discussions particularly regarding how the role has developed in the past. We also discuss future expectations and draw the resulting conclusions (in Chapter 5).

Chart 3.25 Developments strengthened company secretary role (level of agreement)

3.4.2.1 Increasing workload calling for new structures

As a result of the interview process, our overwhelming impression is that the workload for secretaries has increased dramatically over the past years. This is in line with the pressures boards are currently under, regarding performance and compliance. Almost everyone say that corporate governance has become a much more important issue and has had a significant impact on their roles and responsibilities. This heavy workload may lead to changes on how the secretary function is set up organizationally. Two American secretaries, who also assume the general counsel role comment, respectively:

> Given the enormous workload, the secretary function might be separated from the general counsel function going forward as the general counsel is less and less in a position to really perform the role. He has to delegate a significant part of his responsibilities to his staff that, however, do not get the full picture of the function and are neither fully informed nor really accountable for their activities.
>
> It will not be possible to perform the secretary function on a "part-time basis" – as part of the general counsel function.

This is true, of course, primarily in the case of large companies. A British and an American secretary report having just gone through this change – making the secretary a separate function and independent of the general counsel. Secretaries in the United Kingdom, Switzerland, and the Netherlands confirm that creating a separate company secretary function might well be a choice because of the increasing workload; the change is mostly carried out in connection with personnel moves either at the general counsel or the chairman or CEO position. A French secretary who also assumes both functions reports that his company has been undergoing a change by splitting the secretary and general counsel roles due to the upcoming merger with an American company. One interviewee working with a dual board structure who today assumes both secretary functions for the supervisory and the management board sees a good solution in splitting these two roles. And one of the Italian secretaries, where the function has not yet really been implemented but in practice is "handled" by the legal department, concedes that a special internal secretary function can be envisaged given the new, increased responsibilities.

Whether or not the general counsel should be the secretary is controversial. On one hand, a German secretary believes that the head of legal might potentially be "too legalistic and formalistic" to adequately and flexibly support the board. Two British colleagues, on the other hand, cannot imagine a separation of the two roles. One of them clearly expresses this view:

> I would never accept the secretary role without being the general counsel at the same time. The secretary role would not be challenging and interesting enough.

One of the British secretaries we interviewed is in the rather unique position of being an executive director himself. He is convinced that being a member of the board is the best way for the secretary to be more visible and influential, giving him/her a really strong position. The general counsel is the most likely management position to make it possible for the secretary to officially sit on the board; this is definitely not a structure though that represents common practice in other companies.

3.4.2.2 The corporate governance environment makes secretary role more important

There is something of a common understanding among our interviewees, from all countries, irrespective of their legal environments. The changing corporate governance environment is clearly making the secretary role more important. Although the rate and intensity of change differs from company to company, it is clear that change is everywhere. The strengthened position of outside independent directors is changing the responsibilities of secretaries. Outside directors need much more information and support, normally the secretary's responsibility. Networking among other secretaries, therefore, has become much more relevant as one of our American interviewees reported. It is increasingly necessary to share experiences, both good and bad, with colleagues so the job function can be executed more efficiently.

We found a strong tendency for secretaries in France to view their role as being stronger now than before. One French interviewee says that due to corporate governance changes he is taking on more legal and regulatory responsibilities. He also comments that he has needed to have more business understanding than before – processes are becoming more complex and external directors need additional assistance. Another secretary says that the role would be strengthened due to the increasing information requests from shareholders (mainly institutional ones), often in the area of corporate governance. For a third French secretary, the role has become more important mainly because of the company's internationalization. This situation has required extended knowledge of various legal and regulatory systems, making sure that compliance is ensured across all jurisdictions. A German secretary, in charge of running the secretariat for the Vorstand, is experiencing a steady transfer of special responsibilities from the legal department to his unit – primarily in the field of corporate governance.

The growing importance of the secretary role is sometimes the result of a change in the structure of the board. This can entail splitting a combined chairman-CEO into two separate functions or having a fully independent external chairman. Supporting an external, independent chairman creates a fundamental role change for the secretary. A Dutch secretary at a company that recently appointed a fully independent outside chairman for the first time expects his personal responsibilities to increase dramatically. The new chairman will need more support and advice, and as the secretary adds:

> We organized a fairly intensive special induction program for the new chairman – something I never did with this breadth and depth thus far.

One British secretary, whose company also recently moved from having a former executive as chairman to a structure with a fully independent outside chairman, describes the change as follows:

> Today I am playing a major role as "sounding board" for the chairman. I am much more strongly involved in all the activities of the

> board and have a much stronger impact and influence on how the board works. In earlier days, the chairman had a broad network within the company because of his former role as an executive. Today he clearly needs my support.

Many of our interview partners see room for structural improvements in one particular area – their involvement in board committee work.

> Going forward people working with the committees, as their secretaries, must also be involved in the respective day-to-day activities to get better insight, mainly for the very important task of taking the minutes. Only by knowing how things work in practice can the secretary really do a top job.

Secretaries in various jurisdictions express their conviction that they should also be fully involved in compensation/remuneration committee activities. A French secretary refers to the problem in his company; certain compensation decisions have been taken by the respective committee without any "employees" present (no secretary, no HR representative). Decisions made under those circumstances may lack the proper formalities that under today's compliance and control culture, primarily in the context of SOX, could be detrimental. Other secretaries, generally in countries where detailed compensation reporting is a legal requirement, consider a stronger and deeper involvement in executive compensation discussions to be a must. They emphasize that compliance with all the complex reporting requirements in this field cannot be guaranteed if the person drafting a report is not fully aware of the issues. Companies will be well advised to listen to their secretaries when they ask for a deeper involvement with compensation committees.

3.4.2.3 Should secretaries be independent of management?

From our self-completion questionnaire results, we know that only 23 percent of all respondents have experienced an increase in their independence of management (see Table 3.9). This improvement is most frequently reported by secretaries in Other Regions and least frequently by those in the United States and United Kingdom.

Our personal interviews showed that this question cannot be answered simplistically. What does "independence of management" mean? What are the pros and cons of such a change? And is independence at all desirable or even necessary? German secretaries for instance, who most frequently are also the heads of legal departments, normally see no need for such a change. More importantly even, the German legal system does not really allow for an independent secretary; the supervisory board and its chairman do not have any dedicated personnel resources. Other than in Germany, the views of our interviewees regarding their independence – today and in the future – vary significantly across countries.

Most secretaries seem quite happy with their current situation, irrespective of whether they are formally independent of management or not. Some do admit to occasionally feeling the contradictory needs and demands of their efforts to support the independent directors on one side and reporting to the CEO or other management on the other. Many of our interviewees who are not formally independent stressed their singular mind, their clear will, and also the company's commitment to providing independent support and advice to the board. A Dutch secretary is convinced that independence is a question of integrity, not of formal reporting and positioning within the organization. And one of our American interviewees comments along these lines:

> It is the personality that matters. The secretary must have the courage to say unpleasant things if it is necessary in the interests of the company, irrespective of his reporting line.

Nevertheless, an independent secretary can definitely be an asset for the external board members as one of the Dutch secretaries who reports exclusively to the chairman describes:

> My independent position allows for a somewhat more "external view" which I can bring to the board and which certainly adds value to creating the basis for the external directors making more independent judgments.

Or another one, even more specifically, notes:

> The views of the board and of management sometimes differ "by nature" – one looking more at strategic and reputation aspects, the other one more at business and financials. If we exclusively provide "management view information" to the board, there might be important loopholes in the overall picture. It is my responsibility to make sure that documents are more balanced.

And finally, one of our British interviewees points to the more fundamental question: What does the positioning of the secretary tell about whether or not a company is giving the board's independence a "high rating"? He suggests:

> More companies should consider the appointment of a fully independent secretary, reporting exclusively to the chairman. Companies taking the call for independent boards seriously and understanding what corporate governance is all about must go in this direction. Independent directors need an independent secretary.

On the basis of our discussions, and given the information we gained about the personalities involved, we conclude that the secretary being clearly positioned on the management side in no way impedes his/her excellent and objective support of the board. It may, however, make the job even more difficult and challenging. Over time, the debate launched some time ago about the basic principles of independence regarding board members may, nevertheless, be extended to include the corporate governance officer.

4
Analyzing Causal Effects

In the above chapters we have outlined potential causal effects on a case-by-case basis while reporting on the evidence collected through our interviews. In this chapter we present findings from a regression analysis of the quantitative data obtained from our self-completion questionnaire, designed to systematically detect causal relationships. Our analysis is intentionally somewhat exploratory; we wished to exploit the opportunity presented to us in the form of our unique dataset. We also wanted to test for a wide range of causal effects, some of which we knew were unlikely but not inconceivable.

As Figure 4.1 shows, we tested causal effects of three sets of independent variables, namely drivers, general corporate governance setup and company secretary's profile, on three sets of dependent variables:

1. The company secretary setting.
2. The secretary's tasks and responsibilities.
3. The company's corporate governance performance.

Unless indicated otherwise, all causal effects reported are statistically significant at a 10 percent level or higher. It should be noted that the effects reported are essentially of a statistical nature and thus shall always be interpreted in the context of complementary data – most importantly those obtained from the interviews.

4.1 Which factors determine how the company secretary views his/her setting?

In the following paragraphs, we report on those factors that do or do not influence the setting, in which the company secretary operates,

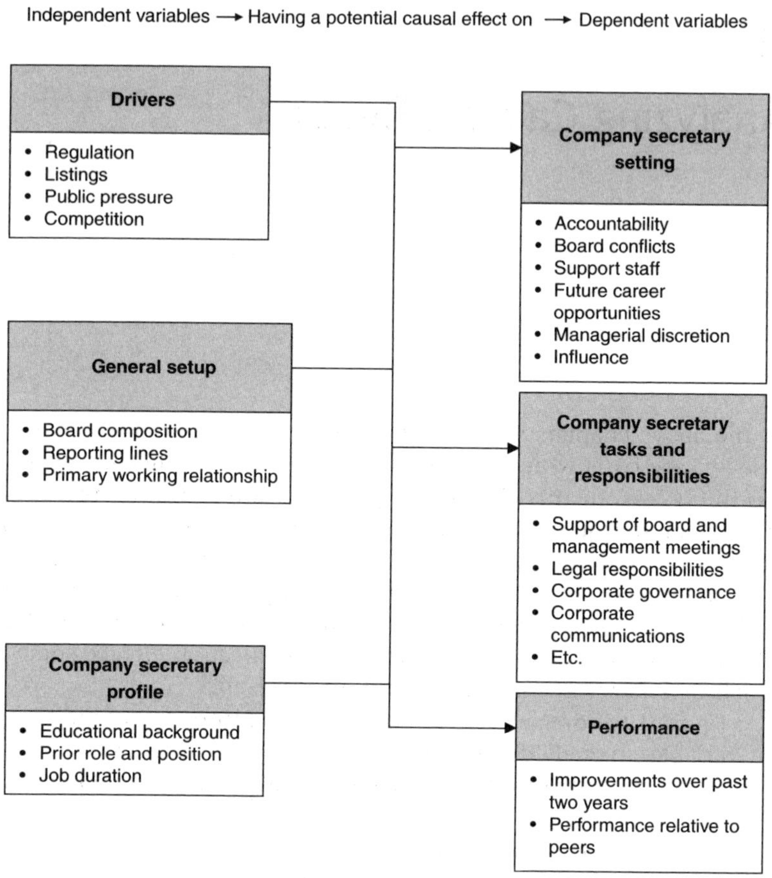

Figure 4.1 Causal effects tested

that is, his/her accountability, the frequency of board conflicts, support staff, and so on.

The influence of corporate governance drivers

The secretary's accountability to the chairman is greater if the legal framework permits executives on the board. In light of a majority of nonexecutive chairmen in our sample (only one-third of our respondents have an executive chairman who in roughly 23 percent of all the responding companies is also the CEO), we ascertain a certain countervailing force against executive power at the board level.

Higher regulatory pressure, as perceived by our respondents, increases the company secretary's accountability to the CEO – not the chairman. This reflects the company secretaries' still predominant primary allegiance to the CEO who often has responsibility for the company's compliance with regulatory requirements. Higher regulatory pressure is also associated with stronger support for the secretary from his/her staff and with an enhanced, self-perceived role of the secretary position overall.

This is verified by the following finding: Requirements from stock exchange listings are associated with greater influence on both the corporate governance structure and the processes. With regard to corporate governance, it also appears that listings are more influential and prescriptive than state- or country-specific legislation.

Whereas continuous public pressure is also associated with greater influence on corporate governance processes, ad hoc public pressure is linked to having a lower influence. This suggests that continuous public scrutiny – rather than selective, opportunistic behavior – drives corporate governance.

The influence of board composition

Overall board composition does not appear to have a significant or coherent influence on the company secretary's setting. In light of our interviews, we conclude that the secretary's working environment is more strongly determined by corporate governance structures and processes and the checks and balances established within the individual company.

Nevertheless, we would like to highlight the following effects found in the data:

1. The secretary's accountability to the chairman is greater if the chairman is also the CEO. Because the chairman-CEO is clearly the authority figure in the company, he/she will also strongly influence corporate governance, making the secretary's accountability to him/her significant.
2. A strengthened secretary's role – in terms of influencing corporate governance processes and structure – is linked to (1) a majority of nonexecutive board members and (2) the existence of one or more executive members who are neither chairman nor CEO.
3. A stronger influence on corporate governance structure is additionally associated with a majority of independent board members.

Effects 2 and 3 both confirm that the significance of the secretary function for corporate governance increases in conjunction with the strengthening of the independent factor on the board.

The influence of the secretary's educational background and professional history

The influence of educational and professional background, overall, on the secretary's setting seems significant and somewhat conclusive.

A business background (which in this case also includes finance and accounting) is associated with a stronger secretarial role, in general, and with a stronger influence on corporate governance structure and processes, in particular. It is also – like an educational background in economics – linked to greater career opportunities.

Company secretaries with legal backgrounds report that, in general, they have a stronger role. In contrast, a "more removed" educational background, such as engineering, is associated with weaker influence on the dimensions of corporate governance. Obviously, having an affinity to the secretary's tasks and responsibilities counts. Trained engineers, for example, are at a disadvantage in a legal and regulatory environment, most likely because they are unable to capitalize on their learned skills.

Job duration also holds significant importance. Respondents who have been on the job longer report greater discretion – both strategically (what he/she does) and operationally (how he/she does it); they also report greater influence on the corporate governance structure.

In contrast to both educational background and job duration, the secretary's prior engagement (e.g., with the current company, one of its subsidiaries, or another company) has no meaningful influence on his/her setting. The secretary's prior functional position (e.g., legal, finance) also appears to have a minor effect. But we did find, for example, an effect from having had a finance position previously: Respondents with that professional history report more strategic discretion, that is, freedom in terms of what they do on the job.

The influence of reporting lines and working relationships

As we expected, the reporting line is a key determinant in the secretary's setting as it influences accountability/allegiance of the secretary as well as the support he/she gets from the chairman. More specifically, a reporting line to the chairman is linked to greater accountability to the chairman and weaker accountability to the CEO. Conversely, a reporting line to the CEO is linked to greater accountability to the CEO and weaker accountability to the chairman. In addition, respondents who report to the chairman receive stronger support from the chairman.

The influence of the secretary's working relationship is similarly significant and conclusive: A primary relationship with the CEO and management in general makes the secretary less accountable to the chairman and more accountable to the CEO. Conversely, a primary relationship with the chairman and the board increases the accountability to the chairman; it decreases accountability to the CEO.

Moreover, respondents who work primarily for the chairman and the board in general report a strengthened role over recent years more frequently. In addition, they receive greater support from the chairman and consider their career opportunities to be greater. Respondents who work primarily for the finance department also report better career opportunities.

Finally, a primary working relationship with the chairman and the board in general increases the secretary's discretion and influence (on both corporate governance structure and processes).

4.2 Which factors shape the secretary's tasks and responsibilities?

The influence of corporate governance drivers

In line with the significance of stock market listings as determinants of the company secretary's setting (see previous section), they also appear to be influential factors with regard to the secretary's tasks and responsibilities. For example, greater importance of listings – as a driver of corporate governance – goes hand in hand with the higher importance of various tasks such as the support of board meetings and committee work, continuous board information, contributions to the annual report, and board evaluation.

The effect of the legal framework is somewhat contradictory. Whether or not executives are allowed on the board has only a minor impact on how individual boards are composed in practice or how they work. Nevertheless, two results should be mentioned:

1. Secretaries working in a legal environment that allows executives on the board report a greater importance of supporting management meetings. This provides evidence of the secretary having a stronger allegiance with management.
2. Secretaries working in a legal environment that does not allow executives on the board report a greater importance of defining corporate governance structure and approach. This points to a significant influence of independent directors on the secretary's job description (i.e., tasks and responsibilities).

The influence of board composition

Overall, the effects of board composition that can be detected lack coherence. This suggests that board structure has little to no influence on the company secretary's tasks. However, some results are insightful and suggest again that the role of the company secretary as "chief governance officer" increases as the independent board members' influence increases:

- A majority of independent board members drives some tasks with specific relevance to corporate governance, such as structure and approach, shareholder information, whistle-blowing, and codes of conduct.
- A majority of nonexecutive board members is associated with greater importance of defining corporate governance structure and approach, and supporting board meetings and committees.

The influence of the secretary's educational background and professional history

In line with the results presented above, we see a conclusive effect of a secretary's educational background. Again we discover an affinity between education and tasks. For example, an educational background in business is linked to greater importance regarding board committee support, informing shareholders, generating visions and ideas, reporting management transactions, and whistle-blowing, as well as defining the corporate governance structure and approach.

Respondents with a legal educational background report a greater importance of legal responsibilities and a greater importance of defining corporate governance structure and approach, formulating codes of business conduct and reporting management transactions. It is also plausible that secretaries with a communications background tend to more strongly emphasize corporate communications in their role.

As one would expect, the secretary's prior engagement (e.g., with the current company, one of its subsidiaries, or another company) has no meaningful influence on the importance of his/her individual tasks and responsibilities.

However, we detect several significant effects of prior positions. Results are somewhat in line with those reported above: Company secretaries tend to report greater importance of those tasks that closely relate to their prior positions. For example,

- Respondents who were company secretaries in their prior position consider the definition of corporate governance structure and approach to be more important.

- Similarly, a prior legal position is associated with greater importance of legal responsibilities, formulating codes of conduct and defining the company's corporate governance structure.

Finally, company secretaries who have been on the job longer report greater importance of three tasks: the continuous information of shareholders, legal responsibilities, and codes of conduct. This result is in line with findings presented above: Longer job duration strengthens the overall position of the secretary who consequently takes on more responsibilities (e.g., in working as a shareholder interface and contributing to corporate governance).

The influence of reporting lines and working relationships

To some extent, reporting lines with strong relations to the secretary's role (finance, legal, investor relations) appear to determine the importance of certain tasks and responsibilities. More specifically, a reporting line to finance increases the importance of supporting board committees (this may specifically be the case for the audit committee); it decreases the importance of generating visions and ideas. The latter also applies to a reporting line to investor relations. Furthermore, respondents with a reporting line to legal affairs consider the support of board evaluation more important.

We see also that the company secretary's primary working relationship clearly determines the importance of tasks and responsibilities, as the following examples illustrate:

- A primary working relationship with the chairman and the board, in general, is associated with greater importance of (1) board information, (2) the support of board meetings, (3) the support of board committees, (4) the support of board evaluation, (5) the contribution to annual reports, and (6) contributions to the annual meeting.
- Primary engagement with legal affairs is linked to lower importance of board information and committee support (which may be delegated to business specialists) and to higher importance of legal responsibilities.
- A primary link to investor relations is associated with lower importance of legal responsibilities but also higher importance of corporate communications.
- The importance of supporting management meetings is obviously higher if the secretary works primarily for the CEO and management in general. That a primary working relationship with the CEO and

management is associated with greater importance of whistle-blowing is likely because management frequently assumes responsibility for whistle-blowing processes, the board generally does not have this responsibility.

Results are, overall, conclusive and reflect a significant congruence between working relationships and certain tasks and responsibilities.

4.3 Which factors influence corporate governance performance?

Our results on key determinants of corporate governance performance are very much in line with those of previous studies. The performance cannot be conclusively linked to certain structures and systems; it is primarily determined by individuals and groups making appropriate strategic decisions and ensuring their stringent implementation.

We would, nevertheless, like to report a few insightful findings. Improvements in corporate governance over the past two years are more frequently reported by

- Secretaries who consider stock market listings to be a stronger driver. Again, this underscores the dominance of listings over other potential corporate governance drivers – including domestic regulation – and reflects their more specific and prescriptive nature.
- Secretaries whose boards have a majority of independent board members. This result points to an almost automatic link between stronger influence of independent directors and improved corporate governance; independence per se is considered by many as the key driver to improve corporate governance.
- Secretaries who are on the job longer. This is not implausible if one takes into account that company secretaries staying on the job for an extended period of time become more influential; they may therefore be better positioned to help improve corporate governance structures. However, this may also be partly attributed to self-presentation bias.

Improvements on a company's corporate governance performance are obviously much easier to achieve if it starts from a low level. Companies with "best in class" governance will, therefore, not rank among the top performers with regard to improvements. Whatever the drivers may be – board composition or secretary profile, for example – these companies may simply have almost nothing to improve anymore in this area.

5 Conclusion – Where Are We Heading?

Making Sense Out of Diversity

Given the huge diversity that our research has revealed, it is highly unlikely that there will be a "standard" company secretary across different industries, ownership forms, or legal frameworks. However, based on our research, we are able to identify the drivers that will shape the options and the "space" in which the role of the company secretary will evolve. This expansion is most likely to involve the more prominent role of a "corporate governance officer."

The legal prerequisites (if existent) are only one side of a corporate governance officer's role. The other side is the business perspective, determined predominantly by the nature of the corporation and its strategy. The corporate governance officer's role is determined by two critical dimensions:

1. The organizational positioning (e.g., reporting line) strongly influences his/her role. There are two main options for the reporting line – the board or the top management. Within these two main options, reporting to the head of either corporate body is a common solution in the business world (i.e., to the chair or the CEO) but reporting to another high-level member of management (i.e., the CFO or the general counsel) is also quite frequent.
2. The other critical dimension is the level of competence assigned to carry out the secretary's responsibilities. The (low or high) level of competence associated with a corporate governance officer strongly influences his/her role and the impact he/she has in the company.

As Figure 5.1 illustrates, we distinguish between four clusters, depending upon the company secretary's reporting line and level of competence. Each cluster has a different job description, different tasks, and ultimately a different corporate governance impact in the boardroom:

The chair's proxy. If a corporate governance officer is assigned responsibilities that require a high level of competence and is reporting to the chair of the board, we call the position "chair's proxy." He/she is the "eyes and ears" of the chair. If the chair is strong, this type of corporate governance officer will be a very important and influential person, perhaps even an "éminence grise" at the head of the company. The chair will delegate the management of compliance and board information gathering to the corporate governance officer. The chair's proxy is also in charge of important board procedures, for example, evaluating the board. Often, this type of corporate governance officer has had a long, successful career in the organization with a strong record as a corporate lawyer, auditor, controller, or business manager. In many cases, it is the corporate governance officer's last career stage before retirement giving him/her a degree of independence and guaranteeing a great deal of organizational experience. Even the most senior executives treat the chair's proxy very respectfully since he/she represents the board in the daily life of the company. The main tasks and goals of this

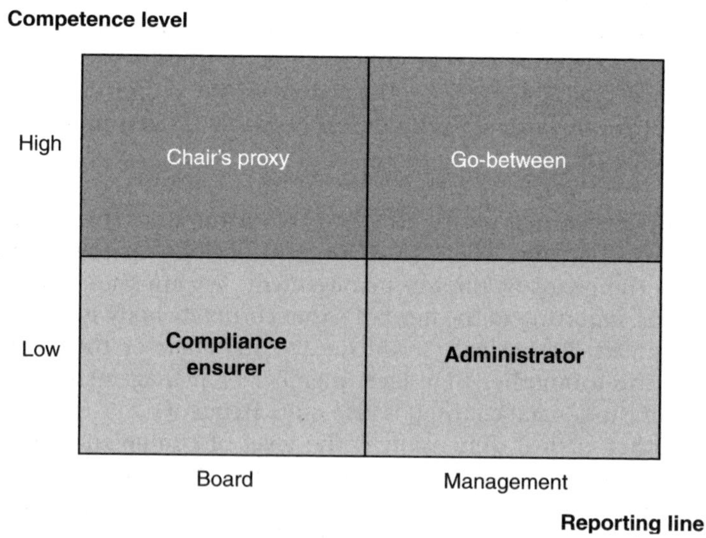

Figure 5.1 Clusters of company secretary roles

type of corporate governance officer are to organize extremely effective board meetings, ensure that relevant information is readily available, and to anticipate any potential issues (to alert the chair if necessary). The chair's proxy reviews all board papers in advance, ensuring quality and completeness of the information. Even without specific instructions by the board, he/she usually knows what reasoning the chair and the board will use on an issue. They are familiar with which specific points to highlight during an upcoming board meeting and most likely also how the board will vote. Therefore, a part of the chair's proxy role is content-oriented: He/she is involved in the discussion and actual writing of the board meeting agendas and in doing so can influence the topics addressed.

The go-between. The go-between is a corporate governance officer who has a high competence level and reports to top management. This type of secretary is a confidant of the CEO and has the task of providing top-level support to the board. He/she supplies the board with information, follows up on their requests, and prepares the necessary board papers. Individual board members might call with specific requests or raise issues or concerns. By addressing their questions with the go-between, the board members know, and even expect, that they will be brought to the attention of the CEO. The go-between's objective is to ensure that the board accepts the CEO's, the management board's, or executive committee's proposals. In doing so, he/she also provides an important "early awareness" function for the CEO regarding issues that board members might bring up during upcoming meetings: He/she must "read" emerging concerns and the changing positions of key people involved, identify objections, and alert the CEO accordingly. This normally requires an extensive network, especially in systems where board members use their own corporate staff to help them prepare for board meetings. In most cases, the go-between will be responsive to the (informal) feedback of board members rather than appear to be on the "Praetorian Guard" of the CEO; the latter behavior bearing the risk of excluding the go-between from noticing the soft and often weak signals on which to rely.

Compliance ensurer. There are also company secretaries who have lower level of responsibilities and competence and are reporting to the board (mostly the chair). We refer to them as "compliance ensurers." In companies with compliance ensurers, the CEO and CFO take care of most of the interaction with the board. Compliance ensurers are typically lower-level managers, primarily with legal expertise in the field of corporate governance; they also prepare other, specific reports for the board. They do not control or influence processes during board meetings and do not provide material impact in the preparation of these meetings. Instead, they respond to individual requests, for example, from the chair and prepare the requested documentation. A vital part of the role is often to keep records of board meetings and governance topics; they also report internally on compliance issues. This involves documenting cases where the company has violated laws or regulations, or has been prosecuted in any way for noncompliance with internal rules. Examples may include violations of codes of conduct, safety regulations, and nonbribery rules. To work efficiently, this type of secretary needs a wide internal information and contact network in areas such as internal auditing, health, safety, environmental departments, and corporate communications. The network ideally extends to all divisions of the company and all its key people.

Administrator. The administrator role comprises no major competencies and is characterized by a direct reporting line to management. The administrator is a lower-level manager, often a staff member of the corporate legal department and only temporarily delegated to the chair's office. As the title suggests, his/her tasks are predominantly administrative and he/she is not involved in setting the agenda, ensuring compliance, or the quality of the information delivered to the board. He/she is just responsible for pulling it all together and sending the board book out in time. The administrator is generally involved in many organizational details; the role comes closest to the most basic and initial company secretary function as described earlier.

Although the research in this field is relatively new and no generally applicable distribution of role frequencies has emerged so far, based on our extensive study – including professional experience and involvement with boards – we suggest the following job function breakdown: Today approximately 25 percent of company secretaries are chairs' proxies, 40 percent are go-betweens, 20 percent are compliance ensurers, and 15 percent are administrators. This is underscored by the fact that boards often have no full-time support staff but have to rely on personnel from the CEO-controlled headquarters. Overall, a majority of the secretaries have considerable competence, have an influential role, and for the most part report to the management.

The companies with compliance ensurers and administrators typically have a corporate history of less influential company secretaries. Over time, their company secretary role is likely to be enhanced and become a more comprehensive corporate governance officer position. In the coming years, we expect the percentage of administrators and compliance ensurers to drop. We expect all four roles described above to continue to exist in the future, but some will increase whereas others decrease in terms of their importance.

5.1 Future dynamics of the corporate governance officer

It is indisputable that there is a deep, fundamental change occurring in boardrooms around the world – a result of the corporate governance earthquake described earlier and its ongoing developments. The company secretary is still in charge of administrating the company's affairs and the board's work, but there has been an enormous expansion in the function's content. The business case for corporate governance also changed and has affected the work at the top echelon of companies. Individual research in this area may vary depending on country or legal corporate governance systems, but we see several significant trends:

Increased workload of individual board members. In most cases, there has been a considerable increase in the quantity and complexity of work for each board member. The workload of already heavily involved board members (i.e., chair) increased as did the involvement and task requirements for regular board members. Some board members claim it has even doubled. The main reasons for this are that there are more board meetings throughout the year, more committee and preparatory work as well as the addition of new tasks.

Increased scope of board duties. The statutory and factual duties of the board as the core corporate governance body have also increased. Scrutiny of top management by the whole (supervisory) board, or at least by the independent directors, has become more important. A meaningful indicator for this is that the dismissal of nonperforming CEOs – some years ago an event which bordered on scandal – has become an issue facing numerous boards today.

Increased reporting to the board. As boards have become increasingly involved and active in myriad issues, the task of reporting to the board has intensified as well. Not only is management providing extensive information to the board (to be on the safe side) but individual board members are also requesting an increased amount and more relevant information.

Increased board work documentation. The documentation of board meetings has grown and became more detailed; today it has to be very precise and reflect the deliberation of every decision – only "sound business judgment" protects companies against shareholder lawsuits.

Board importance has heightened and hence they are more involved in company governance than ever before. Most of these changes have significantly influenced the role of the company secretary (see also Section 3.4.2).

The first and obvious driver for changes in the role of the company secretary is the increased demands board members are faced with today. Few boards feel comfortable with a low level of support. As a result, the function of what has been known as the company secretary will be elevated in terms of hierarchy to full corporate governance officer and it is likely that more support staff will be allocated. Today only a minority of company secretaries have the official title of corporate governance officer although many of them in fact assume this role. One British secretary notes:

> I have a strong position in our company. But I believe that the new title "corporate governance officer" or "governance professional" as currently being introduced in companies in the US would also have a positive effect on the position of the company secretary in other countries. This title gives evidence of a broader perception of the function: getting away from the "bureaucratic administrator" to a high level member of management with responsibility to shape the company's governance structure.

However, beyond the few cases with specific (new) national legislation there is no visible trend indicating that the corporate governance officer will report directly to the CEO or rather the (nonexecutive) chair.

Given the ever-increasing importance of board independence, the question of whether or not the corporate governance officer should be independent of management – thus exclusively reporting to the board and/or the chair – may nevertheless become a topic of interest. We did not find much support, however, when we asked some of our US interviewees about their views on the recently published decision of the UnitedHealth Group (after a broad corporate governance redesign following a major options backdating scandal) to hire a board secretary who will be completely independent of management and separate from the traditional corporate secretary function, which continues to support management. There was also a lack of understanding regarding this move:

> I do not see how that person would handle the support of the board, not being integrated in the organization. If the external, independent

presiding director had to fully rely on that person this would be a disaster.

Despite the strong trend toward strengthening the boards' independence, US companies seem to have no problems with having their corporate secretaries reporting exclusively to the CEO who, of course, is still quite often also the chairman. Also, independent directors do not seem to have a problem receiving their information almost exclusively from management and having a secretary helping them – someone who is fully on management side and is by no means independent.

With the increased importance of board work and ongoing evolution of corporate governance, the role of the corporate governance officer will bring specific attention to three emerging tasks and challenges: (1) the necessity for board information improvements, (2) assurance of internal and external compliance, and (3) managing the complexity of the board governance processes. We will outline them in more detail in the following sections.

5.1.1 Board information improvements

IMD research in the field of board information revealed that board members feel the information they receive is

- Backward looking and untimely instead of forward looking and timely.
- Generated only internally (i.e., by the company) rather than externally.
- Delivered by old-fashioned channels.

The lack of timely, forward-looking information affects strategic decision making, particularly when it comes to technology and product innovations in the company's markets, direct competitors, and other market dynamics.

Now that boards are becoming more involved in corporate strategy and day-to-day business issues, they want and need to receive information earlier – before decisions are made and with adequate time to review materials thoroughly. Future strategic interest issues, for example, technology revolutions in the industry, have to be brought to the board's attention early. As board meeting agendas include an increased number of topics, board members are asking more questions in advance of the meeting. This requires more preparation time prior to meetings; it also means an increase in workload for the corporate governance officer. Secretaries are also increasingly faced with challenging situations: Price sensitive information such as financial results, strategic moves (e.g., mergers and acquisitions), or critical personnel changes are subject to "ad hoc disclosure rules." These are included under most stock exchange regulations and request that such news remain strictly confidential until their official public release. Secretaries have to make sure that board members receive information on such subjects in a timely manner before board meetings. At the same time, they have to prevent any leaks. This can quite often be a real tightrope walk.

Currently, senior management is usually the gateway for information between the board and the company. More than half of the board members we surveyed (in the above-mentioned complementary IMD study) receive 100 percent of their information directly from the company, particularly the CEO and other key officers. This means the people who have the biggest interest in persuading the board of their decisions and plans are in charge of informing board members. Acquiring independent information from impartial sources (i.e., sources external to the company) is still not common practice for most boards.

As to board information channels, the bottom line seems to be that paper dominates and it comes from the CEO. Electronic board libraries containing past board decisions or minutes, or even a comprehensive board information system (BIS) with access to company information databases, do not exist for the most part. Some companies have created online board portals that provide easy access to a wide range of internal (company) and external (e.g., market) data. They also offer sophisticated software tools for data aggregation, comparison, and visualization. But as our interviews showed, a great majority of today's board members are only rarely using such tools. This is a situation that is likely to change over time with board members becoming younger and more familiar with using electronic support for their work.

In order for the boards to perform their crucial role, the corporate governance officer must work to dissolve the board-information-related dilemmas at the top reaches of the company. He/she should assume and defend the gateway position of information between the board and management as well as guarantee that pertinent and unbiased information is forwarded to the board in a timely fashion. This may mean sending executive summaries to the board instead of extensive management or department reports. It can include the provision of information that is more detailed when deemed necessary. The corporate governance officer must ask the board to clearly state its information requirements and priorities and then deliver the information in a format that enables comparability, accessibility, and storage. In very large companies, it might make sense to set up internal board information guidelines – a system that all information providers to the board have to comply with.

Easy access to internal and external sources should additionally be provided. Today's widespread responsibilities of external, independent directors will no longer allow companies to prevent their board members from forming an independent opinion on issues to be decided by the board. Opening up the direct access of board members to high-level managers for collecting additional, supporting information does not only improve the decision-making process but also demonstrates a sound balance of powers. Board members are equally important for the success of the company as the management. The role of the corporate governance officer in this sometimes sensitive and even conflicting "power struggle" may be to act as the door-opener for the directors but not to "control" their information gathering. As one of the US secretaries comments in a very straightforward way:

> Our directors are intelligent and smart enough to make up their own mind, to collect independent views from a lot of internal and external sources and to then make their own judgment.

Such an approach will ensure that the board gets the big picture and that board meetings and the resulting decisions are in the best interest of the company.

5.1.2 External and internal compliance management

Assuming a corporate governance officer role definitely means taking responsibility for external and internal compliance management. The first task of effectively guaranteeing compliance is to assure alignment with external regulatory and quasi-regulatory demands. External compliance means ensuring the company's business is in accordance with regulations and codes of external parties, for example, from states or stock exchanges. It is important that the corporate governance officer keep abreast of the synergies, differences, and upcoming issues of law and corporate governance in all the company's markets. This is crucial to operate successfully in this challenging, complex, and dynamic environment.

Acting as corporate governance officer also involves making sure that the company's self-imposed rules are observed. This is the so-called internal compliance. Most modern companies have implemented business guidelines, corporate values, or codes of conduct, and they promote them extensively to stock markets or other stakeholders. Therefore, for the corporate governance officer, internal compliance is as important as external compliance. Even if there are no strict published guidelines on internal compliance, there are always values that a company does or does not want to pursue and uphold. The corporate governance officer must constantly be aware of these and must use his/her influence to make sure that employees respect them.

Every now and then, major changes in the societal, political, or legal environment occur. The corporate governance officer must anticipate these changes and alert the board when the ground starts to shift. Rather than overwhelming the board with legal formalities, the corporate governance officer should propose how to deal with these changing tides. A forward-looking corporate governance officer might suggest to the board that an internal code of conduct regarding suppliers be implemented before such a code becomes mandatory. He/she might convince the board of the opportunities resulting of the company's reporting on "soft issues," such as environmental and social responsibility; or persuade the board to voluntarily disclose meaningful information on the company's compensation policy before binding rules are issued by regulators or new laws instituted.

5.1.3 The governance process manager

Board work becomes more complex as the board becomes more involved in company affairs and the interaction between board members and management increases. Board committee work must be prepared but must also be coordinated and linked to the overall board responsibility. Today boards are held accountable for making sure that an effective risk management and control system is in place, and that the identified risks are appropriately dealt with. This reaches far beyond the financial domain and includes tax and legal risks, technology risks, and, equally importantly, reputation risks. It also means having internal audits to detect fraud and corruption, checking legal compliance (e.g., in health, safety, and environment, proper due diligence in acquisitions, and so on).

A multitude of people and organizational units within companies are in charge of establishing all necessary rules and guidelines. It is the corporate governance officer, however, who must propose clear and effective criteria for the board and its various committees enabling them to assume their responsibilities in defining and overseeing company risks. He/she must clearly delineate what should be brought to the full-board's attention, what information do board members need, and at what time should they receive it. It is the corporate governance officer's job to make sure that the board work remains transparent and that its members have a shared understanding about the necessary processes.

Despite these considerable responsibilities, it is important that corporate governance officers avoid any appearance of being the decision makers themselves or of assuming any real power. The corporate governance officer is managing the complex process of corporate governance at the highest level of the company. This requires a high degree of discretion due to the important and often sensitive issues involved. Ultimately, however, responsibilities have to remain clear – the board and top management are running the company, not the corporate governance officer, as highly qualified and strongly empowered as he/she might be.

5.2 Where shall we go? What has to be done?

The evolving world of corporate governance has brought considerable change to companies worldwide. It has clearly grown beyond the legal dimension. For successful companies, sound corporate governance is essential to both board and company performance; at its best it is also a source of competitive advantage. The corporate governance officer plays a key role in this.

Significant challenges ahead

As companies continue to grow and globalize, they become increasingly complex and from that situation, the basic need for a governance process manager is emerging. Legal expertise is important and helpful but mastering the complex processes at the head of a company requires different and much broader skills.

Corporate governance is not static. It is subject to constant change. New influencing factors and stakeholders may have additional impact on the corporate governance officer's role in the future. As these changes cannot be foreseen, the corporate governance officer must exercise his/her role with expertise and accuracy; they must also have a forward looking and flexible mindset. Despite any changes in the future, the role of corporate governance officer will continue to evolve into a top executive position – one that ensures sound corporate governance, and with the ultimate goal of supporting successful business performance. One of our American interviewees described the perspective in a very concise way:

> The biggest challenge for the boards over the years to come is to find an appropriate balance between compliance and strategy. And it will

> be one of the secretary's challenges to influence processes in a way that leads to finding this balance. The biggest struggle must be to add value to the business.

Another high-level US secretary pointed to the impact of new shareholders' expectations that change gradually from a strict financial view to more long-term success considerations:

> The "ESG" view (environment, society, governance) will influence board behavior mostly in a positive way but will also make some activities of the board – and ultimately also of the secretary – more challenging. AGMs, for instance, will become less predictable, requiring much more flexibility and broader knowledge.

Many companies will be confronted with the need to adapt their structures and to further develop their governance standards. The corporate governance officer will be called to exercise his/her influence when it comes to ensuring that the substance of a governance structure prevails over form. In the long term, effective and successful corporate governance is not a question of checking boxes but living up to high professional and ethical standards.

Ready for the tough choices?

Increasingly, the corporate governance officer will have to confront dilemmas making the role more demanding and sometimes quite critical. As discussed earlier, dilemmas arise mostly from the corporate governance officer's positioning within the organization. Conflicts can manifest themselves between board and management, between the chairman and the CEO or between individual board members – any one of which can put the secretary in an awkward position. The question of his/her independence from management may suddenly become an issue; clearly established rules under normal circumstances may not weather the storm.

The times of a "legal-only" and primarily administrative company secretary are over in most global companies. The new challenges and dilemmas make the job more interesting and rewarding but also riskier. Now the job also demands plenty of "soft skills." In one company, the corporate governance officer we interviewed has taken a different route to her current role: She first assumed the function of corporate governance officer, a job which had been in place for many years, and only later was she assigned the corporate secretary position:

> I see it as a privilege coming from the governance side and moving to the additional secretary role rather than the other way round. This shows that the secretary is no longer an administrative function but a challenging and very interesting assignment.

A high-level corporate governance officer, and member of senior management, embracing the additional role of "company secretary" is a challenging perspective for the future; it is clear proof of the function's increasing importance.

There is, however, one final and crucial comment to make: It is not the board composition or structure, listing, jurisdiction, or corporate governance design which are the ultimate defining factors for the company secretary role. It is the personality of the secretary himself/herself that really counts. This is even more the case with high-level corporate governance officers. Some of our interviewees express their personal views:

> When I retire the new secretary may shape the role completely differently, depending on his personality and his educational and professional background.
>
> Strong personalities will be strong secretaries. Weaker people will play a less important role.

The overall importance of the function is increasing. More boards will realize how important it is to position the secretary appropriately within the hierarchy; they will listen to him/her when it comes to defining and organizing governance issues. However, at the end of the day the best corporate governance rules do not make a company successful. People matter – not structures. This is true for the boards as well as for the secretary. In the future, there will be tough choices for company secretaries as they face numerous and challenging complexities. Boards will also be confronted with serious issues and decisions – one of the important of which will be selecting the right person as their corporate governance officer.

Appendix

A.1 Interview guide

The Role of the Company Secretary

Opener:

Briefly emphasize the need for and relevance of this study:
Corporate governance has become increasingly complex in the wake of financial scandals and regulatory changes. This has had a particularly marked effect on the role of the company secretary who is in a "unique position to provide value to...Chairmen and Boards of Directors by being [the] company's Chief Governance Officer" (American Society of Corporate Secretaries & Governance Professionals).

This study aims to shed light on key trends in corporate governance with a particular focus on the challenges and role of the company secretary.

Clarify key terms (Company Secretary, Board etc.)
NB. This interview guide provides the basis for semi-structured interviews conducted for the purpose of this study. It provides guidance without being prescriptive – giving the interviewer the freedom to phrase, segment (and skip) questions appropriately.

1. Company background	
Question	*Probes/remarks*
1.1 Provide information about company background (provided it could not be obtained from desk research).	– Industry – Number of employees – Size (market capitalization/annual revenues/total assets) – Legal structure
2. Reporting line	
Question	*Probes/remarks*
2.1 What department/function/ corporate body do you report to?	– Chairman of the BOARD – Head of Investor Relations – Head of Legal Affairs – CEO – Head of Finance/Chief Financial Officer – Other, please specify

3. Qualification for the function	
Question	*Probes/remarks*
3.1 What is your educational background	– Business – Economics – Engineering – Legal – Communications/journalism – Other, please specify
3.2 What is your personal qualification/professional history	– Prior position/function (legal, public affairs, operations, etc.) – Prior engagement (another company, subsidiary of current company, current company etc.)
3.3 How long have you been with your current employer?	–
3.4 How long have you been company secretary in your current company?	–

4. Company secretary's positioning within the organization	
Question	*Probes/remarks*
4.1 What is your hierarchical position and title?	–
4.2 What resources/dedicated staff are at your disposal	–

5. Board organization and board work (provided it could not be obtained from desk research)	
Question	*Probes/remarks*
5.1 How is your board organized?	– One-tier/two-tier board – Executive/nonexecutive Chairman – Executive/nonexecutive directors – Independent directors
5.2 Describe existing board committees (members, special functions)	– Audit Committee – Nominating/corporate governance committee – Compensation/remuneration committee – Other, please specify
5.3 How often do the full board and these committees convene?	–

6. Legal and regulatory environment	
Question	*Probes/remarks*
6.1 What are the key characteristics of your company's legal and regulatory environment?	– Domestic/global – Stock exchange listings – Special regulators
7. Company secretary's responsibilities	
Question	*Probes/remarks*
7.1 What are your responsibilities in general?	– Discuss job description and other assignments
7.2 What are your responsibilities with regards to board meetings?	– Agenda drafting – Preparation of documents – Participation in meeting – Minutes – Follow-up
7.3 What are your responsibilities with regards to informing board members?	– Special information tools – Role of the company secretary with drafting information – Role of management/chairman with defining content
7.4 What are your responsibilities with regards to board committees?	– General support for committees, also outside meetings – Meetings: Agenda, participation, minutes – Secretary role in which committees?
7.5 Who assumes the secretary function in committees, in which you – as a company secretary – are not involved?	–
7.6 What are your responsibilities with regards to shareholders?	– AGM: Convocation, proxy statements, other legal issues, shareholders' requests, proposals, logistics, activities during the meeting, follow-up – Other responsibilities (informing shareholders, contributing to annual reports, etc.)
7.7 What are your legal responsibilities?	– Specific responsibilities beyond corporate governance and compliance
7.8 What are your regulatory responsibilities?	– Reporting to special regulators

7.9 What are your responsibilities with regards to corporate communication?	–
7.10 What are your specific responsibilities in the field of corporate governance?	– Corporate governance design, reporting – Board evaluation – Sarbanes-Oxley Act (certification, reporting) – Compliance – Code of business conduct and ethics – Corporate responsibility – Whistle-blowing – Other, please specify
8. Key trends and outlook	
Question	*Probes/remarks*
8.1 What changes occurred over the past years with regards to your position, responsibilities, etc.?	– Changes in general board work – Changed role or positioning of the company secretary – Impact of new directors' independence requirements on role of the secretary: information, support
8.2 What developments do you expect in the future?	– Changes ahead (for general board work/for secretary role) – Increasing independence requirements for board members and the impact on secretary work – New job description, new positioning, new title – Career opportunities for the secretary
9. Special issues	
9.1 What loyalty conflicts (between board and management or chairman and CEO) did you experience/might you envisage?	–
9.2 How strong is the need for an "independent" company secretary?	–

A.2 Project description

The following project description was added to the mailed self-completion questionnaire to provide contextual information and clarify our terminology.

Project description, research method and glossary

Project description

Professor Ulrich Steger, Director of IMD's Building High Performance Boards program, and Gertrud Erismann-Peyer, IMD Executive in Residence and former Company Secretary of the Swiss financial services group UBS AG, are carrying out empirical research into the role of the company secretary. The aim is to:

1. Identify new challenges that company secretaries are facing given the tightening of legal and regulatory requirements.
2. Obtain a better understanding of the role of company secretaries in the field of corporate governance.

Research method

- Interviews with 70 to 80 company secretaries of large international, listed companies in the US, the UK, Germany, France, Italy, the Netherlands, Spain, Switzerland and some northern European countries.
- A questionnaire covering a broader segment of the global economy: small and medium-sized companies, family businesses, non-listed companies, companies in other jurisdictions than those covered by the interviews, etc.

Glossary

Interviews conducted so far show a broad variety of roles and responsibilities assumed by company secretaries. For the purposes of this survey the following definitions should apply:

- BOARD should be understood as the supreme corporate body of the company, responsible primarily for defining strategy and appointing and supervising management, irrespective of whether the company has a one-tier or a two-tier board structure.

  Main terms used: Board of Directors, Supervisory Board, Aufsichtsrat, Verwaltungsrat, Conseil d'administration, Consiglio di amministrazione.

(Note: The survey does not target so-called Management Committees, Executive Boards, Vorstand, Directoire, Direzione Generale, etc.)

- COMPANY SECRETARY should be understood as a function incorporating a broad variety of corporate activities assumed on behalf of and/or in support of the BOARD in its above-described meaning, be it full time or in addition to other assignments.

Main terms used: Company or Corporate Secretary, General Secretary, Secretary to the Board of Directors, General Counsel.

A.3 Self-completion questionnaire

The Role of the Company Secretary

There have been significant developments (tightening of regulatory standards in particular) in the area of corporate governance over the past years. These developments are likely to have affected the role of the company secretary. We have sent you this questionnaire because you – as a company secretary (whether in title or not) – can substantially contribute to a better understanding of the main trends in corporate governance and the challenges facing the company secretary. For the purposes of this study:

- COMPANY SECRETARY should be understood as a position incorporating all corporate functions to support the BOARD. See Glossary.
- BOARD should be understood as the supreme corporate body of the company, responsible primarily for defining strategy and supervising management. See Glossary.

We will be happy to send you the results of this study upon its completion.

IMD has outstanding expertise in corporate governance research. We guarantee strict confidentiality. Please simply indicate your personal opinion and perception in response to the following questions.

1. Please rate the following items in terms of how strongly they have affected your company's approach to corporate governance.

	① = **Not at all** to ⑤ = **Very strongly**				
Domestic regulation (in country where headquarters are)	①	②	③	④	⑤
Stock exchange listings	①	②	③	④	⑤
Ad hoc public pressure	①	②	③	④	⑤
Continuous public pressure	①	②	③	④	⑤
Competition (e.g. capital markets)	①	②	③	④	⑤

2. Does the legal framework in which your company operates allow executives on the BOARD?

☐ Yes ☐ No

3. Please indicate your company's BOARD characteristics by marking the boxes below. (Mark all that apply.)

☐ Chairman is an executive – **Please mark if he/she is also the CEO:** ☐	☐ BOARD includes one or more executive members who are neither chairman nor CEO
☐ Majority of BOARD members are nonexecutive	☐ Majority of BOARD members are independent
☐ BOARD includes employee representatives	☐ BOARD includes government representatives

4. What is your educational background? (Mark all that apply.)

☐ Business	☐ Legal
☐ Economics	☐ Communications/journalism
☐ Engineering	☐ Other, please specify

5. In which company did you work immediately prior to your current role as COMPANY SECRETARY?

☐ Subsidiary of my current company	☐ My current company
☐ Another company	☐ Other, please specify

6. Which positions did you hold prior to your current role as COMPANY SECRETARY? (Mark all that apply.)

☐ Legal	☐ Finance
☐ Public affairs, communications	☐ Strategy
☐ Operations	☐ Other, please specify

7. For how long have you been COMPANY SECRETARY in your company? (in years)

8. Who do you as COMPANY SECRETARY report to? (Mark all that apply.)

☐ Chairman of the BOARD	☐ CEO
☐ Head of Investor Relations	☐ Head of Finance/Chief Financial Officer
☐ Head of Legal Affairs	☐ Other, please specify

9. Who do you as COMPANY SECRETARY primarily work for? (Mark all that apply.)

☐ CEO	☐ CEO and also management in general
☐ Chairman of the BOARD	☐ Chairman of the Board and also the BOARD in general
☐ Investor relations	☐ Finance
☐ Legal affairs	☐ Other, please specify

10. To what extent do the following statements match your situation as COMPANY SECRETARY in your company?

	① = Not at all to ⑤ = Great extent				
As COMPANY SECRETARY, I am primarily accountable to the chairman of the BOARD	①	②	③	④	⑤
I occasionally find myself in the middle of a conflict between management and the BOARD	①	②	③	④	⑤
As COMPANY SECRETARY, I am primarily accountable to the CEO	①	②	③	④	⑤
I have enough staff supporting me in my tasks. **Please specify the number of supporting staff:**	①	②	③	④	⑤
Recent developments (scandals, regulation) have clearly strengthened my role as COMPANY SECRETARY	①	②	③	④	⑤
I typically get enough support from the chairman of the BOARD	①	②	③	④	⑤
This job gives me significant future career opportunities within my company	①	②	③	④	⑤
I have significant freedom in terms of how I interpret my role as COMPANY SECRETARY (i.e. what I do)	①	②	③	④	⑤
I have significant freedom in terms of how I fulfill my tasks (i.e. how I do the things I do)	①	②	③	④	⑤
I have a strong influence on my company's corporate governance structure (e.g. existence of BOARD committees, BOARD composition)	①	②	③	④	⑤
I have a strong influence on my company's corporate governance process (e.g. information flow, agenda setting)	①	②	③	④	⑤

11. Please rate the following responsibilities in terms of their importance in your role as COMPANY SECRETARY in your company.

	① = **Not at all** to ⑤ = **Very important**				
Supporting BOARD meetings (preparation, minutes, follow-up, etc.)	①	②	③	④	⑤
Supporting management meetings (preparation, minutes, follow-up, etc.)	①	②	③	④	⑤
Keeping BOARD members informed on an ongoing basis (e.g. regular information packages)	①	②	③	④	⑤
Supporting BOARD committees	①	②	③	④	⑤
Contributing to annual general meeting (formal issues, content, etc.)	①	②	③	④	⑤
Keeping key shareholders informed on an ongoing basis	①	②	③	④	⑤
Contributing to annual reports (e.g. corporate governance part)	①	②	③	④	⑤
Taking legal responsibilities	①	②	③	④	⑤
Engaging in corporate communications	①	②	③	④	⑤
Defining corporate governance structure and approach	①	②	③	④	⑤
Supporting BOARD evaluation (e.g. questionnaire design, data analysis)	①	②	③	④	⑤
Formulating codes of business conduct and ethics	①	②	③	④	⑤
Whistle-blowing (helpline, monitoring, etc.)	①	②	③	④	⑤
Generating visions and ideas	①	②	③	④	⑤
Reporting on management transactions (e.g. purchase/sale of shares and options)	①	②	③	④	⑤
Other (please specify)	①	②	③	④	⑤

12. In which of the following BOARD **committees** do you **act as secretary?** (Mark all that apply.)

☐ **No** secretarial role in any committee	☐ Remuneration/compensation committee
☐ Nomination committee	☐ Corporate governance committee
☐ Audit/compliance committee	☐ Other, please specify:

13. Please evaluate your company's **corporate governance** performance by answering the questions below.

	① = **Clearly below average** to ⑤ = **Clearly above average**				
My company's corporate governance performance relative to that of its peers is	①	②	③	④	⑤
	① = **Not at all** to ⑤ = **Great extent**				
My company's approach to corporate governance has improved over the last two years	①	②	③	④	⑤

14. Which of the following improvements in corporate governance structure and processes have occurred over the last two years in your company? (Mark all that apply.)

☐ CEO is no longer chairman of the BOARD	☐ The majority of BOARD members are now independent
☐ New BOARD committees (e.g. audit, corporate governance) have been created	☐ Only independent members are now on the audit committee
☐ The COMPANY SECRETARY has become more independent of management	☐ A code of conduct has been designed and implemented
☐ Other, please specify:	

A. Please indicate the **industry** your company operates in:

☐ Energy	☐ Financial services
☐ Pharmaceutical	☐ Food and beverage
☐ Automotive	☐ Chemical
☐ Technology/ Telecommunications	☐ Other, please specify:

B. Please indicate the **country** in which your headquarters are located:

C. Please indicate the **size** of your company:

Employees (approximate number):

Market capitalization (approximate figure):

Total assets (approximate figure):

D. Is your company publicly listed?

☐ Yes, please specify the location of its main listing:	☐ No

E. Please provide additional information about secondary listings by marking the boxes below. (Mark all that apply.)

☐ New York Stock Exchange/ NASDAQ	☐ London Stock Exchange

F. Is your company family owned?

☐ Yes	☐ No

G. Is your company a subsidiary?

☐ Yes	☐ No

H. How many subsidiaries does your company have?

I. Please describe the **ownership structure** of your company by marking **one** of the boxes below.

☐ Shares are owned by one shareholder only	☐ Shares are largely owned by a few, dominant shareholders
☐ Company has a broad shareholder base (dispersed ownership)	☐ Other, please specify:

J. Please indicate your **age**:

☐ Under 40 ☐ 40 to 50 ☐ 51 to 60 ☐ Above 60

Thank you for completing this survey. If you would like to receive the results of this survey, please provide us with your e-mail address.

My e-mail address is: ______________________________

Please fax your completed questionnaire to **+41 21 618 0641** or mail it to:

Gertrud Erismann-Peyer
IMD – International Institute for Management Development
P.O. Box 915
Chemin de Bellerive 23
CH-1001 Lausanne
Switzerland

Additional References

Cadbury Report, *Financial Aspects of Corporate Governance* (London: Gee Publishing, 1992).

Greenbury Report on Directors' Remuneration (London, 1995).

Hampel Report on Corporate Governance (London: Gee Publishing, 1998).

Institute of Chartered Secretaries and Administrators, *Duties of a Company Secretary – Best Practice Guide* (London: Institute of Chartered Secretaries and Administrators, 1998).

Institute of Chartered Secretaries and Administrators, *Specimen Job Description for the Corporate Governance Role of the Company Secretary*, ICSA Guidance Note 021001 (London: Institute of Chartered Secretaries and Administrators, 2002).

OECD Principles on Corporate Governance, first published in 1999, last amended 2004 (Paris, OECD Publications, 2004).

Society of Corporate Secretaries and Governance Professionals, *The Corporate Secretary – Duties and Responsibilities. What Does a Corporate Secretary Do?* (New York: Society of Corporate Secretaries and Governance Professionals, online publication), other publications (corporate minutes, current board practices, surveys available at www.governanceprofessionals.org)

Steger, U. "Beyond Preventing Crime – Where Does Corporate Governance Really Add Value?" *Perspectives for Managers*, No. 101 (Lausanne: IMD, 2003).

Steger, U. (Ed.) *Mastering Global Corporate Governance* (Chichester: John Wiley and Sons, 2004).

Steger, U. and Amann, W. *Corporate Governance – How to Add Value* (Chichester: John Wiley and Sons, 2008).

Steger, U. and Frigast, C. "Corporate Governance in Private Equity Companies: Can It Add Value?" *Perspectives for Managers*, No. 122 (Lausanne: IMD, 2005).

Steger, U. and Krapf, H. "Corporate Governance in Global Companies – Content Not Structure as the Main Driver" *IMD Working Paper*, No. 2003-3 (Lausanne: IMD, 2003).

Ward, J. (Ed.) *Unconventional Wisdom: Counterintuitive Insights for Family Business Success* (Chichester: John Wiley and Sons, 2005).

Glossary

Note: A majority of our readers will be familiar with most of the following terms. By providing some short explanation of terms used in the book we aim to avoid misunderstandings, mainly due to the different interpretation of terms in various jurisdictions. For some terms we also provide their very specific use in this book

Term	**Definition/Explanation**
Board	Supreme corporate body of a company, responsible primarily for defining strategy and succession planning (appointment/dismissal) for, and supervision of, management.
Board of directors	Term often used for the "Board" as defined above, as opposed to the board of management.
Company secretary	Function responsible for a variety of activities assumed on behalf of and/or in support of the Board.
Corporate bodies	Term used for the highest authorities of a company, normally the Board (in one-tier structures) or the Supervisory board and the Management board (in two-tier structures).
Corporate governance officer	Emerging new term for highly qualified Company Secretaries with a broad scale of responsibilities.
Corporate secretary	American term for Company Secretary.
Directors' dealings	Purchase and/or sale of the company's stock by members of corporate bodies or some other high-ranked corporate officers.
Executive board	Corporate body responsible for the day-to-day management, mostly in two-tier structures.
Executive committee	Term used for organizational structures with various mandates and responsibilities; for example, management committee (mostly in

Continued

Continued

Term	Definition/Explanation
	one-tier structures), committee of the chairman (mostly in two-tier structures, often also called presidential committee), special board committee with authority to take urgent decisions between ordinary board meetings (mostly in the United States).
Executive director/Executive board member	Board member assuming an executive role and having an employment relationship with the company.
Executive meeting	Term used in some companies for meetings of a selected number of directors (executive or external) to deal with specific issues, mostly of urgent nature and between ordinary meetings. In other companies, term also used for meetings of the nonexecutive directors.
Executive session	Meeting of the nonexecutive or nonmanagement directors.
External director	Board member without employment contract with the company.
General counsel	Chief Legal Officer, Head of the Legal Department, often also assuming the Company Secretary role.
Independent director	External board members who do not have relevant personal and/or business relationships with the company.
Insider list	List of people in a company having specific insider knowledge (board members, members of top management, selected specialists).
Internal director	Board member having an employment contract with the company.
Management board	Term used for the corporate body responsible for the day-to-day management, mostly in two-tier structures.
Management transactions	Purchase and sale of company's stock by defined members of the supreme corporate bodies. In many jurisdictions companies are required to report such transactions to the stock exchange.

Continued

Term	Definition/Explanation
Nonexecutive director	Board member not having an executive function within the company – as opposed to "executive director."
Nonmanagement director	Board member who is not a member of executive management. In two-tier structures he/she might be employed (e.g., full-time chairman) but not part of the executive management.
One-tier board	Board combining executive and nonexecutive directors in one corporate body, with no legal separation of duties.
Principal–agent theory	Theory dealing with problems of conflicting interests between agent (e.g., management wants to maximize power and personal income) and principal (stockholders want to e.g., maximize their assets) and mechanisms to align those interests.
Proxy statement	Document to be provided to US shareholders in view of the AGM, containing agenda items for discussion/approval, as well as a detailed corporate governance report.
Proxy voting	Possibility for shareholders to cast their votes for the AGM by instructing a representative to vote on their behalf, mostly in writing.
Supervisory board	Supreme corporate body in two-tier board structures, with authority and responsibility for appointing and supervising the members of the Management board.
Two-tier boards	Two top boards characterized by legal separation of supervisory function (supervisory board) and management function (management board).
Unitary board	Term used for one-tier boards.
Vorstand	Management board in German companies, completely separate from the Supervisory board.

Index

"administrator", *see* company secretary – types of secretaries
allegiance, 63–9, 147
Anglo-Saxon countries, 1, 5, 6, 34, 44, 98, 105, 106
annual general meeting of shareholders (AGM), 118–22
Asia, 2, 23, 24, 25, 30, 34, 35, 36, 37, 39, 48, 50, 51, 56, 61, 64, 90, 91, 99, 104, 105, 113, 115, 118, 123, 133, 134, 135, 138
audit committee, 4, 39, 42, 90, 98–9, 115, 135, 151
  see also board committees

board
  characteristics and composition, 33–5
  executive and independent board members, 36–9
  executive and nonexecutive chairmen, 35–6
  independence, *see* independence – board
  influence on company secretary setting, 147
  influence on company secretary's tasks and responsibilities, 150
  influence on corporate governance, 152
  internal organization, 39–43
  meetings, 41–3, 76–87
  working methods, workload, 137–8, 157
board committees, 39–41, 134–5, 162
  meetings, 41–3
  secretaries' involvement, 93–103, 109
  support, 90–3
  see also audit committee; compensation committee; corporate governance committee
board evaluation, 110–13
board information, 87–90, 157–61
  improvements, 159–61
board support, 74–90
  ensuring compliance, 75
  information, 87–90, 157–61
  meetings, 76–87: agenda and supporting documents, 77–81; executive sessions, 85–7; follow-up, 85; minutes, 83–5; secretary role during, 82–3
  planning of board activities, 75
  support of chairman, 74, 81–2
  support of individual directors, 75–6
Britain, *see* United Kingdom
British Companies Act, *see* UK Companies Act

career (secretary), xix–xx, 45–54
  educational background, 45–7
  future career opportunities, 51–4
  job duration, 50–1
  professional background / history, 47–50
causal effects, 145–52
  influence of board composition, 147, 150
  influence of corporate governance drivers, 146–7, 149
  influence of reporting lines and working relationships, 148–9, 151–2
  influence of secretary's educational background and professional history, 148, 150–1
  significance level, 145
  tested, 145–6
chairman-CEO function, 4, 28, 32–3, 35–7, 61, 63, 64–7, 133, 134
chairman's/presidential committee, 40, 42, 96, 100, 101–2
"chair's proxy", *see* company secretary – types of secretaries

checks and balances, 4–5, 36, 39, 85–6
Chief Executive Officer (CEO), 2–4, 33, 55–6, 148–9, 155, 160
  see also chairman-CEO function
code of business conduct and ethics, 113–14
  see also codes of conduct
codes of conduct, 5, 133, 162
  design and implementation, 135–6
companies, *see* types of companies
company secretary, xviii, 1, 5, 43–130, 145–52
  accountability, 62–3
  allegiance, 63–9
  background, *see* career
  board committees (involvement of secretary), 93–103: audit/ compliance committees, 98–9; compensation committees, 99–101; nominating and corporate governance committees, 95–8
  challenges, xx, 163–5
  codification: in Australia, 8; in Europe, 8; in general, 44; in Russia, 9; in Spain, 8–9; in Switzerland, 7–8; in United Kingdom, 6–7; in United States, 7
  discretion, 58–60
  effects on role, 138: corporate governance environment, 140–2; independence of management, 142–4; workload, 139–40
  hierarchical positioning, 49–50, 165
  loyalty conflicts, *see* conflicts
  recent developments influencing, xxiii–xxiv, 157–8
  reporting lines, 55–7
  resources, 69–71
  role / positioning of the secretary, 6–9, 153
  secretary's setting, *see* causal effects; determinants
  support from chairman, 57–8
  tasks and responsibilities, xx–xxiii, 71–4, 149–52: board support, 71; committee work, 90–103; corporate communication, 129–30; corporate governance, 103–17; legal responsibilities, 126–7; management support, 117–18; regulatory and compliance responsibilities, 127–8; shareholders, 118–26; vision and ideas, 130
  types of secretaries, xxv–xxvi, 153–7: administrator, 156; chair's proxy, 154–5; compliance ensurer, 155–6; go-between, 155
  working relationship, 60–2
  see also board committees; board support; causal effects; corporate governance; determinants; minutes; shareholders
compensation committees, 39–40, 42, 99–101
compliance and regulatory responsibilities, 127–8
compliance committees, 98–9
  see also audit committee
"compliance ensurer", *see* company secretary – types of secretaries
conflicts, 63–9
  between board and management / chairman and CEO, 64
  company secretary's involvement, 63–9
corporate communication, 129–30
corporate governance, 3–5, 103–17, 163–4
  drivers, 26–33, 146–52: competition, 31; influence on company secretary setting, 146–7; influence on company secretary's tasks and responsibilities, 149; influence on corporate governance performance, 152; listings, 30; public pressure, 31–3; regulation, 26–9; stock markets, 30–1
  dynamics and structure, xviii–xix
  recent research and literature, overview, 9–10
  see also corporate governance committees; corporate governance officer; corporate governance performance; corporate governance – secretaries' involvement

corporate governance committees, 39–40, 42, 94, 95–8
corporate governance officer (CGO), xxiv, 5, 43, 153–65
challenges, xxvi–xxvii, 163–4
dilemmas, 164–5
future dynamics, 157–63
job description, xxvii–xxix
roles, xxv–xxvi, 153–7, 159
tasks and challenges, 159–63: board information improvements, 159–61; external and internal compliance management, 161–2; governance process manager, 162–3
corporate governance performance, xxiii–xxiv, 132–8, 152
improvements, 132–8: CEO is no longer chairman, 134; design and implementation code of conduct, 135–6; independent board members, 134, 135; new board committees, creation of, 134–5; other changes, 136–8
overall governance performance, 131–2
see also determinants
corporate governance – secretaries' involvement, 104–17
board evaluation, 110–13
codes of business conduct and ethics, 113–14
reporting, 106–10, 123–4
Sarbanes-Oxley Act, 116–17
structure and approach, 104–10
whistle-blowing, 114–16
corporate responsibility committees, 40, 101
corporate secretary, *see* company secretary

determinants
of company secretary setting, 145–9
of company secretary's tasks and responsibilities, 149–52
of corporate governance performance, 152
see also causal effects
discretion (as to task fulfillment and role interpretation), 58–60
document distribution, 79–80
electronic distribution, 80
domestic regulation, *see* regulation
dual mandate, 32–3
see also chairman-CEO function

employees on boards, 35, 37, 38, 41, 81, 135
executive board members, 36–9
see also executive directors
executive chairman, 35–6
executive committees, 40–1, 103
executive compensation, 31, 100, 142
executive director, 33–4, 40, 110, 140
executive meeting, 41–2, 66, 68
executive sessions, 85–7, 112
external compliance management, 161–2
external directors, 69, 76, 79, 87

family-owned companies, 21, 22, 25, 26, 30, 36, 38, 39, 48, 52, 61, 95, 96, 105–6, 125, 130, 132, 134, 136, 138
finance / investment committees, 40, 101
France, 18, 19, 28, 32–3, 34, 35, 36, 37, 38, 43, 44, 47, 59, 65, 68, 72, 73, 75, 78, 84, 89, 92, 97, 98, 99, 100, 101, 102, 107, 112, 118, 119, 124, 125, 140, 141, 142

general counsel, 47, 55, 56–7, 66, 73, 82, 107, 114, 118, 126–7, 139–40
Germany, 4, 18, 19, 32, 34, 35, 36, 37, 38, 41, 42, 43, 44, 47, 55–6, 60, 66, 68, 72, 73, 78, 81, 83, 92, 99, 100, 102, 106–7, 109, 112, 115, 118, 119, 120, 124, 129, 135, 140, 141, 142–3
"go-between" secretary, *see* company secretary – types of secretaries
governance process manager, 162–3
government representatives on boards, 35

headquarters location, 18, 22–3

independence
  boards / board members, xii–xiv, 28–9, 36–9, 158–61
  company secretary, xiii, 140, 142–4, 158
  committee members, 39, 135
  information, 87–9
  majority of board members, 37, 134
  see also independent directors
independent directors, 4, 38, 39, 41, 43, 85–6, 87, 141, 143, 144, 149, 152, 157, 159
insider trading list, *see* management transactions
Institute of Chartered Secretaries and Administrators (ICSA), 13, 127
internal compliance management, 161–2
internal organization of board, 39–43
  board meetings, 41–3
  committees, 39–41
interviews, 16, 18–22
interview guide, 166–9, 170
Italy, 18, 19, 34, 36, 38, 39, 43, 44, 45, 79, 92, 99, 100, 118, 119, 140

lead director, 4, 68, 111, 136
legal responsibilities, 126–7
listed companies, 23, 24, 26, 35, 38, 39, 46, 61, 69, 70, 77, 90, 92, 94, 95, 101, 104, 105, 113, 118, 120, 123, 125, 128, 132, 135, 138
  see also non-listed companies
listings, 21
  influence on corporate governance, 30
  standards, 28
loyalty conflicts, *see* conflicts

management board, 5, 8, 75, 109, 140
management support, 117–18
management transactions (reporting on), 128–9, 150
minutes
  annual general meeting, 120–1
  board, 83–5
  board committees, 92–3, 96, 98–9

the Netherlands, 18, 19, 34, 38, 44, 53, 68, 73–4, 81, 85, 87, 88, 92, 100, 107, 111, 115, 119, 140, 141, 143
New York Stock Exchange (NYSE), 21, 23, 28, 30, 42, 59, 107, 113, 114, 115, 134
nominating committee, *see* corporate governance committee
nonexecutive chairman, 4, 35–6, 40
nonexecutive director, 33–4, 54, 110
non-listed companies, 21, 24, 39, 61, 77, 94, 95, 113, 123, 132
  see also listed companies
nonmanagement directors, 86

one-tier board, 4, 33–4
  see also unitary board
Other Regions, 23, 24, 25, 35, 36, 38, 39, 48, 51, 56, 64, 91, 94, 100, 104, 106, 113, 115, 126, 132, 133, 134, 135, 136, 138, 142
ownership structure, 22, 24

presidential committees, *see* chairman's committees
Principal–Agent Theory, 2
project description, 170–1
proxy statement, 109, 120, 123, 124
proxy votes, 122
public pressure, xviii–xix, 147
  influence on corporate governance, 27, 31–3

recent developments, 130
  company secretary's role, 138–44
  corporate governance performance, 131–8
  individual changes, 134–8
regulation, 5, 6, 30, 75, 110, 138
  and compliance responsibilities, 127–8
  influence on corporate governance, 26–9
remuneration committees, *see* compensation committees
reporting lines, 55–7, 153–6
risk committees, 40, 101

Sarbanes-Oxley Act (SOX), 4, 31, 103, 116–17, 142
self-completion questionnaire, 16–17, 22–5, 172–7
shareholders, 27–8, 118–26
  annual general meeting, 118–22
  annual reporting, contributing to, 123–4
  direct contacts with shareholders, 124–5
  share register, 71, 122–3
significance levels, 145
Society of Corporate Secretaries and Governance Professionals, 103
stock markets
  influence on corporate governance, 27, 30–1: competition, 31; listings, 30
strategy committees, 40, 101
study design
  method, 15–17: mixed method design, 15–16; interviews, 16; self-completion questionnaires, 16–17; significance levels, 17, 145; statistical techniques, 17
  samples, 18–25: interviews, 18–22; self-completion questionnaires, 22–5
  scope and framework, 14–15
subsidiaries, 23, 25, 38, 48, 54, 96, 105, 109, 125
supervisory board, 4, 5, 8, 42, 44, 66, 75, 109, 140
Switzerland, 7, 18, 19, 30, 32, 34, 38, 42, 43, 44, 59, 60, 67, 71, 73, 76, 80, 81, 92, 99, 100, 102, 107, 115, 118, 119, 121, 129, 140

tasks and responsibilities (of the secretary), *see* company secretary – tasks and responsibilities; determinants
two-tier boards, 33–4, 35, 36–7, 42–3, 65, 66, 86, 102
types of companies
  bigger companies, 48, 56, 57, 62, 63, 129, 134, 135
  dispersed ownership, 22, 23, 24, 92, 94–5, 99, 105, 113, 118, 129, 132, 136
  dominant shareholder, 24, 25, 38, 125, 132
  large companies/corporations, 30, 38, 48, 50, 71, 86, 90, 95, 101, 113, 122, 130, 132, 139, 160–1
  one shareholder only, 24, 92, 95, 113, 125, 136
  see also family-owned companies; listed companies; non-listed companies; subsidiaries

UK Companies Act, 6, 13, 44, 127
unitary board, 33–4, 36, 49–50, 61, 65, 66, 86
  see also one-tier board
United Kingdom, 1, 4, 6–7, 18, 20, 23, 24, 25, 29, 30, 31, 34, 35, 36, 37, 38, 43, 46, 48, 50, 52, 53, 54, 55, 56, 61, 67, 71, 73, 75, 78, 79, 81, 82, 83, 87, 88, 90, 91, 94, 95, 97, 99, 100, 101, 104, 105, 107, 108, 109, 110, 111, 112, 114, 115, 118, 121, 123, 125, 126, 127, 128, 132, 133, 134, 135, 137, 138, 139–40, 141, 142, 143–4, 158
United States, 1, 2, 4, 5, 6, 10, 16, 18, 20, 23, 24, 25, 26–7, 28, 30, 31, 32, 34, 35, 36, 37, 38, 39, 40, 43, 44, 46, 48, 50, 52, 55, 56, 61, 64, 66, 67, 68, 69, 71, 72, 73, 75, 78, 79, 81, 83, 84, 86, 87, 89, 90, 91, 94, 95, 97, 99, 100, 101, 104, 105, 108, 109, 112, 113, 114, 115, 117, 118, 120, 123, 124, 127, 129, 132, 133, 134, 135, 138, 139–40, 142, 143, 161, 163–5

Western Europe, 18, 22, 23, 24, 25, 31, 34, 35, 36, 38, 39, 46, 48, 50, 55, 61, 64, 90, 91, 92, 94, 95, 98, 99, 100, 104, 105, 106, 112, 113, 115, 135
whistle-blowing, 114–16
working relationship, company secretary, 60–2